The Paralation Model

The Paralation Model

Architecture-Independent Parallel Programming

Gary Sabot

The MIT Press
Cambridge, Massachusetts
London, England

Printed and bound in the United States of America.

Library of Congress Cataloging-in-Publication Data

Sabot, Gary Wayne, 1963-

    The paralation model.
    Originally presented as the author's thesis
(Ph.D.--Harvard, 1988).
    Includes index.
    1. Parallel programming (Computer science)
2. Computer architecture. I. Title.
QA76.6.S216 1988   004'.35 88-9320
ISBN 0-262-19277-2

Contents

List of Figures

Preface

The *paralation model* consists of a new data structure and a small number of operators. The model has two main goals. As a model, it must be high level and abstract. It should ask programmers to describe an algorithm, not every detail of the algorithm to hardware mapping. This leads to programming languages that are easy to use for general application programming. On the other hand, the constructs of the model must be easy to compile into efficient code for a variety of architectures (for example, MIMD or SIMD processors; bus-based, butterfly, or grid interconnect; and so on). An inefficient programming language, no matter how expressive and easy to use, cannot gain widespread acceptance.

The methodology that the paralation model uses to achieve these goals is to make explicit and transparent the costs of both processing and communication. The distinction between computation and communication, along with a careful treatment of locality and synchronization, leads to a model that can serve as a precise tool for a programmer while simultaneously supplying a compiler with an abundance of useful information. The model is both universally powerful and irreducible.

The paralation model accommodates a number of kinds of locality, including locality based upon shapes. The shape facility can be used to improve the layout of data onto processors. It can also be used to build new language paradigms on top of the paralation model. For example, paralations shaped like APL arrays, or like CONNECTION MACHINE LISP xappings, can be defined and manipulated in a convenient and appropriate manner.

Most of the programming examples in this book are written in PARALATION LISP, a language based on the model. A number of compilers for PARALATION LISP have been written. PARALATION LISP code can currently be run in parallel on the 65,536 processor Connection Machine® Computer or serially on any implementation of COMMON LISP. The book includes a short (two pages long) operational semantics for a TINY PARALATION LISP. By executing this code, the interested reader can experiment with the paralation constructs.

Acknowledgments

In the course of developing the paralation model, I was fortunate enough to receive guidance and encouragement from an almost embarrassingly large number of people, two of whom stand out because of their roles as mentors. To begin with, my advisor Harry Lewis wisely encouraged me to focus my research on abstract, machine-independent issues. With only a little prodding, he waded through endless drafts of documents describing my research, returning feedback on both the research and on my abuse of the English language. Discussions with Guy Steele concerning the constantly changing semantics of the paralation model and PARALATION LISP resulted in my learning much about the nature of languages, clean and abstract language semantics, and implementation techniques. Perhaps most importantly, Guy gently but firmly taught me how to focus myself on the interesting abstract aspects of a problem. Guy has been immortalized in the form of a Guy-simulation in my head, which at appropriate times shouts things like, "I don't care about the implementation; what are the semantics of the construct!".

I am grateful to Guy Blelloch for a number of reasons. To begin with, he was the first person who really used PARALATION LISP. His feedback on the language and on the model has been most helpful. In addition, perhaps out of enlightened self interest, Guy B. took the time to optimize portions of the PARALATION LISP compiler, greatly speeding up the execution of a number of constructs.

Advice, attention, and encouragement also came from the other members of my committee, Tom Cheatham, Tony Oettinger, and Michael Rabin, as well as from Michael Berry, Marvin Denicoff, Richard Feynman, Danny Hillis, Sam Kendall, Charles Leiserson, Bill McKeeman, Howard Resnikoff, John Rose, Norman Rubin, Jack Schwartz, Steve Smith, Larry Snyder, Dave Waltz, and Skef Wholey. My thanks also to Lindsay Hotvedt and Eyal Yaari for proofreading. The incredible environment (incredible people, computers, and food) made available to me by Thinking Machines Corporation made the process of implementing PARALATION LISP both intellectually and gastronomically satisfying. I am most grateful to Thinking Machines for giving me the opportunity to work and perform research in such a stimulating setting.

Finally, I want to thank my entire family for their love and support, especially Mom, Dad, and my brother Jay. I am grateful to my Dad for providing encouragement, guidance, long nights of editing, and innumerable toys.

This work was supported in part by the Defense Advanced Projects Research Agency under Navy contract #N00039-83-C-0105.

The Paralation Model

Chapter 1

Introduction

1.1 The Need for a Parallel Model

A parallel computer consists of a large number of conventional computer processors collected into a single device. Parallel computers have a tremendous potential for speed. For example, one might believe that one thousand processors can be up to one thousand times faster than a single processor, given an appropriately parallel program. There are many important computer applications that require such speed. But it can seem impossibly difficult to program parallel computers—the various processors get in each other's way instead of doing useful work. This book proposes a way of programming parallel computers that is easy to use and will work for many different parallel computer architectures with any number of processors, from one to billions.

This chapter begins with a nontechnical introduction which summarizes the motivation for this research. The introduction is followed by an overview of the paralation model.

1.2 A History of Computers

The end of World War II marks the beginning of the era of the modern computer. The transition period contained several interesting architectural solutions to difficult computational problems. One such problem was encountered during the Manhattan Project. It involved simulating an implosion in order to calculate how much energy would be released during the detonation of an atomic bomb. The researchers made use of a room full of devices they called "computers," which, as a group, formed a parallel computer [MN82, Fey85].

1

Each "computer" processor consisted of a Marchant calculator (a mechanical desktop calculator capable of multiplication, addition, and so on) and a human calculator operator. The operators sat at tables and communicated with each other both through speech and by passing colored index cards containing intermediate calculated results. The "program" for this parallel computer consisted of separate written instructions, one for each operator, that described the calculation she was to perform and how the operator should interact with the operators near her. Bugs in these programs resulted in a roomful of confused people. But the speed advantage of utilizing an army of people rather than a single person outweighed such problems; important tasks that could have taken days could now be performed in hours. The human operators could ignore simple mistakes in their written instructions because they were able to understand what the programmer meant to write.

In the postwar era, two-legged "computers" were replaced by electronic computers. Given absolutely precise instructions, a group of tubes, transistors, or integrated circuits could operate more accurately, and much faster, than a human with a calculator. Since a single computer processor was extremely expensive, parallel architectures were unheard of. The task at hand was to make the serial computer faster, by improving the basic components, and to make computers easier to program by developing high-level languages.

As a by-product of advances in technology, computer processors became both smaller and less expensive. Eventually, collecting a number of the small and inexpensive serial processors into a single, extremely fast computing device became technologically and economically feasible. The problem became one of organization: How would the processors be organized and programmed to perform useful tasks? This difficult problem is encountered in any large organization, such as a committee, army, or government. How can one prevent the components of such an organization from getting in each other's way without sacrificing flexibility and speed?

Given the apparent difficulty of the new problem of multiprocessor organization, many designers focused on the old and familiar problem of improving single processors. New miniaturization, cooling, and architectural techniques resulted, but recently further gains by these techniques have become quite expensive. And no matter how fast the designers made a single processor, it seemed as if one could make an even faster machine by bundling many such processors together.

The difficulty of organizing and programming parallel machines slowed progress into parallel computing, despite its promise. Meanwhile, the most visionary single processor designers began to see a barrier at the end of the tunnel: the limitations of physics. The speed of light and the phenomenon of quantum mechanics appeared to draw a line: a limit on the speed and size of a single computer processor. Of course, the line may still be far off, and there is yet much room for technology (both in electronics and in other domains) to exploit in the improvement of single processors for any kind of computer.

Given that parallel architectures may provide a way of building extremely fast computers, an important issue arises: What is the relative cost effectiveness of the "push the serial technology" approach, which makes ever faster and more expensive single processors, compared to the parallel approach, which groups together many processors of any desired speed or cost? Suppose a serial machine could be made to run one hundred times faster by adding one hundred more serial processors, thus creating a parallel computer. It would then cost one hundred times as much as it originally did (ignoring the cost reduction from the learning curve encountered during continued mass production of a single type of processor). No one would want to build or program such a parallel machine if the serial machine could be sped up one thousand times for the same price, simply by improving the underlying technology.

My own belief is that it is asymptotically less expensive to build a parallel computer than an equally powerful serial computer (and that parallel computers can be just as easy to program as serial computers). This belief will be tested empirically in the next few years, as microprocessor technology–based designs begin to proliferate. One reason to expect parallel machines to outperform serial machines becomes evident when one contrasts the efficiency with which they utilize the basic building blocks of computing, switching devices. Parallel computers can be built from the same basic switching devices as serial computers (both processors and memory), but parallel architectures can keep a much higher percentage of those switching devices active performing useful work [Hil86].

1.3   An Insatiable Need for Speed

One might ask why faster computers are even needed; today's computers are thousands of times faster than earlier computers. The practical answer is that there are many problems that require days or weeks to solve on whatever machines are currently available, and a machine that could turn the same job around in minutes would be more than welcome. This is currently the case in many simulation applications, such as circuit simulation, weather prediction, and wind tunnel simulations. A more ethereal view would be that as one achieves the ability to compute at a certain speed, new computational problems begin to appear at the edge of feasibility. Thus, problems that previously could not be solved in centuries on old computers can suddenly be solved in days or months, but new and interesting problems are encountered that require centuries on even the latest and fastest computer.

A computer's reach always seems to exceed its grasp. The concept of a general parallel computer has a matching property: One can add more processors. For many parallel architectures, there is no theoretical limit to the number of processors, just as there is no theoretical limit to the amount of memory that can be included in a von Neumann architecture computer. Of course, any actual parallel computer will have built-in limits, based upon its design (for example, the number of processor address lines available) and its technology (for example, bandwidth limitations).

Some current problems that seem to cry out for faster computers include simulation (of weather, wind tunnels, proposed electronic circuits, atoms or molecules in materials science), signal processing (cryptography, stock market analysis, voice recognition), transaction processing (many airline reservations being made at once), database searching and document retrieval (for example, list all the newspaper articles that discussed parallel computers last year), and of course artificial intelligence, which attempts to program computers to solve problems that are thought to require intelligence [Win77]. The brain itself seems to be a parallel device, made up of billions of slow (compared to current computer technology) processors called neurons.

1.4   A Multitude of Designs

There is currently a multitude of proposed or actual parallel computers. Each is organized in a radically different way. Some, the MIMD (Multiple Instruction Multiple Data) designs, permit each processor to perform different independent tasks simultaneously (like the "computers" of the Manhattan Project). Others, the SIMD (Single Instruction Multiple Data) designs, restrict the parallel processors to performing identical tasks; all the processors simultaneously obey a single stream of instructions from a drill sergeant–like program. (The MIMD/SIMD terminology was introduced in [Fly66]). It certainly seems easier to program such a focused and obedient computer, because it is easier to write a single list of instructions than to write many different lists, especially when the lists must interact with each other.

Programmability is only one part of cost-effectiveness. Another part concerns the inherent power of the processors. Is a SIMD design as powerful as MIMD? Are there tasks that MIMD can perform that SIMD cannot? Another interesting set of questions concerns the degree of parallelism: Is it better to have one million tiny, slow, inexpensive processors or one hundred big, fast, expensive processors? How many SIMD processors does it take to do the work of a MIMD processor?

An important dimension along which parallel designs may differ involves communication between processors. Do all processors have a telephone that enables them to talk to any other processor? Can a processor only talk to the processors that are sitting next door to it? Perhaps all processors talk to a single memory or archive, thus communicating indirectly through a shared memory. Which approach is most powerful, or most cost-effective?

1.5 The Programming Problem

There are many different ways to build a parallel computer. Unfortunately, each way seems to require a different programming technique. There are tradeoffs in the design of serial computers, yet all such machines can be programmed in familiar high-level languages like Pascal, Fortran, Cobol, and LISP. The high-level nature of such languages hides the precise nature of the underlying serial machine. Can something similar be achieved on parallel computers? Some researchers believe that the same serial languages and programs can be used on parallel machines without modification.

1.5.1 Analogy to Cooking

In many ways a program is like a recipe and processors are like cooks. Amateur cooks are familiar with the adage "too many cooks spoil the broth," and yet large catering halls manage to make efficient use of many cooks. The problem arises not from having too many cooks but from asking them to follow a recipe designed from the start to be for a single cook. There is no general, simple way to convert a single-cook recipe into a recipe for many cooks. Of course, there are special cases, such as when a particular part of a recipe tells the cook to chop one hundred onions—one hundred cooks could certainly cooperate for that task. But in general, one must look at the food the recipe was designed to produce and create a new, parallel recipe, free of conflicts between cooks. A new style, notation, or language must be created for expressing such recipes; a direct emulation of the old serial recipe style would simply lead to the creation of new serial recipes. The main issue addressed by such a language is not simply how to instruct many cooks to perform individual, separate tasks, but how to get them to communicate and cooperate so that their individual efforts are not wasted.

1.5.2 Previous Extensions to Traditional Languages

Given that traditional serial programming languages are not sufficient for general parallel programming, the next best thing is to add extensions to current languages, thus addressing the problems of parallelism. Many researchers have done just that, for example, by inventing their own parallel versions of Pascal [PCMP83, Ree84, Pot85]. Historically, many of these extended languages have had several problems.

The first problem with the extended languages is that they are often closely tied to a particular parallel architecture—the one available to the language's author, the one that created his need for a parallel language. It is as if the designer had extensive experience in one kind of kitchen and had produced a recipe language that cannot be used in another kitchen that happened to have a different layout or type of equipment.

The second problem is that many of the languages are hard to use (see Chapter 10). The concepts addressed by the extended languages are based on particular computer parts, not the problems encountered by a programmer. To return to the cooking analogy, the programmer must say "insert onions into spout B12 of the veg-o-matic and press the red button," rather than the higher level, problem-oriented, machine-independent instruction "chop the onions." The high-level instruction can be compiled into lower-level instructions, with no loss in efficiency, by a translator familiar with any target kitchen.

Finally, the concept of extending a single language locks one into the disadvantages of that base language. A more general approach would be to design a set of notation-independent extensions that can be used with several different base languages.

1.5.3   All-New Languages

Several new languages have been proposed that can be used just like conventional languages, but with the promise that compilers for the language will be able to extract all available parallelism from the program automatically, without explicit parallel advice from the programmer. This is possible because certain features of traditional languages, such as side effects, have been eliminated, thus making the language easier to compile.

The difficulty with this approach is that the parallelism of the original application problem may not be present in the text of the final program because the programmer was not asked to think about it. In fact, a "good" serial programmer, one who writes programs that execute quickly on single processor machines, tends to write programs with little inherent parallelism. The tricks and techniques that speed up algorithms and programs on serial machines turn out to cripple parallel machines. These techniques (which have nothing to do with the issues of functional programming or permitting side effects) are inherent in the text of a program, not in the problem the program solved.

One example of this would be a program that smoothes noise out of an array of samples by simply replacing each element by the average of itself and several of its neighbors. This operation certainly can be performed by a parallel algorithm: each element gathers the values of its neighbors, sums them, and divides by the appropriate number. However, a serial program to perform this task would probably not work in this way. Rather than compute a new sum at each element, it would compute a single sum from all of its constituents only once, at the start of the algorithm. After that, it could calculate each subsequent sum by adding in a new value and subtracting the oldest value, as if the summing mask were sliding around the array. This algorithm runs faster than a serial simulation of the parallel algorithm, because it performs fewer additions. Unfortunately, it is difficult to find any parallelism in the serial algorithm, and it therefore would not easily make use of parallel hardware. Thus, although serial languages fit the style of programming to which people have become accustomed, they do not match general parallel hardware. They encourage a programmer to obscure inherent parallelism, instead of encouraging the programmer to program in a way that can fully exploit parallel hardware.

1.6   Solution: An Abstract Set of Extensions

This book describes a model for parallel programming called the *paralation model*. One of its most important goals is to be easy to use for general problem solving. A programmer should be able to describe any type of application problem without needing to know what type of computer the program will eventually run on. The model must provide tools that address the problems of the programmer. On the other hand, languages based upon the model must be easy to compile, in a transparent and efficient manner, for a broad range of target computer architectures. Efficiency (more precisely, asymptotic time and space efficiency, and number of processors) is important because it is necessary for speed, and speed is the driving force behind the original need to program parallel, rather than serial, machines.

The paralation model consists of a new data structure and a small, irreducible set of operators. The model can be combined with any base language to produce a concrete parallel language. The model has two main goals. The first is to lead to languages that are easy to use for general problem solving. The second is to lead to languages that can be transparently compiled into efficient code for a variety of target architectures.

1.7   Paralation Model Overview

The paralation (a contraction from "PARAllel reLATION") model is an abstract model that consists of a single data structure and three carefully chosen operators. The model is algorithmically universal, compatible with a variety of base programming languages, and is machine-independent. Despite its high-level nature, the model does not sacrifice efficiency, specificity, or transparency. The space and time complexities of a paralation program can be calculated analytically, given a description of the target architecture, just as they can for conventional von Neumann programs. By adding the model into any base language, one can create an architecture-independent parallel language.

1.7.1   Data Structures

The central data structure is the *field*, which acts much like an array of objects. The concept of a *paralation*, which is a group of fields, carefully defines field locality, or nearness between field elements. Thus, the programmer is encouraged to describe an important characteristic of the application problem. Since the compiler can make use of the locality information, a programmer can write communication-efficient programs.

1.7.2   Operators

The *elementwise evaluation* operator allows programs to be executed independently in every site of a paralation. This is how parallel computation is performed in the model. Data can be moved between paralations with the *move* operator, which acts like a powerful parallel assignment statement. The pattern of communication is described by a *mapping*, which can be specified by supplying source and destination key fields to the *match* operator. Move uses the concept of *combining* (similar to APL's notion of reduction) to resolve collisions between data values. The colliding values can be reduced according to *any* (possibly user-defined) two-argument function. For example, a group of colliding numbers can be reduced with the arithmetic MINIMUM operation; colliding matrixes can be reduced with MATRIX-MULTIPLY.

1.7.3   Strategy

The paralation model can be compiled efficiently onto a variety of architectures because it draws distinctions between key issues that might be addressed by different types of hardware. The distinctions are general in that they apply to any parallel computer that contains processors and wires to interconnect them. The distinctions center on a separation between computation and communication. The model is careful not to draw distinctions that concern the MIMD or SIMD nature of processors or the precise nature of the interconnections between processors.

Instead of the difficult and often infeasible task of deducing missing information, a paralation language compiler has the simpler task of ignoring any portions of the readily available information (based upon the distinctions) that are not relevant for the target hardware. For example, a compiler for MIMD hardware can take advantage of the lack of synchronization possible during elementwise execution, but a compiler for SIMD hardware is free to ignore this information and synchronize on every function call.

In addition to simplifying the task of the compiler, the key distinctions drawn by the paralation model serve another, equally important purpose. The purpose is to make the model precise and expressive. The result is that a paralation language helps the programmer to understand more clearly the parallel nature of a problem domain. In comparison, a language that does not draw these distinctions, such as conventional serial languages, can encourage the programmer to ignore important parallel issues. Finally, the precise nature of the model means that an algorithm that is easily analyzable can be turned into a program that is also easily analyzable. Each of the language constructs consumes time and resources in a simple, well-defined manner. There are no hidden factors. Thus, the model can express an algorithm without distorting its space or time complexity. Programmers are familiar with these properties because they are common to most serial languages (for example, Pascal and Fortran are transparent; Prolog is comparatively opaque, due to the heavy use of backtracking in its control structure).

1.7.4 Implementation Status

PARALATION LISP is a language that embeds the paralation model in COMMON LISP [Sab87d, Sab87b]. A compiler for the language exists; it can produce output code for a serially simulated multiprocessor, or it can output code that runs on the Connection Machine computer, a massively parallel computer containing up to 65,536 processors. A second compiler for PARALATION LISP is under development by Guy Blelloch (see Section 7.2.1). Chapter 6, along with Appendix A and B, contains a simplified but complete implementation of PARALATION LISP which can be executed on any implementation of COMMON LISP, thus allowing the interested reader to experiment with PARALATION LISP. Section 4.7 describes the syntax of PARALATION C, for which an implementation is under development.

1.8 Claims

The goals of the model can best be summarized by a list of claims. The chapters of this book support the thesis that these claims are true.

- The paralation model is superior to other models because it distinguishes between processing and communication; it makes explicit and transparent the costs of both.

- The paralation model is compatible with most conventional programming concepts. It can be used with many base languages. Conventional structured programming, complexity analysis, debugging, correctness proof, and other techniques are fully applicable to paralation programs.

- The paralation model has an efficient implementation on a variety of feasible parallel architectures. Although hardware concepts such as processors and interconnection networks are not an explicit, programmer-visible part of the model, they played an important role in shaping the tools that make up the model.

- The paralation model allows the user to be specific about synchronization and locality. Therefore, a compiler can easily determine, when optimizing for a particular target architecture, where synchronization and data alignment are *not* required.

- The paralation model is simple and has well-defined semantics.

- The paralation model is easy to use for general problem solving. It permits the expression of algorithms and their inherent parallelism at a high level of abstraction.

- The paralation model is a precise tool that will reveal new approaches to old problems that were known to be amenable to parallel solution, such as breadth-first search, as well as revealing parallel approaches to problems that might initially appear to be inherently serial, such as A* search.

- The paralation model provides a framework for future research and growth: new, more specialized languages can be defined on top of the model, inheriting its architecture-independence and semantic clarity.

Chapter 2

Description of Model

2.1 Notation

The details of the paralation model are presented in a notation based upon COMMON LISP. Any base language could have been used, such as a mathematical notation or a pseudo-Algol. The model makes no commitments on issues such as storage allocation (dynamic or static), typing strategy, or the particular operations that can be applied in parallel.

The LISP notation, however, has one important advantage: examples in this notation can be tested on my LISP-based implementation, PARALATION LISP. (A PARALATION C is currently under development.) LISP was used for the initial implementation for a variety of reasons: One was that the parallel hardware available to me was easiest to manipulate from within a LISP-based notation. Another was the helpful programming environment on dedicated LISP workstations. A final reason was that LISP excels as a tool for writing programs that manipulate programs, partly due to the fact that programs are represented as lists, and partly because of the power of LISP's built-in macro facility.

The body of this chapter begins with a brief summary of LISP notation as it is used in this book. ([SFG*84] is a complete reference to the COMMON LISP language; [Tou84] is a more tutorial introduction to the basic concepts of LISP which would be helpful for the reader who is unfamiliar with LISP.) Then, the paralation model is described. The description consists of three sections: The first corresponds to the model's central data structure, the second to the elementwise evaluation operator for parallel computation, and the final section introduces the model's communication operators. Communication operations are syntactically divided into two parts: match and move (see Section 4.4).

2.1.1   Lisp Notation

LISP is based around a data structure called a *list*. A list is simply a sequence of items. For example, this is a list of three names:

```
(moe larry curly)
```

Lists can themselves contain lists, and they are written simply by nesting parentheses. Conveniently, LISP programs are themselves written and represented as lists. The first item in such a list is the function that is to be called; the remaining items are its arguments. Evaluating a program always returns a result, which can be ignored if it is not needed. The following program adds 10, 20, and 15 together, returning 45. Notice that the function being called, +, is the first item on its list; it comes before its arguments, not between them as in most languages.

```
(+ 10 20 15)
  ⇒ 45
```

In addition to functions corresponding to the conventional math functions, COMMON LISP has a number of built-in special forms (thirty-two of them) and macros (rewrite rules; can be thought of as special forms). For example, setq is a special form that can be used to set a variable to a new value:

```
;; set x to 9
(setq x 9)
;; find the value of x
x
  ⇒ 9
```

defun is a macro that can be used to define new functions. The following program defines a function called double that takes one numerical argument and returns double its value.

```
(defun double (number)
  (* 2 number))
```

LISP has a number of conditionals; one of the simplest is if:

```
(if (> number 0)                         ;; condition
    (print "it was bigger than 0")       ;; then clause
    (print "it was not bigger than 0")) ;; else clause
```

This brief summary of LISP should give the reader enough knowledge to be able to puzzle through the various programming examples in this chapter, given the text that surrounds and explains each of them. There are a number of additional

V-TIME	V-SAMPLE
0	.245
1	.329
2	.398
...	...
$n-1$	$sample_{n-1}$

USER-NAME	ID-NUM	DISK-USAGE
massar	0	2320
donna	1	2081
gls	2	3987
george	3	2319
rose	4	1934
zippy	5	40

Figure 2.1: Two unrelated paralations

linguistic features of COMMON LISP that are used in the examples but are not directly discussed, such as keyword arguments, the distinction between `let` and `let*`, and the generality of the `do` iteration construct. COMMON LISP programmers will understand and appreciate the use of these features. The choice of variable and keyword names, along with the English comments, should make their purpose (in the context of a specific example) apparent to novice LISP programmers. However, the glossary in Appendix C contains more general descriptions of several of these LISP constructs for the interested reader.

2.2 Data Structures

Most languages make available data structures that hold sequences of objects, such as arrays and lists. The paralation model adds a new sequence data structure called a `field`. In PARALATION LISP, a field element can contain any type of object, including numbers, characters, and even fields. The concept of a *paralation* carefully defines field locality ("nearness" between field elements) so that the programmer can write communication-efficient programs. These data structures can be briefly defined as follows: A paralation is a set of related fields. One of these fields is a distinguished *index* field, which enumerates the sites of the paralation. The ith site of a paralation contains the ith field elements of the fields of the paralation; the index field at that site has value i. To create a paralation, one must create an index field. Additional data fields can then be grown around the index field. Each of these additional fields has a pointer to the index field of its paralation.

Two *paralations* are illustrated in Figure 2.1. The first contains two fields, each with n elements. One field, bound to the LISP symbol V-SAMPLE, contains voltage samples. The other field, V-TIME, contains the time at which the associated sample was taken. The second paralation has three fields that describe the users of a computer system.

Ordinary sequences, such as arrays, are created and stored independently of any other sequences. However, a field can be created "near" another field. What this means is that each element of the first field is stored near the element of the second field with the same index—the two fields are aligned. For example, the fifth element of the first field is near the fifth element of the second field. This elementwise locality is guaranteed between two fields if the fields are in the same paralation.

In Figure 2.1, this is illustrated by each element in V-TIME being drawn horizontally right next to the corresponding element of V-SAMPLE. Each such horizontal row in the figure represents a site in the underlying paralation. A site is simply the place where all values in a paralation that have the same index are stored. Intuitively, all values at a single site are near each other. In the figure, site 1 of the left paralation stores both the V-TIME value of 1 and the V-SAMPLE value of .329. This intrasite locality is called *elementwise* locality.

Paralation sites that have nearby indices (and are in the same paralations) are near each other. This nearness is based upon the concept of shape. Paralations of any shape can be constructed. Thus, the sites of a particular paralation might be arranged in the form of a four-dimensional grid, a ring, a butterfly, a pyramid, or even as a double helix. The typographical layout of Figure 2.1 makes it appear that element 0 of both V-TIME and V-SAMPLE is near element 1 of either field and far from element $n - 1$ of either field. One might imagine that the paralation is a one-dimensional grid that has a linear locality. However, this need not be the case; the paralation model draws a distinction between the indexing of paralation sites and their intersite (shape) locality properties. Unfortunately, in drawing a field on paper one invariably implies a table or grid shape. Nevertheless, by default, a paralation has no inherent shape. Shape locality must be explicitly described by the programmer. Chapter 8 discusses ways of describing shape. Unless the facilities discussed in that chapter are used, paralations are shapeless.

One might imagine an unshaped paralation to be a soup bowl and the sites to be noodles floating in the soup. Even though the noodles might be ordered (perhaps it is alphabet soup, so the noodles' names can be alphabetized, or perhaps each noodle has a numerical index), one cannot tell how physically close one noodle is to another from their names alone. A shaped paralation, which can only be created using the facilities in Chapter 8, is like a bowl of soup that has been frozen after the noodles have been placed into useful positions.

The third and most distant type of locality is interparalation locality: Sites and values in different, unrelated paralations are far from each other regardless of their indices. Sites in V-TIME's paralation, shown on the left side of the page, can communicate with each other more easily than they can with sites in USER-NAME's paralation, shown on the right side of the page.

2.2.1 Properties of Fields

A field is a group of values that is stored in a paralation, one in each site. A field assigns a specific value to each site of a paralation. If the values are regarded as colors, each field in a single paralation is a separate coloring of the same sites. Another way to think of a field is as a collection of objects that is given shape and structure by the field's underlying paralation. The value of a field at a particular site, an element of the field, is a *field value*.

Every field in a paralation necessarily has the same size: that of the underlying paralation.[1] One implementation of these data structures on a massively parallel machine with general processors, local storage, and general communication would equate a paralation site with a processor, a paralation with a group of nearby processors, and a field with a slice through the memory contents of a group of processors.

2.2.2 Properties of Paralations

A paralation is a vector-like collection of sites. The purpose of a paralation is to provide a structured place to allocate fields. A user program manipulates fields, but never handles a paralation object directly; any field of a paralation can serve to designate the paralation. Given a field, the index field of that field's paralation can be retrieved. The index field enumerates the locations of the paralation, like the V-TIME and ID-NUM fields in Figure 2.1. An index field is just like any other field; it just happens to contain a set of useful values (the indices). One cannot tell from looking at a field's values whether the field is an index field or just happens to contain the same values as an index field. However, if one retrieves the index of a field, and the very same field is returned, then the field must have been an index field. The fact that the index values impose an order on the sites of a paralation does *not* mean that the sites are stored in any particular corresponding physical shape or arrangement.

Paralations are created by the function `make-paralation`. It takes a specification that describes the length of the desired paralation as its argument, creates the paralation, and returns its index field. For example:

```
(make-paralation 1000)
   ⇒ #F(0 1 2 3 4 5 6 7 ... 999)
;;⇒ denotes evaluation
```

The above call creates a paralation with 1000 sites. It returns as its result the index field of the paralation, which enumerates the locations of the paralation

---

[1] The *size* or length of a paralation refers not to any physical measurement of shape but to the number of sites in the paralation.

from 0 up to 999. (The #F field printing style shown above is analogous to the
#A array printing style of COMMON LISP.) Note that it is impossible to determine
from the concise printed representation used here alone if two fields are in the same
paralation, or are in different paralations that just happen to have the same length.
This is similar to the way that one cannot tell whether two lists share structure or
not from the standard printed representation. More verbose printing formats can
present this hidden information, but this usually turns out to be unnecessary in
practice.

2.2.3   Index Coordinates

The result of `make-paralation` is an index field. This index field can be used,
along with the `elwise` operator described below, to create other fields in the new
paralation. Given any one of the possibly many fields in a paralation, a program is
able to retrieve the original index field by using the `index` function. If two fields are
in the same paralation, their index fields are the same (the standard COMMON LISP
equality function, `eql`, returns t if its two arguments are the same). For example,
suppose `f1` and `f2` are fields in the same paralation:

```
f1 ⇒ #F("any" "data" "at" "all")
f2 ⇒ #F(FOO NIL BAR QUUX)

(index f1)
   ⇒ #F(0 1 2 3)

(eql (index f1) (index f2))
   ⇒ t

(eql (index f1) (make-paralation 4))
   ⇒ nil
```

2.2.4   Reading of Fields

The PARALATION LISP reader can parse the #F syntax as input. However, a new
paralation is created for every field as it is read in:

```
(setq f '#F(a b c))
(setq g '#F(a b c))
(eql (index f) (index g))
   ⇒ nil
;; f and g are in different paralations that happen to have the
;; same length, 3
```

2.2.5 Locality Description is Pragmatic

Knowing that the paralation programmer adheres to certain locality conventions, a paralation compiler can map data onto processors in a way that efficiently accommodates communication. In and of itself, however, the locality of the paralation model has no *semantic* content: the programmer can lay out data structures onto paralation fields in any desired fashion. The point is that certain ways of laying out data (those that relate a problem's inherent locality to the intrasite, intersite, and interparalation locality of the paralation data structures) can lead to faster programs. Locality is merely a pragmatic concept that can lead to communication-efficient programs. Similarly, paging performance in a serial computer usually is much better if multidimensional arrays that are stored in row-major order are scanned in row-major order rather than in column-major order. This is true even though in many languages the concept of array storage order has no semantic content. There is no semantic content because any array element can be accessed simply by supplying its coordinates, and there is usually no way for a user to conclusively prove which storage order a language implementation is using.[2]

2.3 Elementwise Evaluation

The purpose of elementwise evaluation is to execute the enclosed code or program, the *body*, in parallel. Elementwise evaluation takes a list of symbols and a program as its arguments. The symbols are elementwise variables. Each must be bound to a field, and all of the fields must be in the same paralation. The result of the elementwise evaluation is a new field in the same paralation. At each paralation site, this result field contains the value produced by *independently* executing the program at that site, using that site's field values where the field names are mentioned. For example, one could add 1 to each element of a field as follows:

```
;; p5 contains the data
(setq p5 '#F(0 1 2 3 4))

;; make a new field whose elements are those of
;; p5 with 1 added to each
(elwise (p5) (+ p5 1))
   ⇒ #F(1 2 3 4 5)
```

The particular form the elwise takes in LISP necessarily reflects LISP's storage allocation strategy. Each time elwise is invoked, it allocates a new field. The

---

[2]However, some languages contain constructs like COMMON LISP's :displaced-to, or Fortran's COMMON, EQUIVALENCE, IDENTIFY, and alias array constructs, whose behavior does depend upon the underlying storage order.

programmer is not asked to pay attention to the problem of deallocating fields
because in LISP the automatic garbage collector is responsible for such details. If
elementwise evaluation were combined with a lower level base language, storage
allocation and deallocation would have to be handled in an appropriately explicit
manner.

That is all there is to `elwise`, which really is quite simple. This is due, in
part, to the simplicity of parallel computation itself; the real complexity in parallel programming arises in orchestrating communication and cooperation between
processors. The simplicity of `elwise`, combined with the precise locality properties
of the paralation data structures, means that `elwise` can easily be compiled into
efficient code for a variety of architectures. The next few subsections simply expand
upon the consequences of these semantics.

2.3.1 Side Effects

The body of `elwise` is a program, and no restrictions are placed upon what the
program may do. The model makes no restrictions upon its base language. For
example, the body may contain assignment statements:

```
;; p5 was not changed by the last example
p5
    ⇒ #F(0 1 2 3 4)

;; change it this time!
(elwise (p5) (setq p5 (- p5 1)))
    ⇒ #F(-1 0 1 2 3)
p5
    ⇒ #F(-1 0 1 2 3)
```

2.3.2 Synchronization

Elementwise evaluation makes a single, simple synchronization guarantee: Elementwise evaluation terminates and returns its result only after all the paralation sites
have finished executing the program. This provides freedom for the implementation
of elementwise evaluation on a variety of architectures. An attempt to detect an
evaluation order among the paralation sites is defined to be an error. For example, if a program causes two sites in a paralation to attempt to set the same serial
value during the same `elwise` (perhaps hoping that the last side effect to occur will
persist), that program is in error.

The following synchronization example demonstrates one way to apply a field of
functions to a field of data (`elt` is a COMMON LISP function that takes a sequence,

such as a `list`, `array`, or `field` and a number i, and returns the ith item of the sequence):

```
(setq p (make-paralation 5))
(let ((data (elwise (p) (elt '(0 3.14 5 10 100) p)))
      (operator (elwise (p)
                   (elt '(sin cos 1+ 1- identity) p))))
  (elwise (data operator)
    (funcall operator data)))
  ⇒ #F(0.0 -0.99999887 6 9 100)
```

Thus, the first `elwise` returns a field whose ith element is the ith element of the list (0 3.14 5 10 100). It simply coerces the list of numbers (`data`) into a field of numbers in p's paralation. The second `elwise` does the same thing for a list of COMMON LISP functions. The final `elwise` applies the functions to the data using `funcall`, a standard COMMON LISP function.

Interestingly, a similar operation could have been performed with a just a single `elwise`:

```
(setq p (make-paralation 5))
(elwise (p)
  (funcall (elt '(sin cos 1+ 1- identity) p)
           (elt '(0 3.14 5 10 100) p)))
```

The second version is a better implementation because it does not introduce unnecessary synchronization between paralation sites. The first version suggests that each `elwise` must complete before the next can begin. For example, the first version required all the field values of `data` to be calculated (by the first `elwise`) before the field values of `operator` are calculated, and only after *all* `data` and `operator` items had been calculated could the final `elwise` begin to apply `operator`s to the `data` values.

In general, it is both clearer (more descriptive of the application) and more general to leave an `elwise` in factored form rather than distribute the `elwise` by separately applying it to each of the body `forms`. A factored `elwise` can always be distributed by a compiler for hardware that requires the extra synchronization; a distributed `elwise` can be changed into factored form only if a detailed program analysis verifies the correctness of the transformation.

2.3.3   `elwise` Errors

Given that `elwise` does not make any guarantee about synchronization between paralation sites as they execute the `elwise` body, the question arises of how to deal with conflicting side effects between sites. The solution is to define such behavior as an error. Any `elwise` body that would permit a program to discern in which order the various sites execute their programs is in error. For example, the following program attempts to have the variable `the-winner-is` set to a, but it also attempts to set it to b. This is an error.

```
(setq the-winner-is nil)
(setq p '#F(a b))

;; ERROR in this elwise
(elwise (p)
  (setq the-winner-is p))
```

This example illustrates how more than one paralation site can attempt to set the same location. Another way the same type of error can occur is if one site sets a location and another site reads it, within the same `elwise`. In the following example, the first site of the paralation puts something into the variable `bad-mailbox` at the same time that the second site is attempting to copy `bad-mailbox` into the variable `output`:

```
(setq output nil)
(setq bad-mailbox 'no-mail)
(setq p '#F(a b))

;; ERROR in this elwise
(elwise (p)
  (if (eql p 'a)
      (setq bad-mailbox 'a)
      (setq output bad-mailbox)))
```

Defining this behavior as an error means three things:

1. No valid paralation program contains such an error.

2. If a program contains such an error, the effects and results are completely undefined by the paralation model.

3. No implementation based upon the model is *required* to detect such an error, although it is desirable for it to be detected if it is reasonable and feasible to do so.

In a formal sense the problem of detecting this type of `elwise` error is decidable in any program that terminates. (One strategy that involves time-stamping is discussed in Section 7.3.5.) However, the cost of actually performing this detection can vary greatly among different architectures. Therefore, it is necessary to be "precisely vague" about the result of the `elwise` error in order to maintain the model's architecture-independence. (COMMON LISP defines a similar class of errors which implementations are not responsible for detecting.)

Of course, an implementation on a particular architecture, with a particular base language, is free to define legal effects and results for computations that are illegal in the pure model. For example, an implementation might indicate that anywhere from none to all of a collection of colliding serial side effects (up to one per paralation site in an `elwise`) are actually executed. The implementation might indicate that the side effects that are executed can take place in an unspecified serial order. In such an implementation, a read from a serial location that has been side effected elementwise might return the original value, or it might return any one of the values that the colliding side effecting forms attempted to store there. The point is that a program that takes advantage of such a guarantee is not a legal program according to the paralation model.

A programmer who depends upon the guarantee sacrifices portability. In general, elementwise constructs that attempt to read data produced by other sites should be replaced by an invocation of PARALATION LISP's communication function, `<-`, which is described below in Section 2.4. Elementwise constructs that cause colliding side effects should be replaced by a call to `<-` (pronounced "move") that makes use of an appropriate collision combining function.

2.3.4 Lexical Designation of `elwise` Variables

`elwise` takes a list of symbols as one of its arguments. These symbols designate the variables that should be treated in an elementwise fashion when the body is executed. The scope of this behavior is lexical. When an elementwise variable occurs textually within its `elwise`, it is compiled in a special way: each paralation site receives its own field element rather than the entire field.

One might imagine a dynamic version of `elwise`, call it `elwise-d`, that would take a single designation field rather than a list of symbols. The body of this proposed `elwise-d` would treat a variable elementwise if at run-time it contained a field in the same paralation as the designation field. The language APL has this kind of dynamic behavior. In APL, any variable is treated as a parallel variable if it happens to contain an array. APL does not need a paralation designator because there is no concept of paralation-like locality.

The lexical behavior of `elwise` has several advantages over the dynamic behavior of the hypothetical `elwise-d`. First of all, one can tell at a glance which variables are lexically elementwise, because the list of symbols is textually immediately above the body. A dynamic approach requires one to deduce the contents of a variable in order to understand which are elementwise. Unfortunately, the contents of a variable might be changed in an obscure corner of a program. One must trace the actual dynamic flow of control rather than the static lexical structure of the program. This makes it difficult for humans to understand the program and difficult for compilers to optimize it.

The second advantage of lexical behavior is that it makes it easy for a programmer to treat a parallel quantity as a scalar, which is often useful in the manipulation of hierarchically nested parallelism (see Section 4.2). Consider the following example:

```
(setq p (make-paralation 3))
    ⇒ #F(0 1 2)
(setq x p)
    ⇒ #F(0 1 2)
(elwise (x p)
  (cons x p))
    ⇒ #F((0 . 0) (1 . 1) (2 . 2))
```

Both x and p contain the exact same field. If elwise is informed that both should be treated in a parallel fashion, an elwise call to cons them together elementwise does just that.[3] But what happens if one of the two lexical designators is left out?

```
(elwise (x)
  (cons x p))
    ⇒ #F((0 . #F(0 1 2)) (1. #F(0 1 2)) (2 . #F(0 1 2)))
```

Since p is not an elementwise variable, a mention of p in the body refers to the entire contents of p. Therefore, each site of the paralation conses its element of x to the contents of p. This behavior would be difficult to duplicate with the proposed elwise-d, because it would attempt to treat x and p in the same manner, since they happen to dynamically contain fields (actually a field) in the same paralation.

2.3.5   elwise and the Lambda Expression

elwise is reminiscent of a lambda expression. A lambda expression contains a program and a list of variables. When a lambda expression is applied to values, it binds the variables to the values (that is, the formal parameters are bound to the actual parameters) and executes the program. When elwise is executed, every site in its paralation executes the program on its own local set of actual parameters. When a variable not bound by a lambda expression is used in its program body, a value is taken from the surrounding context. Similarly, since every site in a

---

[3]cons returns a dotted pair containing its arguments. A dotted pair is the basic building block used to construct lists: a list is a dotted pair containing a first item and a list of the remaining items, or nil for the end of a list.

paralation independently executes the program, each site retrieves the value of any non-`elwise` variables (that is, serial variables and constants) independently from the surrounding serial context. Thus, serial values are implicitly coerced to parallel. Finally, an `elwise` is similar to a lambda expression in that its program body can contain *any* type of computational expression. For example, in PARALATION LISP, elementwise calls to `let`, `setq`, `eval`, `make-paralation`, or even `elwise` are both feasible and useful.

One difference between lambda expressions and `elwise` expressions is that in

`(lambda (x) x)`

the two `x`s refer to the same thing, while in

`(elwise (x) x)`

the first `x` refers to a field and the second, during elementwise execution, to the individual elements of the field. In this, the analogy between `lambda` and `elwise` breaks down.[4] Of course, when `elwise` execution is over, the individual `x` field elements are reassembled into a field in the involved paralation. This leads to an important difference between `lambda` and `elwise`. Although both of the examples above are in a sense identity functions, there is a subtle difference. The `lambda` returns the very same value `x` that was passed to it. On the other hand, the `elwise` accepts an `x` (which must be a field) and returns a new field in the same paralation as `x`. Although this result field contains the very same elements as `x`, it is a different field than `x`. Nevertheless, `lambda` and `elwise` are similar because they share an important, basic feature: both operate in a lexical manner, binding and unbinding data to names, rather than by statically storing data in named storage locations.

2.4 Communication with Mappings

The paralation model introduces two new functions that allow communication between the sites of paralations: `match` and `<-`. Together, the two functions perform a matching operation that acts like a powerful parallel assignment statement. These are perhaps the most important functions in the paralation model. An example involving dictionary lookup is used to explain communication between paralations; it is illustrated in Figure 2.2.

Suppose a paralation contains two fields, `dword` and `dmeaning`. Each site in this paralation serves as a definition; the paralation is a parallel dictionary. Given a field `word` in a text paralation, one might want to create a new field in the text paralation, `meaning`, containing the definitions of the text words.

---

[4]The binding shorthand presented in Section 2.6.3 eliminates this difference by allowing the user to rename the elementwise variables.

MEANING?	WORD
	a
	twonky
	was
	a
	machine

DWORD	DMEANING
a	determiner
ate	verb, ingest
boy	noun, child
twonky	noun, creature
twonky	noun, television set
was	verb, is

Figure 2.2: Dictionary Lookup

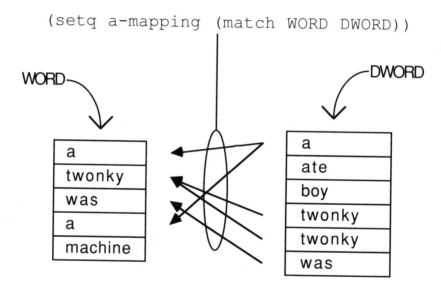

`(setq a-mapping (match WORD DWORD))`

Figure 2.3: Match creates a mapping

2.4.1 Match and Mappings

Figure 2.3 shows the function `match` being called with `word` as a destination key and `dword` as a source key. `match` is a function that computes and returns an object called a *mapping*. A mapping can be thought of as a bundle of one-way arrows that connect certain sites of the source paralation to certain sites of a destination paralation. Two sites are connected if their key field values are the same. In the dictionary example, an arrow connects a dictionary site to a text site if the value of `dword` at the dictionary site is equal to the value of `word` at the text site. Note that not every possible pattern of arrows can be a mapping; only patterns that represent a correspondence between two fields can be computed by `match` (this is discussed further in Section 5.6.3).

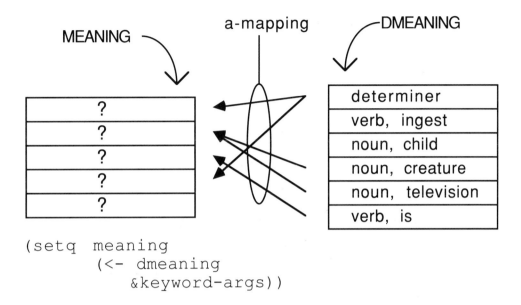

```
(setq  meaning
       (<- dmeaning
           &keyword-args))
```

Figure 2.4: Move moves a field through a mapping

The purpose of a mapping is simple, and is illustrated in Figure 2.4. With the help of the move function, a mapping can accept as input any field in the same paralation as its original source key. Move simply pushes this source data field into the tails of the mapping's arrows, causing an interesting object to pop out of the heads of the arrows: a field that is in the same paralation as the destination key. The elements in this field are calculated based upon what arrived over the arrows. If a single arrow arrives at a destination site, it is clear what that element's value should be. Of course, in many cases, arrows can conflict. Simple rules govern the resolution of the conflicts.

The simple case where multiple arrows leave a site (the same word occurring several times in the text) is handled as illustrated in Figure 2.5: Each arrow carries a conceptual copy of the source site's data. This situation occurs when a word in the dictionary is needed by each of several occurrences in the text.

The more complex case occurs at the destination, where either multiple or zero arrows can arrive at a site. This corresponds to the situation when a dictionary contains multiple (or zero) definitions of a word that occurs in a text, such as "twonky" (or "machine").

When zero arrows arrive at a destination site, the site plucks its default value

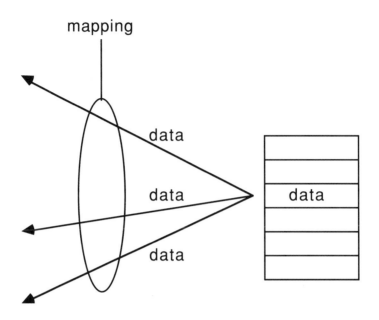

Figure 2.5: Concurrent Read

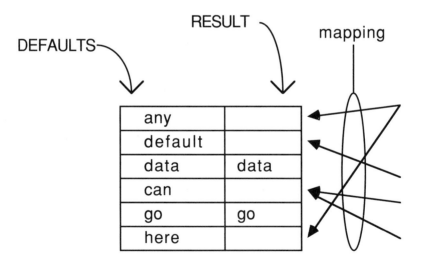

Figure 2.6: Default values can be supplied in advance

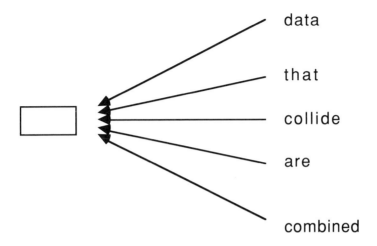

Figure 2.7: Collisions are resolved with combining

from a field of defaults supplied to move. This is shown in Figure 2.6, where two sites had no incoming arrows. The field of defaults is an optional argument to move; if no default is supplied, but one is needed, an error is signalled.

Combining

The most important case involves conflicts between multiple arrows arriving at a destination site. The colliding values are resolved according to an induced reduction tree and a two-argument combining function. Any desired combining function can be specified by the user (including user-defined functions), but move selects the reduction tree. As with the field of defaults, the combining function is an optional argument to move; if it is needed, but was not specified, an error is signalled.

Figures 2.7 and 2.8 illustrate the construction of a reduction tree. The colliding arrows are pinched together, two at a time, until only one arrowhead remains. When two values collide at a node in this tree, the output is calculated according to the user-supplied combining function. Thus, repeated application of the combining function reduces many values into one. The <- function can pinch together any pairs of arrows that it wishes: no particular associative pairing is guaranteed. However, the index order of the incoming data is maintained; arrows cannot leap over other arrows and combine out of order.

Given the uncertainty over the precise reduction tree that will be used, what types of combining functions are useful? Associative functions form one class, because they produce the same result for any reduction tree. For example, + always

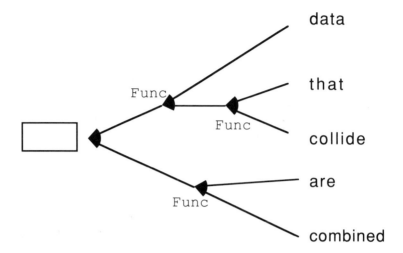

Figure 2.8: Induced reduction tree

sums a group of colliding numbers, while `max` always picks the largest. Similarly, `string-append`, `logical-or`, and `matrix-multiply` can serve as combining functions.

It turns out that nonassociative functions can also be used to combine colliding data in a useful way. For example, consider the `arb` function, which accepts two arguments and arbitrarily returns either the first or the second. When applied to a number of colliding values, all of which happen to be "X", this function always returns X. When applied to a group of prime numbers, it always returns a prime number. `arb` is not associative because it is not true that:

`arb(arb(x, y), z) = arb(x, arb(y, z))`

However, one cannot even say that:

`arb(x, y) = arb(x, y)`

since one side may return **x** and the other **y**. Of course, if one refers to sets of possible returned values rather than to actual values (thus changing the equality to an equivalence relation), one could then say that `arb` is associative in this limited sense. Alternatively, one might define an associative combining function as a function such that given any set of inputs and corresponding outputs, one cannot infer anything about the pairing structure of the particular reduction trees that were used to compute the outputs.

Another interesting nonassociative function is the LISP function `cons`, which accepts two values and returns a structure, called a dotted pair, which contains the two values. For example:

```
(cons 'a 'b)
   ⇒ (a . b)
(cons (cons 1 2) 3)
   ⇒ ((1 . 2) . 3)
(cons 1 (cons 2 3))
   ⇒ (1 . (2 . 3))
```

Combining with `cons` can be useful during debugging. For example, suppose a program uses + as a combiner with <-, and the field returned by <- seems to contain an incorrect sum at a particular paralation site. In order to debug it, the programmer will probably want to know what numbers went into the incorrect sum. One way to find this out is to change the combiner from + to `cons`. The field returned by <- will then contain, at each paralation's site, a dotted collection of the numbers going into that site's sum. The particular associative pairing is unpredictable, as illustrated by the two ways of `cons`ing the integers 1, 2, and 3 shown above. For the purposes of debugging, however, the position of the parenthesis does not matter; the programmer only cares about what numbers are present. Thus, depending on how it is used, a nonassociative function can be "effectively" associative because of the way in which its results are viewed.

2.4.2 Interaction Between Destination Sites

Combining conceptually occurs separately at each destination site. One might imagine that <- begins by creating a field in the destination paralation that contains, at each site, a list of the values arriving at that site. These values are then elementwise reduced into a single value according to the combining function. Since each destination site performs its own reduction, it is possible that two destination sites with the exact same key will use two different associative pairings for the reduction. If the combining function is not associative, the sites could calculate different result values even though they have the same value in the destination key field of the mapping.

If an application required one, a match-like operator that provides a guarantee that destinations with identical keys all use the same associative pairing could be implemented (in a time and space efficient manner) in terms of the less restrictive match and elementwise evaluation operators.[5]

---

[5]One efficient implementation of <- on certain kinds of parallel hardware is to extract the

Like elementwise evaluation, move makes a simple synchronization guarantee: After all of the data in the arrows has been delivered to the newly created destination field, the move terminates.

2.5   Code for Dictionary Lookup

The following code implements dictionary lookup in PARALATION LISP:

```
;; text
word  ⇒ #F(A TWONKY WAS A MACHINE)
;; old definition = defaults
old-def  ⇒ #F(NONE NONE NONE NONE NONE)


;; dictionary
dword  ⇒ #F(A ATE BOY TWONKY TWONKY WAS)
dmeaning  ⇒ #F(DETERMINER VERB-INGEST NOUN-CHILD
                NOUN-CREATURE NOUN-TV VERB-IS)


;; combining function
(defun string-min (a b)
  (if (string-lessp a b)
      a
      b))


;; THIS PERFORMS THE DICTIONARY LOOKUP
(setq meaning (<- dmeaning :by (match word dword)
                          :with #'string-min
                          :default old-def))
  ⇒ #F(DETERMINER NOUN-CREATURE VERB-IS
          DETERMINER NONE)
```

The variable word contains a field of the words from the text. old-def contains a field, in the same paralation, of the old definitions of the words, each of which is currently NONE. Similarly, dword represents the dictionary words and dmeaning represents their definitions. Finally, a function is defined, called string-min. It accepts two strings as arguments and returns the lexicographically smaller of the two. It is used in this dictionary lookup example as a combining function—if a word has many definitions, the alphabetically smallest definition is chosen. Although this is an arbitrary way to choose a dictionary definition from competing possibilities, it is illustrative of the power of <-.

---

distinct to-field key values, perform a *single* combining lookup for each key value, and then distribute the combined results for each key to all destination sites containing that key. However, this particular implementation is not required by the model.

The object of dictionary lookup is to create a field that contains the definitions of the words from the text. The actual lookup consists of moving the contents of `dmeaning` by a mapping from the dictionary words (`dword`) to the text words (`word`). The combining function, introduced with the keyword `:with`, is `string-min`; the default is the old definitions, `old-def`. `<-` returns the result, which is then saved away in `meaning`.

2.6 Idioms and Programming Technique

This section describes several useful operations that can be concisely defined in terms of the paralation primitives. They can be thought of as idioms of usage, or as library functions. Later chapters present several other library functions. By showing how these derived operations can be implemented, I hope both to illustrate the operations *and* to demonstrate one style of usage for the paralation primitives. Of course, a compiler is free to implement the derived operations at a lower level than `elwise`, `match`, and `<-`; efficient implementation techniques are discussed in Chapter 7. The library functions presented here are those that seemed useful in PARALATION LISP, and some may therefore reflect the unique features of LISP, such as the way it uses dynamic storage allocation.

2.6.1 Library Function: Value Reference with Vref

The function `vref`, for "Value REFerence," can be used to reduce all of the values in a field into a single value using any combining function. For example, `vref` can sum the numbers from 0 to 4 as follows:

```
(vref '#F(0 1 2 3 4) :with #'+)
  ⇒ 10
```

`vref` can easily be implemented in terms of the paralation primitives, as is shown in Figure 2.9.[6]

Figure 2.10 illustrates the execution of this implementation of `vref`. Working from the inside of the code outward, the purpose of the `elwise` is to create a source key that contains a 0 in each of its elements. A `match` can be performed using this key. Since each of the items in the input field has the same key, this produces a match that connects each of the data items to the same destination, which is exactly what `vref` is supposed to do. The destination key field (the first argument to `match`) should therefore contain a single 0, like this: `#F(0)`. The index field of a paralation of length 1 is just such a field.

---

[6]The `&key` used in this example makes "with" into a keyword argument: The user calls `vref` using the keyword `:with`. For example, `(vref #F(1 2) :with #'+)`

```
(defun vref (field &key with)
  (elt
    (<- field :with with
        :by (match (make-paralation 1) (elwise (field) 0)))
    0))
```

Figure 2.9: An implementation of vref

	<key>	FIELD
	0	0
<result>	<one-paralation>	MATCH	0	1
? = 10	0		0	2
	0	3
	0	4

Figure 2.10: Execution of vref

The match creates a mapping that connects every element of field's paralation
to the single site of the newly created paralation. The <- uses this mapping to
reduce all of field's data values, producing a field in the new paralation. The elt
then plucks the answer from this field. Note that many of the fields manipulated
by this example, as well as the mapping, are never stored in variables or given
actual names. The model accommodates, but does not require, an applicative
programming style.

vref turns a field into a kind of associative memory. For example, one can ask
if a field contains the symbol 'blue:

```
(defun or-func (a b) (or a b))
(setq c '#F(red green blue orange))

(vref (elwise (c) (eql c 'blue))
      :with #'or-func)
   ⇒ T
```

or-func is a utility combining function that is true if either of its arguments are
true. COMMON LISP's built-in or cannot be used directly as a combining function
because it is a LISP macro, not a function. The elwise in the example creates a
field that has a t where items are blue and nil elsewhere; the vref with or-func
simply ors all of this data together. The result of the vref is t if any item was
blue.

The actual vref of PARALATION LISP contains a second keyword argument,

:else, in addition to :with. The value of the else argument is returned if the input field being vrefed contains zero elements. Its purpose is analogous to the :default of <-, but while default has to be a field, else can contain any value.

2.6.2 Library Function: Choose

choose constructs a new field by using selected pieces of an input field. One might design such a function so that it accepts as arguments a field and a predicate, and returns a new field. However, it turns out to be more general to define it as a function that accepts a field of booleans and returns a mapping. The mapping can then be used by <-. The following example selects the odd numbers in the range 0 through 4 and constructs a field to hold them:

```
(setq p (make-paralation 5))
   ⇒ #F(0 1 2 3 4)
(<- p :by (choose (elwise (p) (odd p))))
   ⇒ #F(1 3)
```

Note that the field whose parts are being selected (p) is different from the field that contains the booleans (the result of the elwise), although they both must be in the same paralation. The following elaboration may clarify that:

```
(setq data '#F(a b c d e))
(setq p (index data))
   ⇒ #F(0 1 2 3 4)
(setq bool (elwise (p) (oddp p)))
   ⇒ #F(NIL T NIL T NIL)
(<- data :by (choose bool))
   ⇒ #F(B D)
```

choose maintains the index-based ordering of the input data values. For example, b comes before d in both the input and the output.

How does choose work? Figure 2.11 illustrates one way that it might have functioned in the previous example. (A full implementation of the library function choose in terms of the paralation primitives is presented in Section 6.3.1.) choose simply counts the number of trues (non-nils) in the boolean field and creates a new paralation with exactly that many sites. choose must then create and return a mapping that connects each true site in the input to its own site in the new paralation, maintaining the index-based ordering. One way it can do this is to create a field in the destination that contains the index of each site's t value, and then to call match to create a mapping to that new field from the index of the source data.

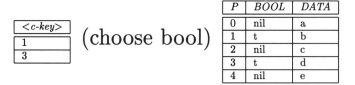

Figure 2.11: Execution snapshot of `choose`

2.6.3   `elwise` Binding Shorthand

It is often the case that one wishes first to create a field and then to perform elementwise evaluation upon it immediately. As a convenience, so that the user does not have to name the variable twice (once in a COMMON LISP `let` and again in an `elwise`), PARALATION LISP allows `elwise` to perform `let`-like binding:

```
(let ((x (make-paralation 6)))
   (elwise (x) (oddp x)))
≡
(elwise ((x (make-paralation 6)))
   (oddp x))
```

Thus, `elwise`'s first argument does not have to be a simple list of symbols. Instead, some of the elements of the list can be a sublist containing a symbol and a LISP form that calculates an `initial-value`. In either case, let us refer to the elements of the list as *field-specs* and to the symbols as *field-vars*.

In this new form, in which a *field-spec* can be either a symbol, as before, or a binding pair, `elwise`'s list of *field-specs* has a dual purpose. The familiar, `let`-like purpose is to evaluate expressions and to lexically bind the values to symbols. The other purpose is the one introduced by the initial, simple form of `elwise`: to designate the variables that are to be treated as parallel quantities (fields) by the body `forms`.

Although the shorthand makes `elwise` syntactically similar to a `let`, there is an important difference: Unlike `let`, `elwise` does not create a new binding for a *field-spec* that is simply an atom (a *field-var*). In this case it is assumed that the named *field-var* already has a value; mentioning it as an `elwise` variable simply changes the way it is compiled within the `elwise`. This is most unlike a COMMON LISP `let`, in which a binding specification that is an atom rather than a pair produces a new binding for that atom with an initial value of `nil`:

```
;; assume no global binding for x
(let (x)
  x)
  ⇒ nil

; BUT:

(elwise (x)
  x)
  ⇒ Error, the variable X is unbound
```

To summarize, the following regular expression defines the full form of an elwise, in which the *field-specs* can be either *field-vars* or *field-var/initial-value* pairs, and an elwise must contain one or more *field-specs*:

elwise ({*field-var* | (*field-var initial-value*)}+) *form**

An elwise of this general form can be converted into an elwise of the simpler form by moving the *field-var/initial-value* pairs into a surrounding let, and replacing each with just a *field-var* in the elwise.

```
(elwise (a
         (b (calculate-b))
         c
         (d (calculate-d)))
  body)
≡
(let ((b (calculate-b))
      (d (calculate-d)))
  (elwise (a b c d)
    body))
```

LISP programmers who are aware of the significance of the ordering of variables to let will recognize that the ordering of the pairs has the same significance. Basically, the binding clauses of a let are evaluated separately and cannot refer to each other. The clauses of a let* are evaluated in order and the right-hand side of a clause can make use of variables defined by earlier clauses. Section A.1 introduces elwise*, which has the same relationship to let* that elwise has to let.

2.7   Fields as Sequences

Most serial base languages already have some type of sequence data structure, such as an array. A useful set of library functions extends whatever built-in sequence functions a base language already has so that they transparently and efficiently operate on objects of type `field`. For example, COMMON LISP has a rich library of sequence functions, such as `sort`, `reverse`, `length`, `concatenate`, `delete-duplicates`, `position`, and so on, as well as a number of different equality predicates. In PARALATION LISP, these functions can be applied directly to fields:

```
(length '#F(this is a field))
  ⇒ 4
```

```
(position 'a '#F(this is a field))
  ⇒ 2    ;; index is zero-based
```

```
(reverse '#F(this is a field))
  ⇒ #F(FIELD A IS THIS)
```

Sequence functions such as these can easily be built-up from the paralation primitives. For example, consider `length` (see also Appendix A):

```
(defun length (field)
  (vref (elwise (field) 1) :with #'+ :else 0))
```

By providing these functions as a library, a paralation language becomes a better tool (possibly better matching the flavor of the base language, if it has a rich set of sequence functions) and provides the compiler with an access point for the optimization of these commonly used functions.

A number of other library functions are discussed and implemented in subsequent chapters.

2.8   Programming Examples

2.8.1   Prime Number Sieve

The following code uses the sieve method of Eratosthenes to create a field containing only prime numbers. Each iteration of the loop locates a single prime number by finding the sieve position (index) of the leftmost t in `candidate-p` using COMMON LISP's `position` function. The primality of the prime is recorded by setting the corresponding location in `prime-p` to t. This is done using `setf`, which is a generalized version of `setq`. `setf`'s first argument describes a place, and the second argument is stored into that place. If the place is simply a variable name, `setf` is equivalent to a `setq`. In this case, the place is the `next-primeth` element of `prime-p`. Finally, all `candidate-ps` at sieve locations that are multiples of the prime are set to nil, because multiples of a prime obviously are not prime. The loop exits when there are no more candidates.

```
;; SIEVE describes the sieve locations
;; CANDIDATE-P is boolean, t if sieve position could be prime
;; SIEVE      = #F(0   1   2   3   4   5 ... n)
;; CANDIDATE-P = #F(nil nil t   t   t   t ... t)    ;;initially

(defun find-primes (n)
  (let* ((sieve (make-paralation n))
         (candidate-p (elwise (sieve) (if (> sieve 1) t nil)))
         (prime-p (elwise (sieve) nil)))
    (do ((next-prime 2 (position t candidate-p)))
        ((null next-prime)
         (<- sieve :by (choose prime-p)))
      (setf (elt prime-p next-prime) t)
      (elwise (sieve candidate-p)
        (when (and candidate-p (zerop (mod sieve next-prime)))
          (setq candidate-p nil))))))
```

The result of calling `find-primes` with a given n is a field in a new paralation (created by `choose`) that is just long enough to hold the primes that are less than n.

```
(find-primes 50)
  ⇒ #F(2 3 5 7 11 13 17 19 23 29 31 37 41 43 47)
```

2.8.2 Set Operations

Just as one can use an array of distinct items to explicitly represent the contents of a set, a `field` that contains no duplicates can also represent a set. This section demonstrates the implementation of `intersection` and `subset` on sets represented in this way. Of course, a base language might already contain these operations in its library of sequence functions.

The representation of sets is that each element of a field represents an element of a set. Each set can be in its own paralation.

```
(setq colors '#F(red green blue))
(setq names '#F(george harry red larry))
```

To intersect two sets, one simply causes each object in one of the sets to discover whether it is also in the second set by using `match` and `<-`; then `choose` can build a new set containing only those elements. Part of the execution of `intersection` is illustrated in Figure 2.12.

COLORS	KEEP-ME
red	t
green	nil
blue	nil

NAMES
george
harry
red
larry

Figure 2.12: Execution snapshot of `intersection`

```
(defun intersection (set1 set2)
  (let ((keep-me
          (<- (elwise (set2) t)
              :by (match set1 set2)
              :default (elwise (set1) nil))))
    (<- set1 :by (choose keep-me)))))
```

By simply exchanging the `t` and the `nil` in the `intersection` function, one could create a `set-difference` function which subtracts `set1` from `set2`.

Another useful set operation is `subset`, which returns true when all elements of a given set are contained in another supplied set. Its implementation is similar to that of `intersection`, except that the field of booleans is now passed to `vref` with a combining function that logically ANDs its arguments together. `subset` is true if and only if all elements of the first set are members of the second.

```
(defun subset (contained container)
  (let ((found
          (<- (elwise (container) t)
              :by (match contained container)
              :default (elwise (contained) nil))))
    (vref found :with #'and-func :else t)))
```

`and-func` is a combining function that logically ANDs it arguments together. `and-func` returns true when both of its arguments are true, and `nil` otherwise. Like PARALATION LISP's `or-func`, is provided because the corresponding COMMON LISP function (`and`) is actually a macro and not a function. These and other combining functions are discussed further in Section 6.3.2.

Chapter 3

Strategy for Harmonizing Conflicting Goals

3.1 Model Versus Goals

The two main goals of the paralation model are:

- To be easy to use for general problem solving.

- To be easy and transparent to compile into efficient code for a wide variety of target architectures.

The methodology that the model uses to balance the tension between these goals is based upon distinctions the model draws between key concepts that *might* be implemented by different types of hardware. This means that information about a variety of different architectural features is accessible to the compiler. As a result, instead of the difficult and often infeasible task of deducing missing information, a paralation language compiler has the simpler task of ignoring any portions of the readily available information that are not relevant for the target hardware. Simultaneously, because the key distinctions are general and abstract, they are able to make the model more precise, expressive, and transparent *without* introducing architecture-based details.

The most important distinction drawn by the model is between general computation and communication. Elementwise evaluation performs computation, move without a combining function performs communication, and move with a combining function mixes computation and communication.

The distinction between computation and communication is rooted in the fundamental difference between processors and wires and in the different types of basic operations that they represent (see the Orthogonality principle in Section 4.4). All parallel computers that I am aware of draw this distinction. However, many proposed parallel programming languages do not draw a corresponding distinction. Due to the general nature of this distinction, the paralation model's ease of use and ease of compilability goals, which may seem to be in conflict, actually mix and aid each other.

3.2   Processing Issue: Synchronization

The concept of processing is associated with the idea of synchronization. The paralation model is very specific about synchronization: synchronization occurs upon entry to and exit from `elwise`. Therefore, the paralation programmer implicitly describes the *minimal* synchronization required by an application through the use of `elwise`. The result is that `elwise` itself is very general in its requirements for synchronization: no requirements are in force when a program body is executed elementwise. This generality can be very useful to a compiler for a MIMD architecture, which can assign separate, unsynchronized processors to each paralation site. On the other hand, a compiler for a SIMD architecture is free to ignore this information and synchronize all processors on every function call. `elwise` is general enough to have a natural implementation on both MIMD and SIMD architectures.

3.3   Communication Issue: Locality

The concept of communication is associated with the idea of locality. The paralation model is very specific about locality. It includes a three-level locality hierarchy: intrasite, intersite, and interparalation localities, representing same location, nearby location, and far location, respectively. In mapping a problem's data structures into the `fields` of paralations, a programmer can use this hierarchy to describe the locality properties of the problem. A compiler for a shared memory architecture might ignore the communication locality information inherent in the paralation data structures, while a compiler for a target architecture whose interconnected processors have their own local memories would use the locality information to map data onto processors in a communication-efficient manner.

Locality is an important characteristic of a parallel algorithm [LM86], yet many parallel languages ignore it. For example, a discrete simulation of a wind tunnel that notes that adjacent samples are somehow three-dimensionally "near" to each other (in terms of expected communication patterns) is preferable to one that ignores this spatial property. Similarly, a model should permit one to say that the airspeed at a particular location in the air tunnel and the temperature at the same location are even "nearer" to each other. When such information is supplied, the compiler can conclude that data structures that are *not* noted to be near each other are unrelated, and each can be stored in whatever area is most convenient for the storage allocator.[1] Thus, the paralation programmer is able to precisely describe the characteristics of the problem, while the paralation compiler is free to use or ignore the locality information.

3.4 Key Distinctions Add Precision

In addition to simplifying the task of the compiler, the key distinctions drawn by the paralation model serve another equally important purpose. The purpose is to make the model precise and expressive. `elwise` describes computation, `<-` without a combining function describes communication (permutation), and `<-` with a combining function mixes communication with computation. The result is that a paralation language helps the programmer to understand more clearly the parallel nature of a problem domain and provides a notation for describing it. In comparison, a language that does not draw these distinctions, such as an implicitly parallel language (for example, dataflow), can encourage the programmer to ignore important issues. Simultaneously, a compiler for a paralation language can easily determine when computation or communication will or will not be needed.

Specificity is important for the programmer. Better and more specific tools encourage a programmer to examine problems from a sharper, closer perspective. This results in a better understanding of the problem and its inherent parallelism. Less precise models discourage the direct understanding of parallelism by offering a single, overly powerful, monolithic tool. For example, the ultimate in lack of precision is to promise to extract available parallelism from programs written in conventional serial languages. The user has no direct way to describe parallel computation or communication among data elements.

Specificity is also important for machine independence. The compiler for any kind of hardware can produce better code when given a more detailed specification. It is easy to ignore extraneous information and compile upward for more powerful and expensive hardware. It is quite difficult to compile in the other direction.

For example, consider an image processing algorithm with an inherent two-dimensional cartesian locality pattern. An imprecise model might not allow the user to describe this locality pattern. The resulting program would then seem to run best on expensive, shared memory type hardware, even though the original problem did not require it. The locality pattern that was obvious to the original

---

[1]The same phenomenon occurs with information about synchronization: Indicating that synchronization takes place upon entry to and exit from elementwise evaluation means that asynchronous execution is otherwise acceptable. Thus, elementwise body code does not have to be synchronized between sites.

programmer is obscured by the imprecise model and, therefore, is hidden from the compiler. A communication operation that the programmer intuitively expects to take a constant amount of time (nearest-neighbor communication) may actually take time that is logarithmic in the size of the target machine's shared memory! A good model permits powerful operations but does not force their indiscriminate use.

3.5   Synchronization Between Processes

A number of programming models and techniques have been developed that address the problem of synchronization between processes (Actors, dataflow [AI83], CSP, Ada rendezvous, and so on). These models can be used to solve a class of problems that often involve the concept of many individual time-sensitive events. The paralation model does not attempt to address this type of general synchronization or to simplify problems that require it (see Section 11.2.1). Rather, the model simply passes the unsimplified, raw problem of synchronization along to the programmer. The simple all-or-nothing barrier synchronization provided by `elwise` is as complex as paralation synchronization gets. Of course, this simple synchronization has universal power, as the definition of `fork` (see Section 5.3.4) and the emulation of the PRAM (see Section 9.2.1) indicate. Perhaps this can allow the paralation model to be used as a platform upon which models that do address process level synchronization can be built (see Section 9.4). In any case, many problems do not require this general type of synchronization (for example, all of the programs presented in this book).

3.6   Types of Parallel Architectures

Parallel architectures can be categorized according to a number of dimensions. The paralation model is insensitive to many of these divisions, but they are presented here so that the same terminology can be used later when compilation techniques are discussed.

3.6.1   Shared Versus Local Memory

To begin with, processors may have either local memory or a shared memory. The difference between these two is not so great. For example, the IBM RP3 [PBG*85] is usually described as a shared memory machine, but each of its processors has a direct line to a portion of memory. Often, shared memory machines provide some sort of per processor local cache; in the IBM machine, this cache happens to be a physical part of the main memory.

To the extent that a shared memory machine permits a program to control the contents of its cache, a compiler can exploit the locality description inherent in a paralation program. In an idealized shared memory machine (no local cache), locality cannot be exploited at all. The problem is that general communication is performed as a part of the basic cycle of the machine, which is undesirable (see Section 7.8).

3.6.2 Nature of Communications Network

Two additional differences between parallel architectures concern the types of communication that are accommodated. First, there is the hardware nature of the communications network. Where are interconnections physically present? In what topological configuration (for example, hypercube, ring LAN, bus, and so on)? Second, there is the firmware control over communication. Can a message be injected into the network with a numerical processor address as its target? If so, what route will it take to its target? Does a precise route have to be calculated and executed by software? What type of switching is used?

As with the local/shared memory issue, a paralation compiler benefits most when it can have a great degree of control of low-level execution details. When local communications take place in shaped paralations (see Chapter 8), the compiler has a great deal of knowledge about communication patterns that can be used in formulating efficient routing patterns. Of course, when general communication is to be performed, it is perfectly acceptable for firmware to take care of all the details of routing messages to their destinations.

3.6.3 Nature of Processors

Another difference between machines concerns the nature of their processors and the manner in which they are controlled and synchronized: MIMD, SIMD, or some mixture of the two (for example, the M/SIMD PASM [SKS81, SSKI87]). For a local memory SIMD architecture, the efficiency of indirect addressing can be an important issue.

It is unclear precisely which type of processor is best suited to the paralation model. A MIMD machine certainly would be easier to compile for, especially when nested parallelism is used (see Section 4.2.1). A MIMD machine also would be able to take advantage of the lack of synchronization possible during `elwise` execution.

However, a SIMD machine might be a better choice as a paralation target because of its simplicity. Using it as a target might uncover efficiencies that are inaccessible to a complicated, powerful MIMD design. The principle is the same one that enables simple RISC (Reduced Instruction Set Computer) machines, with instruction sets that do not intuitively match the constructs of high-level languages, to serve nevertheless as efficient targets (see Section 7.8 and Section 10.4.1).

3.6.4   Abstract Programming Models and Hardware

Different programming models have different goals. One natural result of this is that models vary in their relation to physical hardware. Some serial models, such as the lambda calculus, are extremely abstract, while others, such as the Turing machine, are closely tied to an implementation model. Similarly, some parallel models are closely tied to certain computer architectures. For example, the PRAM can be described as a shared memory MIMD architecture.

The paralation model is abstract and machine-independent. In general, a description of the operation of the paralation constructs should avoid the use of hardware terms (such as processor and communication network) in favor of new terms such as paralation site and mapping. Of course, hardware terms can be used in order to provide an intuitive backdrop to the model by describing possible implementation strategies.

Chapter 4

Compatibility with Conventional Programming Concepts

4.1　Principles of Programming

There is a large body of research concerning the nature and principles of computer programming, computer languages, and software engineering. One would prefer a parallel model that did not force one to set aside that research. However, the programming of parallel computers requires a number of new concepts to address new, previously unimportant problems. The constructs of the paralation model attempt to address those new problems. Fortunately, for the most part, parallel paralation programming seems to be very similar to serial programming. One explanation is that the new problems and their paralation solutions are orthogonal to the valuable old concepts and solutions of serial programming.

In geometry, when two lines are orthogonal, it means that they form a right angle. One can move parallel to one line while remaining stationary relative to the other; the two axes are independent. In computer languages, orthogonality refers to a similar kind of independence. When two functions are independent, they should be controlled by two different mechanisms. This allows one to change one of the functions without affecting the other. For example, the Ada programming language separates the issue of how an argument is used by a procedure (either for input, output, or both) from how argument passing is implemented (passing by reference, value, or result).

The paralation model is designed according to the view that the methods one uses to instruct a single processor to perform a task (such as writing in a conventional programming language) are orthogonal to the methods (such as paralation operators) used to orchestrate cooperation among many processors. As a result, the paralation model is compatible with most conventional programming language concepts. This chapter discusses the relevance of important conventional concepts, such as hierarchical structuring and information hiding, to the paralation model. A number of principles that lead to good serial languages are used to evaluate paralation languages. In addition, the model is shown to be orthogonal to issues of any particular base programming language style or flavor.

4.2   Hierarchical Structure

The construction of large programs is often facilitated by a separation of the program into procedures, functions, or subroutines: modules with carefully defined interfaces. Usually, these modules are grouped hierarchically. Thus, a module can call upon a number of submodules to perform various tasks; the module manages the work of its submodules and each submodule automatically returns control to its manager when it has accomplished its task. Submodules themselves can have subsubmodules, and so on, until one reaches the lowest level, where a module performs a task so simple it does not have to be split up or delegated any further. This type of structure is valuable because it allows separate modules to be written, debugged, and rewritten separately, so long as each adheres to the specification of its interface. In this context, information hiding refers to the fact that the implementor of a module should know nothing more about the program as a whole than the detailed specification of a particular module's interface. By hiding extraneous information, one ensures that a module does not "cheat" and go beyond or around its interface.

Hierarchical structure seems to occur naturally in problems; problem solving tasks can be subdivided naturally into smaller tasks. The benefit of exploiting hierarchical structure is a programming methodology that simplifies the construction and maintenance of large, complex programs. It turns out that the parallelism of a problem can also be exploited in a hierarchical fashion. Structured parallelism enables a program to exploit many levels of parallelism without overwhelming or confusing the programmer, who simply focuses upon the single level of parallelism that corresponds to the task of the current module. The paralation primitives implement a kind of information hiding, because a module does not have to "know" whether it is running in serial or parallel. Of course, if the base language has side effects, it can use them in a way that attempts to pierce the information hiding barrier. This error is analogous to the case when a serial procedure side effects a global variable, piercing the barrier set up by parameter passing conventions.

4.2.1 Simple Nested Parallelism Example

One simple case of nested parallelism occurs when `elwise` is invoked in an elementwise fashion. For example, suppose one had a field full of objects. Each object consists of a name, such as OBJ2, and a description of its attributes. Conveniently, the attributes of a single object consist of a field full of numbers:

```
(setq objects '#F([OBJ1 #F(9 3 2 7 ...)]
                  [OBJ2 #F(0 6 2)]
                  ... ))
```

It is not important for this example to indicate exactly what the objects and attributes actually represent. What is relevant is the modular way in which one can manipulate the objects. For example, one might want to analyze each of the objects in parallel, producing a field containing the results of the analysis:

```
(elwise (objects)
  (analyze objects))
```

At this point, one might want to write the **analyze** function, which takes a *single* object and its attributes and returns its analysis. Here is one contrived thing that **analyze** might do: It doubles all of the numbers in the attribute field, and then returns the sum of the doubled numbers:

```
(defun analyze (object)
  (let ((a (get-attributes object)))
    (vref (elwise (a) (* 2 a)) :with #'+)))
```

Here is another contrived thing that **analyze** might do. This version returns the sum of all of the even numbers in the attributes:

```
(defun analyze (object)
  (let ((a (get-attributes object)))
    (vref (<- a
              :by (choose (elwise (a) (evenp a))))
          :with #'+)))
```

Both of these proposals for **analyze** apply paralation operations to the attributes. The first one doubles the attributes in parallel, then performs a `vref` communication operation. The second executes `evenp` in parallel, then a `choose` and a `<-`, and finally a `vref`. However, the **analyze** function is itself called in parallel from the top-level `elwise`.

Seen in the context of this example, nested parallelism can be seen as a simple and useful tool. The next subsection presents a larger example that uses several

1	2	3
8		4
7	6	5

Figure 4.1: Solved 8-puzzle position

levels of nested parallelism. It is more realistic than these examples and therefore is more complicated. Its value is that it shows in detail how the paralation model can be applied to a problem in artificial intelligence; it does not actually present any new features of the model.

4.2.2   A* Search

A* is a heuristic search algorithm used to explore state-spaces [Nil71]. For example, it can be used to explore the space of possible paths through a number of cities in order to find the shortest (the traveling salesman problem). Another problem to which A* has been applied is a game called the 8-puzzle, a small version of the traditional 15-puzzle.

This section illustrates how state-space search can be executed in parallel using the paralation constructs. This demonstrates how nested parallelism can occur in a real application and shows how the paralation model can be applied to a nontrivial problem. First, the 8-puzzle itself is described, followed by a description of a simplified version of A*. A parallel version of A* is then presented, including PARALATION LISP code. Finally, code for the 8-puzzle is presented, and the nested parallelism in the A*/8-puzzle combination is analyzed.

The 8-Puzzle

The 8-puzzle consists of a square board with nine spaces, eight of which contain tiles. The tiles are numbered one through eight. The object of the puzzle is to go from a given initial permutation of the tiles to the position in Figure 4.1, with the space in the middle, simply by sliding tiles around on the board.

When viewed from a state-space search perspective, the positions in the search space are all of the possible board positions. The problem is to find a path from some given point or node to the point representing the solved board position. A node is directly connected to another node if the corresponding board positions differ by one application of the move operation: sliding a single tile over into the empty space. From any given position, there are several different directly connected positions, or children. Each child itself has several children. If the puzzle is solvable, the goal node is a descendant of the original start node, and the problem is to find the path (sequence of moves) that connects the two. A breadth-first search explores a search space by expanding a node into all of its children, then expanding all of those children, and so on, until the goal is found. The node expansion function in state-space search is often referred to as the *gamma* function. In the case of the 8-puzzle, the gamma function takes a single node and returns a sequence of its successors, of which there can be at most four (one for each tile that can be slid into the blank space).

Restricted A*

The A* algorithm attempts to avoid work by making use of a heuristic that can rate a board position, guessing how far it is from the goal node.[1] Effort can best be applied to nodes that are near to the solution, perhaps only a few moves away from completion, rather than to nodes that are far from the goal. A* works by maintaining a list (called the OPEN list) of the nodes being explored, and these are kept in sorted order based on the cost of the moves each has required so far (in the 8-puzzle, all moves have the same cost: 1) added to a heuristic guess at the cost of transforming the node into a solution. (The sum of these two values is commonly referred to as f', or f-prime. The cost of the moves that have been taken so far is g, and the heuristic value is h'; $f' = g + h'$. The primes refer to the fact that the value is an *estimate* for an unknown value.) In serial A*, the first, "best" node (the one with the smallest f') is taken off and expanded, its descendants are rated, and then they are merged back into the sorted list. This process is repeated until the first node on the sorted list is the goal node, and the search is then over.

A search algorithm that always finds the best path to the goal (when one exists) rather than some other more expensive path is termed *admissible*. In order for A* to be admissible, the heuristic it is used with must satisfy a certain property: its guess must never be larger than the actual cost from a node to the goal. A heuristic that performs careful computations to create an accurate measure of the difficulty of transforming a given node into a goal is not admissible if it can ever overestimate the distance to a goal. On the other hand, a heuristic that always says that a node is 0 moves away from the goal is admissible. The trivial constant zero value heuristic turns A* search into a uniform cost search (a variant of breadth-first search).

In the case of the 8-puzzle, a very powerful heuristic exists [Nil71, page 66]. It very quickly leads a program to produce a solution. However, it does not satisfy the requirement that its guess is never larger than the actual cost from node to goal. Therefore, A* with this heuristic is not admissible; A*'s 8-puzzle solution will not always contain the minimum number of moves possible. The 8-puzzle heuristic is made up of two parts. The first is the sum of all of the tiles's Manhattan distances

---

[1]For simplicity, the A* algorithm presented here is restricted in that it ignores cycles in the search space. The full A* algorithm maintains a list of nodes that have been expanded, called CLOSED, and does not waste effort reexploring nodes that are on that list.

to their positions in the goal node. (A Manhattan distance measure simply adds the x-distance and the y-distance: it measures the distance between two points when one cannot move diagonally.) The second part is a sequence score. One looks around the perimeter of the square, scoring 2 points for each tile that is not followed by its proper successor; then, 1 point is added if a tile is in the center. Thus, the first part of the heuristic calculates the work to move a tile directly to its destination; the sequence score takes notice of the difficulty of exchanging tiles that are out of order.

A* search is useful because it allows one to apply effort selectively to the many possible paths that could be explored. Parallelism can help us to explore more paths more quickly. For example, breadth-first search, which explores all descendants, seems to be an excellent candidate for parallelism: simply recurse elementwise to explore all descendants in parallel. To illustrate, suppose a function BF (breadth-first) takes a field full of nodes and is responsible for exploring them and their descendants. If any node in the field is a goal node, BF terminates. Otherwise, it elementwise expands each node into a field of children nodes, regroups by concatenating the daughter fields back into a single, long field, and tail recurses upon itself:

```
(BF #F(START-NODE-1-1))
(BF #F(SUCCESSOR-NODE-2-1 SUCCESSOR-NODE-2-2  ... SUCCESSOR-NODE-2-n))
(BF #F(SUCCESSOR-NODE-3-1 SUCCESSOR-NODE-3-2  ... SUCCESSOR-NODE-3-n))
and so on, until goal is found
```

The A* algorithm, on the other hand, seems inherently serial: at each step, a single node is expanded into its descendants. The A* algorithm is able to use the leverage provided by a heuristic to avoid work that the breadth-first search algorithm seems to blunder into. Fortunately, a closer look at A* reveals that the power of parallelism is compatible with the selectivity of A*.

Parallel A*

A* works by applying the minimum unit of work possible in a blind fashion (applying gamma to a single node) and then regrouping before working again. In a serial machine, that unit of work happens to be 1. In a parallel machine, however, more work can be done at once. The first step in parallelizing A* is to recognize that several nodes can be taken off the sorted OPEN list and expanded in parallel. The number of nodes in this field of removed nodes is related in some way to the number of processors available. Elementwise, these removed nodes are expanded into successor nodes by the gamma function, and then a heuristic rating function is called upon each successor node.[2] Finally, the descendants of the removed nodes are merged back into the sorted list[3] (thus using parallel communication to regroup in preparation for continued search), and the process is repeated. At each step of the algorithm, all processors are working on nodes that come from the front end of the sorted list; no processor is wasting its effort by continually exploring a dead end. Thus, parallel A* mixes the features of serial A* with those of breadth-first search.

There is one important difference between serial and parallel A* involving termination. Serial A* terminates as soon as it finds itself removing goal node from the front of the OPEN list. Since the OPEN list is sorted, the first node must be the best node on it, and therefore it represents the best path to the goal, and A* algorithm can terminate. However, parallel A* removes several nodes from the front of OPEN. Even if one of these is a goal node, it might not be the best possible goal node, since it is not necessarily the very first node on OPEN. Therefore, parallel A* must keep track (cumulatively) of the best goal node that has been removed from the head of OPEN to date. It can terminate only when that best node is better than the very first node on OPEN.

The following code implements the core of parallel A*. To begin with, the basic data structure is a state-space node:

```
(defstruct (node)
           state
           g h-prime f-prime
           parent
           operation)
```

The `state` part of a node contains a description of the position of the node in the problem's state-space. For example, in the 8-puzzle it might contain a field describing the positions of the various tiles. The gamma operator fills in `g`, `h-prime`, and `f-prime` and therefore rates the node. The remaining two fields are also filled in by the gamma operator. `parent` contains the state of the parent of this node and `operation` is the precise operation or game move that was required to create this node from the `parent`. (Most of this information is not used by the restricted A* algorithm presented here.)

COMMON LISP's `defstruct` automatically provides a constructor for nodes, `make-node`, and a number of accessor functions such as `node-state`, `node-parent`, and so on. (By default, `defstruct` names the accessor functions by concatenating the structure name, `node`, with the various slot names.) Before presenting the

---

[2]If one expected many parent nodes to produce identical children, and the heuristic were an expensive operation, one might want to remove any duplicates from the successor list before elementwise calling the heuristic on it.

[3]Removing duplicates as a side effect.

A* code, it is necessary for two more support functions to be defined. The first is `node-less-p`, which is true when its first argument's f' rating is less than its second argument's f' rating:

```
(defun node-less-p (n1 n2)
  (< (node-f-prime n1) (node-f-prime n2)))
```

The second function is a combining function that accepts two nodes and returns the better one (the one with the lower f' rating, that is, the lowest estimated cost from start to finish):

```
(defun pick-better-node (n1 n2)
  (if (node-less-p n1 n2)
      n1
      n2))
```

The main entry point to the A* code is `parallel-a*`, which accepts a `start` node, a `gamma-operator` function (which must take a node and expand it into a field of successor nodes), and a `goal-p` function that takes a node and returns true if it is a goal. It is assumed that the gamma operator elementwise calls the heuristic rating function on the nodes that it produces before it returns them.

`parallel-a*` begins by initializing `open` to a field in a paralation of length 1, containing the `start` node. `best-goal` is initialized to be a node of infinite cost (it will later be replaced by the first real goal to be found). Finally, the main `loop` is entered. Each iteration plucks nodes off of `open`, expands them, rates and then sorts the successors, and finally merges the successors back into `open`, checking for termination.

```
(defun parallel-a* (start gamma-operator goal-p)
  (let ((open (elwise ((p (make-paralation 1))) start))
        (best-goal (make-node :f-prime infinity)))
    (loop
      (let ((nodes-to-expand
              (subseq open 0 *max-nodes-to-expand-at-once*)))
        (setq open (subseq open *max-nodes-to-expand-at-once*))
        (let* ((goal-node-ps (elwise (nodes-to-expand)
                               (funcall goal-p nodes-to-expand)))
               (a-good-goal
                 (vref (<- nodes-to-expand :by (choose goal-node-ps))
                       :with #'pick-better-node
                       :else nil)))
```

```
(when a-good-goal
  (setq nodes-to-expand
        (<- nodes-to-expand
            :by (choose (elwise (goal-node-ps)
                                (not goal-node-ps)))))
  (when (> (node-f-prime best-goal)
           (node-f-prime a-good-goal))
    (setq best-goal a-good-goal)))))
(when (or (zerop (length nodes-to-expand))
          (< (node-f-prime best-goal)
             (node-f-prime (fref nodes-to-expand 0))))
  (if (< (node-f-prime best-goal) infinity)
      (return best-goal)
      'failure))
(setq open (parallel-a*-step
            open nodes-to-expand gamma-operator))))))
```

The main loop begins by using a COMMON LISP sequence function to pull the best nodes off of open. An alternative way to do this would have been to use the paralation library function choose to pull off nodes with indices less than *max-nodes-to-expand-at-once*. In any case, a field containing these removed nodes is stored in nodes-to-expand, and open is rebound to a field containing only the remaining nodes.

The next step is to check nodes-to-expand to see if any goal nodes are on it, using the user-supplied goal-node-p function in an elementwise fashion. If any goal nodes are found, vref will place the best one in a-good-goal (the combining function pick-better-node simply returns whichever of its two argument nodes is the largest according to node-less-p), the goal nodes will be removed from nodes-to-expand, and best-goal will be updated appropriately.

At this point, parallel-a* checks for the termination condition: When best-goal is rated better than the best node on nodes-to-expand, it can be returned as the result. If there are no nodes to expand, and no goal with a non-infinite cost has been found, failure is returned. Finally, the last line calls parallel-a*-step, which is responsible for returning an updated version of open.

```
(defun parallel-a*-step (open nodes-to-expand gamma-operator)
  (merge 'field
         (sort (expand (elwise (nodes-to-expand)
                               (funcall gamma-operator nodes-to-expand)))
               #'node-less-p)
         open
         #'node-less-p))
```

parallel-a*-step begins by expanding each node on nodes-to-expand using the user-supplied `gamma-operator`. The result of calling the `gamma-operator` on a single node is a field of nodes; the result of the elementwise call is a field of fields of nodes. `expand` is a paralation library function that flattens the top level of that structure, returning a field of nodes. (It has nothing to do with the gamma expansion of a state-space node into successor nodes; `expand` simply happens to have a similar name). `expand` is presented in more detail in Section 5.3.3; for now, this brief example will suffice:

```
(expand '#F(#F(a b) #F(c) #F() #F(d e)))
  ⇒ #F(a b c d e)
```

Returning to `parallel-a*-step`, the nodes returned by `expand` are sorted according to their heuristic ratings and are then merged with the already sorted `open` nodes, thus producing the final result.

Nested Parallelism in Parallel A*

Stepping back, one can see that there is a three-level nesting of parallelism in the simple algorithm described above. At the top level is the field of removed nodes, the `nodes-to-expand`. The gamma node expansion operator is called elementwise on this field. Each individual invocation of the gamma operator produces several daughter nodes; in fact, it produces a field of daughter nodes. Gamma was responsible for heuristically rating these successor nodes, and it does so in parallel. Thus, the gamma operator, which itself was called elementwise, internally calls the heuristic rating function elementwise on its output. Interestingly enough, in the case of the 8-puzzle, the heuristic function itself uses yet another level of elementwise computation.

Each of the 8 tiles in a node elementwise performs the following calculation to calculate its Manhattan distance metric from two elementwise variables:

```
(+ (abs (- my-x-coordinate my-x-coordinate-in-solution))
   (abs (- my-y-coordinate my-y-coordinate-in-solution)))
```

The sequence score can be implemented by using `<-` to obtain the successor tile in the next square over, and then `elwise` to calculate each tile's contribution to the sequence score:

```
(if (and successor-tile              ;; if there is a successor
         (< successor-tile my-tile)) ;; tile, 2 points if
    2                                ;; in wrong place
    0)                               ;; otherwise 0 points
```

The sequence score is elementwise added to the Manhattan distance, `vref` is used to sum the scores over the squares, and 1 is added if the center is occupied.

If one assumes that R nodes are removed at each A* step, and each produces D daughter nodes, parallel A* for the 8-puzzle is able to productively apply $R * D * 8$ paralation sites (processors) to the problem. The program itself is not complicated by this nested parallelism; in fact, it is simplified by it! The heuristic was described above and is written in a natural style (it is omitted for the sake of brevity). The heuristic is written to solve the rating problem for a single node containing 8 tiles; it is oblivious to the fact that it will be called in parallel for many nodes. The gamma operator accepts a single node, produces several successors in parallel, and then elementwise calls the heuristic on those successors. That is a natural implementation of node expansion. In fact, both a `gamma-operator` and the rating heuristic can be written by taking their serial counterparts and turning their loops into invocations of `elwise` (and array reference into `<-`). Naturally, although the gamma operator is written to expand a single node, `parallel-a*` can and does call it elementwise on each of the removed nodes.

If one were to attempt to describe a parallel A* in a model that did not allow the nesting of parallel constructs, one of two things would happen. The most likely is that a single level of parallelism would be chosen as the most fruitful and the others abandoned. In this case, the removed nodes would be expanded in parallel and the remaining parallelism would be serialized unnecessarily. Alternatively, the programmer would have to implement a mini-language that does accommodate nested parallelism on top of the existing language and then would use that mini-language to implement A*.

Applicability of Parallel A*

One can imagine that in some search space the rating heuristic might be so accurate that a serial A* implementation would be able to dive down directly toward the solution. The very first node on `open` would always be on a path to the best goal node, so no time would be wasted exploring paths that look better at first than they actually turn out to be. In such a space, the work that is performed by the "extra" processors in a parallel implementation is not really necessary. However, whenever state-space search is applicable to a problem, the heuristic is usually less precise and is often "fooled" (when a heuristic cannot be fooled, it is usually called an algorithm!). Parallelism will speed up the search in such a space.

4.2.3   Machine-Tied Models Do Not Naturally Accommodate Problem Structure

Machines normally have a fixed number of physical processors, arranged into some sort of fixed hierarchy (for example, all processors may be the same, or some may be more powerful than others). Problems, however, can be quite dynamic in their need for processing power and in their structure. A model that is tied to a particular architecture can inherit the static nature of hardware and restrict the programmer.

For example, imagine an associative memory programming model designed for SIMD machines, such as the one discussed in [Pot87]. A program might consist of repeated cycles of broadcasting both a data pattern to be matched and a subprogram to be executed by the processors that found a match. But what language is used for writing the subprograms? If they cannot be written in the full associative language, the model cannot naturally accommodate the hierarchical structure of problems—it is tied to the one-level nature of SIMD hardware. That is, nested parallelism is not readily accessible in a language that is not recursively embedded in itself, because such a language cannot concisely express the parallel execution of parallel tasks. It is important to note that permitting the programmer to nest selection constructs, such as pattern matchers or conditionals, is *not* the same thing as a recursive embedding. Nested selection statements in SIMD languages is usually just a notation for the logical conjunction of several boolean conditionals.

In a language without a self-embedding, program modules cannot be written in a manner oblivious to whether they will be executed in parallel or serially, since modules used in parallel cannot use parallel language constructs themselves. Thus, the expected module calling pattern becomes a hidden part of a module's specification, violating the principle of information hiding. Information hiding and hierarchical structure are important tools that can be used to conquer complexity; languages that lack them can allow the details of the problem to overwhelm the programmer.

In addition to hindering dynamic control flow patterns, hardware can also discourage the use of dynamic data structures. For example, consider writing a program that used nested parallelism, such as the A* search program, in a PRAM language that requires the programmer to explicitly assign tasks to processors. A large part of the user's application program would actually consist of a storage allocator, a tool whose functions are trivially performed by the primitives of the paralation model. Flat models are just as powerful as self-embedded models. After all, computer architectures are flat, yet they can be used to implement the self-embedded paralation model. The point is that flat models make it difficult to solve problems in a hierarchical manner, and hierarchical decomposition is perhaps the best tool programmers have for attacking and simplifying complexity, complexity that might otherwise be overwhelming.

4.2.4 Inherited Locality

Elementwise locality promises that the field values at a particular paralation site are near each other. Inherited locality indicates that this is true for any kind of field values, including numbers, structures, and even fields. For example, consider the following code:

```
(setq p '#F(A B C))
(setq sub-p (elwise (p) (make-paralation 10)))
   ⇒ #F(#F(0 1 ... 9) #F(0 1 ... 9) #F(0 1 ... 9))
```

Inherited locality means that each of the lettered sites A-C would be near the storage used to represent the elements of the corresponding 10 long subfield. Thus, the user might picture the locality relationship as follows:

| A, #F(0 1 ... 9) | B, #F(0 1 ... 9) | C, #F(0 1 ... 9) |

Inherited locality is given that name because each object inherits the locality properties of the object that created it, along with any finer substructure that it itself contains. Another name for the same phenomenon might be "contagious locality," although that term does not capture the unidirectionality of the creator/created relationship. As a result of inherited locality, objects that create fields can easily communicate with the elements of those fields. The base case is when the user directly executes a `make-paralation`; the elements of the returned index field can easily and efficiently be accessed with `elt` or `vref`.

Inherited locality is a consequence of the elementwise locality of the paralation model interacting with the allocation of fields during nested parallel execution. Logically, it should have been discussed in Section 2.2. Pedagogically, it is more appropriate to discuss it here, after both elementwise evaluation and nested invocations of elementwise evaluation have been introduced.

Inherited locality takes place in both shaped and unshaped paralations. Returning to the alphabet soup analogy of Section 2.2, one might imagine that some of the noodles floating in a soup actually contain miniature soup bowls of their own, in which miniature noodles are floating.

4.3 Programming Style

This section describes two programming styles using serial examples and briefly describes how the paralation model is compatible with them. The next chapter demonstrates this compatibility in more detail with a programming example based on Quicksort.

```
procedure up-x-over-y(x,y : integer);
 begin
  up(x);
  over(y);
  writeln('total distance moved was ', sqrt(x*x + y*y))
 end;

procedure up(var length : integer);
 var i : integer;
 begin
  for i := 1 to length do
    up1;
 end;

procedure over(var length : integer);
 begin
  while length > 0 do
   begin
    over1;
    length := length - 1;
   end;
 end;
```

Figure 4.2: Accidental side effecting in contrived Pascal

Many popular serial computer languages permit the use of side effects upon data structures. A side effect occurs when a variable contains a value and that value is changed. This imperative operation reflects a corresponding basic operation in which a von Neumann processor modifies the contents of a particular address in its memory. Side effects have the unfortunate property that they can hinder modular programming, because modules that have no explicit interface can communicate by side effecting variables or memory space that they share. Often, the result is a hard-to-find bug. Each module expects to have private use of the variable and is "surprised" when its value is unexpectedly changed by the other module. Obviously, programmers can write clear and correct programs that use side effects. The example in the next section has been chosen to illustrate some of the pitfalls that lie in wait for the programmer who uses side effects, not to criticize the careful use of the imperative style.

4.3.1 Side Effecting Example

Consider the contrived Pascal example in Figure 4.2. The main procedure, up-x-over-y, takes two integers x and y as arguments and causes some sort of robotic arm to move up by x and over by y. Finally, it calculates and prints out the total distance moved. It performs the movement by calling procedure up.

The up procedure simply calls up1, x times. It accepts its argument x by reference, not by value. This means that instead of giving the procedure a copy of the value of x, Pascal gives it a pointer to the memory location of x; length points to the same storage as x. In this simple example, there is no obvious motivation for the programmer to do this. However, when a parameter is a large value, such as an array or a dynamic memory structure, reference parameters are often used for efficiency: Pascal passes a small pointer rather than copying a large structure. The programmer's quest for efficiency causes no problems in procedure up, but procedure over is a different matter. The author of over uses its length variable as a counter, moving the robotic arm over1 and decrementing length until it contains zero. This, of course, sets y's value to zero, so that up-x-over-y prints out an incorrect estimate of the total distance moved.

4.3.2 Applicative Style

A functional approach to the same problem would not store and restore information in variables but would simply direct information flow through function calling. It is impossible for the same type of unexpected interaction to occur between the functions of a functional program because they can communicate only by the values that they explicitly supply as arguments and the values that they explicitly return as results. A true functional language does not have a general assignment operator in it; the example in Figure 4.3 is written in a functional subset of LISP. (Pascal is inappropriate because of its lack of a functional, value-returning if.)

The main advantage of the side effecting, imperative style comes from its obvious and close ties to hardware: side effecting programs can be extremely efficient. It seems that the functional method is inefficient, because in order to slightly modify a large structure like an array, one must create an entirely new structure; there is no way to side effect the original. The inefficiency inherent in modifying large structures can be crucial to an application. Consider a functional database program that would be forced to copy its entire database in order to change one piece of data in it! Of course, researchers are looking into ways of eliminating the problem [AT80]. It has been persuasively argued that functional programs have an advantage over side effecting programs in that they are usually easier to write, verify, and analyze [Ste78]. Finally, if every piece of data has its own processor, copying of data becomes a constant time operation. This partially defuses the efficiency criticism:

```
(defun up-over (x y)
  (sqrt (+ (sqr (up x)) (sqr (over y)))))

;; over is similar to up, and is omitted
(defun up (x)
  (cond ((= 0 x) 0)          ;; if x is zero, return zero
        (t (up1)             ;; otherwise move up 1 units
           (up (1- x))       ;; then move up x-1 more units
           x)))              ;; finally, return distance moved
```

Figure 4.3: Functional version in LISP

copying an entire database may not be entirely infeasible.

4.3.3   Language's Influence on Style

Both of these programming styles have their advocates. Neither style is clearly
superior; both have coexisted for years. In some ways, the side effecting Pascal
example is a ludicrously bad example. No advocate of the imperative style would
feel a desire to write code like that; the issue of the efficiency of copying a value
of constant size versus passing it by reference would be instantly categorized as
irrelevant in comparison with the potential problems of that approach. But at one
time such a blatantly low-level style was common practice, and the facilities of some
older programming languages can subtly encourage such a bad style. Modern serial
languages, such as Ada, provide facilities that fully accommodate both styles.

Unfortunately, many parallel languages forcibly encourage the programmer to
continually side effect data contained in parallel structures. For example, although
Pascal permits the dynamic creation of arrays, Parallel Pascal [Pot85] does not permit the dynamic creation of parallel arrays. This makes it difficult for a function to
return a fresh parallel data structure—the programmer must implement a dynamic
storage allocator. Because of the static nature of Fortran, most parallel languages
that build upon Fortran do not accommodate dynamic creation of parallel arrays.
Even a language based upon LISP, which alone can be used in a functional manner,
can leave out important facilities. For example, the *Lisp language [Thi86b] does
not perform any parallel garbage collection. As a result, a dynamic parallel data
structure (that is, one that persists outside of the scope in which it was created)
is never automatically deallocated. It turns out to be easier to acknowledge this
limitation by creating and using a few permanent data structures in a side effecting
style rather than to attempt to use a functional style and become bogged down in
the task of explicitly deallocating the intermediate data structures (or running out

of memory in the middle of a computation).

Thus, parallel languages seem to be recapitulating the history of the serial languages, going though the same interim stages, concerns, and shortcomings. For example, early serial programs had to know exactly how much physical memory was available, but many modern programs make liberal use of virtual memory. One might expect that a similar transformation will occur concerning the visibility to the programmer of the number of processors in a parallel machine and perhaps the precise type of communication interconnections that are directly implemented by hardware.

The paralation model, however, is compatible with base languages of any processing style: `elwise` can be used either for its result or for its side effects. It is neutral on the topic of imperative versus functional programming. That is, with an appropriate base language, programs can be written as tools that accept collections of parallel data and return new computed data, or as tools that modify collections of data with side effects.

4.4   More Principles of Programming

While language design is admittedly an art, there are a number of design principles to which useful conventional programming languages tend to adhere. Some of these principles, many of which have the flavor of Occam's Razor, are described in this section, in order to show that the paralation model is compatible with conventional design principles. Of course, the user does not need to be aware of the principles in order to benefit from the fact that a language adheres to them. The principles were formulated by Bruce MacLennan and are quoted from [Mac83].

- Simplicity: A language should be as small and simple as possible. It should contain the minimum number of concepts with simple rules for their combination.

The paralation model consists of a data structure and three operators. The data structure is the field; the relationship between fields is defined by the concept of a paralation. Parallel calculations are performed by the first operator, elementwise evaluation. Communication is performed by the joint action of the second and third operators, match and move. Thus, communication is syntactically divided into two parts. This separation clarifies the difference between describing a communication pattern and actually using it. The paralation primitives can be used in any combination. Thus, communication can transfer fields, and match and move can be called elementwise. Thus, no rules for permissible combinations have to be memorized. A stark serial example of the simplicity rule can be found by comparing the simple and elegant Algol 60 language with the large and unwieldy PL/I.

- Regularity: Regular rules, without exceptions, are easier to learn, use, describe, and implement.

Fields can contain any type of data. The elementwise evaluation operator may be wrapped around any program code. Match can be applied to any two fields, using any equality predicate. Move can be used with any combining function, mapping, and source data and default fields. This kind of regular generality has proved itself to be extraordinarily useful in the serial world. For example, consider the mathematical expression. It allows any number of variables and operations to be combined in a general fashion. Compare that to the severely limited way in which arithmetic operations can be described in assembly languages, which usually permit a limited set of two operand arithmetic operations to be applied to a pair of processor registers or perhaps to the contents of memory locations.

- Orthogonality: Independent functions should be controlled by independent mechanisms.

The paralation model draws a key distinction between computation and communication. Elementwise evaluation controls computation alone, move without a combining function controls communication, and move with a combining function mixes the two operations. This distinction is important because the costs of using computation and communication can be independently varied in the design space of parallel computers. For example, some parallel computers have powerful processors and weak communications networks. The paralation model does not call out for some sort of ideal, "balanced" computer design [Par86]. An application that does not require a great deal of communication can be described with the paralation primitives in a way that permits it to be used efficiently on a computer with a weak communications network.

A serial example of this principle is found in parameter passing. Parameters can be used to supply values to a procedure, and they also can be used to return values (via side effecting) from a procedure. On the other hand, parameters can be implemented by passing values or by passing pointers to values. Pascal and C mix these two issues, but Ada separates them. The result is that the user specifies how a procedural parameter is to be used, and the compiler is free to use the most efficient of the applicable parameter passing methods.

- Zero-One-Infinity: The only reasonable numbers are zero, one, and infinity.

The paralation model contains three types of locality, loosely corresponding to the order of the number of communications hops (wires) required for communication between two paralation sites. Intrasite locality, or elementwise locality, requires zero hops. Intersite communication within a paralation requires a small number of hops (related, by a slowly increasing function, to the size of the paralation). Finally, interparalation communication can require an unbounded number of hops.

In serial languages, an obvious application of the Zero-One-Infinity principle occurs in the types of arrays that are permitted. One can easily imagine languages with no arrays, languages with one-dimensional arrays, and languages with multidimensional arrays. A language that permits arrays with dimensions of only one, two, or three, however, would violate the principle. Specifically, it requires the user to remember an arbitrary number. Furthermore, it encourages the user to think in a certain multidimensional way but then erects an arbitrary barrier to this type of thinking.

- Preservation of Information: The language should allow the representation of information that the user might know and that the compiler might need.

Through the use of paralations and mappings, the paralation programmer can express the locality information that is crucial to compiling communication-efficient programs. Chapter 8 discusses paralation shape, which allows the programmer to describe precisely the intersite locality pattern in a paralation. For example, the sites of a paralation might be arranged in a grid, a pyramid, or a butterfly.

The serial description of floating point precision is an example of this principle. A description that specifies the precision of a variable in terms of the number of digits that must be represented preserves the user's knowledge in a useful form. A less detailed description, such as the C language's long, or a description in terms of the number of machine words on a particular architecture (for example, double precision), discards useful information in favor of highly specific information that could have been derived from more general preserved information.

- Localized Cost: Users should pay only for what they use; avoid distributed costs.

The algorithm underlying a program that is explicitly written for a shared memory machine may not require shared memory hardware, but that fact is not preserved by the program. In contrast to that, due to its adherence to the preservation of information principle, the paralation model does not require the user to pay for a computer with baroque capabilities not inherently required by the user's application. Similarly, elementwise evaluation does not inherently require communication; a shared memory model that requires communications for elementwise-like operations is assessing a cost for a service that is actually not needed. Such a model necessarily proposes an ideal type of balance between communication and computation hardware for efficient execution. Instead, the ideal balance should be controlled by the user's application code and the various instruction mixes that a compiler might produce from it.

A serial example of the localized cost principle occurs in an iteration construct in which the loop control variables can be modified by the body of the loop. Consider the following loop:

```
j := 1;
n := 10;
for i := 1 to square_root(n) step j * j
 begin
  j := j * 2;
  call_some_procedure;
 end;
```

When a language's semantics allows loop control variables to be modified by a loop's body, compilers for that language are forced to reevaluate loop control statements after each loop iteration, unless the compiler or optimizer can prove that it does not have to reevaluate them. Although most loops do not modify their control variables, every user of the loop construct is forced to pay the price of reevaluation. In the case of the loop above, it is likely that `square_root(n)` will be called once each iteration (because `call_some_procedure` might change the value of `n`). Aside from the cost of unnecessary reevaluation, the inclusion of this sort of construct causes confusion, since it is difficult to tell how many iterations a loop will actually take. Thus, a misguided attempt to give the user extra power and generality can backfire and make a language both less efficient and harder to use.

- Portability: Avoid features that are dependent on a particular machine or a small class of machines.

The paralation model is useful on any machine that contains processors and permits communication between the processors; all parallel machines that I am aware of fall into this class. The model is independent of processor type (MIMD versus SIMD) or network topology. This independence is a natural consequence of the principles of information preservation and localized cost. Almost all modern high-level languages adhere to the portability principle in that they can be efficiently compiled for any von Neumann computer.

- Structure: The static structure of a program should correspond in a simple way with dynamic structure of corresponding computations.

`elwise` is a static, lexical construct. Code that is lexically within an `elwise` is executed in parallel, relative to the paralation of the elementwise variables (which themselves are specified lexically, in the header of the `elwise`). The written form of `elwise` helps a programmer to visualize how a parallel program will execute. A programmer can use the macroscopic perspective, viewing a particular `elwise` as a module, a magic box that performs certain array-like calculations and returns a result. Alternatively, the microscopic perspective allows one to debug `elwise` code as if it were conventional serial code, simply by imagining its execution at a single paralation site. The lack of communication between sites during an `elwise` enforces the correspondence between these simple viewpoints and the possibly complex reality that is visible only to the language implementor.

One serial illustration of this principle arises in structured control flow statements, such as if-then-else conditionals. The importance of structure is reflected in the way programmers use indentation to display the static structure of programs.

- Information Hiding: The language should permit modules designed so that (1) the user has all of the information needed to use the module correctly, and nothing more; (2) the implementor has all of the information needed to implement the module correctly, and nothing more.

The operators of the paralation model permit modules to be written independently, oblivious as to whether they will be used serially or in parallel (elementwise). Conversely, a module can use another module in parallel *without* having to know how that other module operates internally. This, of course, is not true of programming models that are not self-embedded.

The classic serial example of information hiding is ordinary function calling, which passes arguments to a function, treated as a black box, and accepts the returned result. Just as indiscriminate use of serial side effects can pierce the barrier, indiscriminate and incorrect use of elementwise side effects can also pierce the information hiding barrier.

- Labeling: Avoid arbitrary sequences more than a few items long; do not require the user to know the absolute position of an item in a list. Instead, associate a meaningful label with each item and allow the items to occur in any order.

Most parallel models contain some sort of communication operation that is based upon numerical addresses. Implicitly, this requires the programmer to know the absolute (or relative) position of data in a numerical address space. On the other hand, communication in the paralation model makes use of a special object called a mapping. Mappings are created based upon equality between data keys stored in fields; the data can be of any type. The user can match between any appropriate collection of labels. If the labels happen to be numeric, the compiler can detect that and produce code that is just as efficient as code that could be produced from the use of a communication operator that is limited to numerical keys. A serial example of the labeling principle is the case statement, a modern descendant of the computed goto statement.

- Automation: Automate mechanical, tedious, or error-prone activities.

The move operator automates the fan-in and fan-out trees implicit in the use of a mapping, while the `elwise` operator automates the creation of parallel loops and especially of nested parallel loops. Broken trees and fencepost errors are among the bugs that are avoided; simultaneously, the compiler can choose the most appropriate and efficient implementation (for example, general parallel communication, hash tables, indirection through serial pointers, and so on). The same advantages arise from the use of structured looping constructs in serial languages.

- Abstraction: Avoid requiring something to be stated more than once; factor out the recurring pattern.

This principle is embodied by `elwise`. Its parallelism consists of extracting a procedural pattern that can be executed in many places at the same time. The very concept of a procedure or subroutine is itself an illustration of the principle of abstraction. In fact, any high-level language construct can be thought of as a pattern that has been factored into an idiom because of its general utility.

Obviously, the principles are not independent of each other. For example, preserving information is a part of maintaining portability; orthogonality is a part of regularity. Thus, a language that concentrates on adhering to only a few of the principles may benefit from a synergistic effect and end up adhering to the other principles.

4.5 Program Complexity

When evaluating different programs for solving a problem, one often uses running time as a basis of comparison. Running time depends upon many factors, including the particular kind and type of input to the program being timed, the quality of the compiler and target computer, and, of course, the intrinsic time complexity of the algorithm that underlies the program. Normally, running time, either average or worst case, is measured as a function of n, which measures the size of the input problem.

In the theoretical analysis of algorithms, the growth rate of the running time of an algorithm relative to its problem size is recorded in what is known as "big-oh" notation [Knu76, AHU83]. Big-Oh notation allows one to ignore minor constant factors, thus simplifying complexity calculations. For example, instead of saying that a program takes $7.5n + 8$ seconds, one can say that the time complexity of the corresponding algorithm is $O(n)$. The memory space required for program execution can be measured in a similar manner. A transparent language makes it easy to calculate the time and space complexity of a program by examining the text of the programs. If a language is not transparent, the complexity of a program can be measured only by laboriously tracing every detail of its execution.

Complexity notation assumes that a single processor is available and that time is measured by some primitive, basic, *unit-time* operations, such as assignment statements, basic mathematical calculations, and so on. The growth function depends upon precisely how powerful those basic operations are. For example, although a single memory access is often treated as a unit-time operation, in some cases it is necessary to treat it as an operation that requires time that is logarithmic in the number of memory locations that can be addressed. This more detailed approach takes into account the fact that a larger memory asymptotically requires a logarithmically larger word size and a correspondingly deeper memory address decoding tree.

The simplified, constant-time addressing approach is used when the time to decode an address is irrelevant; it assumes that the word size is fixed, as it is in most machines. In the analysis of high-level algorithms (that is, those that do not concentrate on low-level bit-manipulation), the constant view is almost always used. It hides the implementation of large scale memory addressing from the programmer by burying it in the cycle time of the computer, thus greatly simplifying order calculations. It is feasible because memories large enough to accommodate problems of size n are relatively easy to build.

4.5.1   Parallel Complexity

At best, a parallel machine with k processors can divide the running time of a program by the constant k. However, this type of improvement is not reflected in the big-oh notation because k is a constant factor. When discussing the maximal speed of a parallel algorithm, it is more convenient to analyze its execution on a machine where the number of processors grows as the size of the problem grows. For example, one might analyze an algorithm for execution on a target machine with n processors, or even n^2 processors.

Parallel complexity calculations, like their serial counterparts, depend upon the precise operations that are designated as primitives. In general, the same kind of processor operations are designated as primitive. Since the machine-wide memory address decoding circuitry has been replaced by a communications network, however, the choice of a constant-time or logarithmic viewpoint should be reexamined. In particular, one must decide how to measure the cost of communication. Some theorists use a detailed approach, which acknowledges that as communication takes place among more processors in a larger address space, logarithmically more time will be taken. Others use an approach reminiscent of the standard serial approach to memory addressing and designate communication as a basic operation that takes a constant unit amount of time. Of course, models that do not draw a distinction between communication and computation do not have to take a stand on this issue, but such models are inherently less precise and therefore less transparent.

The constant-time communication view hides from the programmer the hard- ware difficulties involved in building a large scale communications network. Currently feasible large communication networks (that is, thousands of nodes) seem to have at most logarithmic connectivity. It therefore seems that the complexity of communication should not be ignored. In fact, a constant time approach squashes locality, an important distinction, into its constant factor; local and global communication both take the same amount of time. This viewpoint is appropriate for shared memory computers that also ignore this distinction.

The preservation of locality distinctions is a feature of the paralation model because it leads to ease of use (clarity), efficiency on any architecture, and transparency. Therefore, the remainder of this work employs the logarithmic point of view. Any choice of viewpoint makes assumptions about the target architecture; logarithmic communication time is simply chosen as a target that can be achieved by feasible hardware. There is no overriding physical reason why some other function, such as $\sqrt{n}$, is not used instead. One can easily change assumptions and calculate the corresponding complexity function without redoing an entire analysis, simply by keeping the communication and computation costs separated when describing an algorithm. Thus, one might say an algorithm takes $O(\log n)$ calculation time on $O(n)$ paralation sites, plus $O(1)$ matches and moves for communication.

4.5.2 Complexity of Paralation Programs

Paralation programs are transparent because their complexity can easily be calculated. The worst case running time of an `elwise` in a paralation of size n is simply the worst case when the body is executed serially at any one of the paralation's sites, assuming n processors are available. The space required is simply the sum of the space required by all of the paralation sites. The complexity of execution at a site is calculated either in the conventional, serial manner, or by recursing on this method if paralation constructs are nested. Finally, the complexity of communication (either match or move) between paralations with a maximum size of n is $O(\log n)$ multiplied by the complexity of the combining function.

The $O(\log n)$ communication metric does not differentiate between mappings that connect two paralations and mappings that connect a paralation to itself because the difference disappears into a constant factor. However, imagine a paralation whose sites are arranged into the shape of a two-dimensional grid. There should be a lower cost for local communications within such a paralation, such as communication to the north, than for a more general communication pattern.

Local communication requires a concept of shape, which is presented in detail in Chapter 8. However, the time complexity implications of shape can be summarized here: A shape has certain built-in mappings that connect nearest-neighbors; when move is used with these mappings, it takes a constant amount time, plus time proportional to the logarithm of the largest number of collisions at a paralation site, to execute.[4]

Of course, this constant time viewpoint assumes that the hardware has sufficient interconnectivity to implement the nearest neighbor connections in constant time. This assumption can be violated. For example, a paralation program running on a computer with a two-dimensional grid network might make use of hypercube-shaped paralations. The grid hardware will take exponentially more time to execute communications in a hypercube-shaped paralation than hypercube hardware would because the diameter of the grid is $\sqrt{n}$ while the diameter of the hypercube is $\log n$.

This communication slowdown is similar to the slowdown that occurs in virtual processing: A machine slows down to simulate a capability for which it is lacking appropriate hardware. If no wire directly connects the implementation of two paralation sites, messages between them are routed over several wires. If not enough processors are available, each processor performs the work of several, and the communication wires of that processor handle the communications leaving that clique of processors. Just as in most cases virtual memory can be ignored when it is not thrashing, virtual processing can be ignored when it is not thrashing (or, more graphically, choking).

The paralation model can be transparent because it allows the user to precisely describe what is to be done, and key aspects of how it is to be done (that is, when to communicate, when to process, locality, and so on). Implicitly parallel models that do not allow the user to describe such details necessarily obscure the cost of programs. For example, a loop unwinding compiler might promise to extract parallelism from an ordinary serial program, but usually there is no simple mental model that indicates which loops the system can or cannot parallelize. The user must understand how the compiler works in minute detail; the system is not transparent. Most users will be unable to calculate the amount of extractable parallelism in a source program without timing its actual execution.

Automated program verifiers can make use of a technique called symbolic execution. Rather than execute a program, they prove theorems about what the result of executing the program must be like. Analogously, it is more reliable, universal, and general to calculate symbolically the cost of using a construct than to measure its cost during an actual execution. For example, a serial loop with n iterations multiplies the cost of its body by n. With a transparent language, a symbolic execution of a program fragment in the mind of the programmer can quickly and easily produce an accurate estimate for its eventual cost during an actual, fully detailed,

---

[4]Simple shapes like grids have mappings with no collisions, but complex shaped paralations can also be created.

program execution. Consider the prime sieve presented earlier in Section 2.8.1:

```
0  (defun find-primes (n)
1    (let* ((sieve (make-paralation n))
2           (candidate-p (elwise (sieve) (if (> sieve 1) t nil)))
3           (prime-p (elwise (sieve) nil)))
4      (do ((next-prime 2 (position t candidate-p)))
5          ((null next-prime)
6           (<- sieve :by (choose prime-p)))
7        (setf (elt prime-p next-prime) t)
8        (elwise (sieve candidate-p)
9          (when (and candidate-p (zerop (mod sieve next-prime)))
10           (setq candidate-p nil))))))
```

Assuming there are n processors, it can be analyzed as follows: Lines 1, 2, and 3 take constant time. The loop of line 4 is executed once for each prime that is in the range $2..n$. According to [HW60, Chapter 22], this is $O(n/logn)$; call that number p. The body, which consists of lines 7–10, takes constant time. The calculation of next-prime, which is performed once for each of the p loop iterations, is performed by a call to position, which is equivalent to a simple vref. Finally, upon exit from the loop, line 6 is executed, which performs a choose and a <-. Therefore, the cost of the whole algorithm is $O(p \times \texttt{computation} + p \times \texttt{vref} + 1 \times \texttt{choose} + 1 \times \texttt{move})$. If all communication operations take logarithmic time, this becomes $O(p \log n)$, or $O(n)$. If communication operations are treated as constant time operations, the algorithm is $O(p)$, or $O(n/\log n)$.

4.6   Conventional Programming Dilemmas

The noise-smoothing problem of Section 1.5.3 points out a dichotomy between efficiency and speed. Efficiency concerns the ratio of operations performed to the minimum number strictly necessary to solve a problem. Clearly, the parallel noise-smoothing algorithm performs many more additions than the serial algorithm, and in some sense these extra additions are unnecessary. On the other hand, speed is based upon the absolute amount of time a computation requires for completion on a given computer with a fixed number of processors. The speed viewpoint indicates that in the time a computation takes place, there is a fixed number of computation cycles available (number of processors multiplied by time). In order to maximize speed, one would like to keep the ratio of number of cycles used to number of cycles available near to 1.0, even if calculations are performed that may not be strictly necessary.

The paralation model is a tool to be used for writing precise programs. It allows one to describe algorithms. However, it does not attempt to discover its own optimal algorithms; the paralation model does not promise to do the work of the programmer. Given a certain fixed number of processors, different algorithms might be appropriate (either optimizing efficiency or speed) for different amounts or kinds of input. In fact, this is commonly the case in program libraries. For example, consider parallel operations on large sparse matrixes. Such operations can certainly be performed in an inefficient manner by applying a naive or dense matrix algorithm along with support from virtual processor facility. Of course, most of the virtual processors will manipulate zeroes, which is a waste of computational resources. This is not a shortcoming of the model; this is a fact of life that was also true in the serial world. Another example can be found in sorting. The utility of a particular serial sorting algorithm depends upon the number and initial order of items to be sorted and upon the precise nature of a machine's memory hierarchy (for example, size of memory, disk, and tape, paging strategy, etc). Thus, bubble sort is appropriate for sorting lists that are almost in order, quicksort is appropriate for larger jobs, and external sorting techniques are applicable for extremely large jobs.

The need to change algorithms as one begins to make use of lower levels of the memory hierarchy is reminiscent of the need to change from naive matrix algorithms to sparse algorithms when extensive (but unnecessary) use is made of the virtual processing "hierarchy." When different kinds of input require different algorithms, both paralation and serial programmers must describe the various algorithms and then write code to select an appropriate algorithm for any given input.

Similarly, knowledge of the precise nature of the communication network, the physical processors, and the virtual processor facility that underlie an implementation of a paralation language may push a programmer toward solving a problem using one or another parallel algorithm. The paralation *notation* is architecture-independent. However, particular *uses* of that notation may reflect a programmer's expectations about the target machine. It has been suggested [Sny87] that a compiler for any type of architecture might be able to make use of type declarations in which a programmer declares that a particular segment of a program has been written with certain target characteristics in mind. Thus, when a compiler for a SIMD machine encounters a procedure that was written for a MIMD machine and declared as such, it might choose to emulate a MIMD machine rather than compile the code conventionally and make inefficient use (that is, keep a low percentage busy) of the SIMD processors.

4.7 Other Base Languages: C Example

In order to clarify which of the concepts described in this book are paralation concepts and which are artifacts of the LISP-based notation, this section presents a brief description of a C-based paralation language.[5] It demonstrates that although the paralation model has a strict world view about parallel concepts, it has no commitment to other orthogonal language concepts. Portions of a PARALATION C simulator have been implemented using an object-oriented dialect of C called C++ as a base language. Since PARALATION C is a language under development, it is likely that further changes and evolution will take place before the implementation is completed.

4.7.1   Data Structures

First, a family of `field` types are added to the base language. `field(t)` is a type that can contain a field of objects of type `t`. For example, the following declares a variable that can contain type `field(int)` (without allocating any space for the field's contents):

```
field(int) f;
```

Fields in PARALATION C share many of the properties of C arrays, such as the way that individual elements are addressed via brackets. In addition, conventional C pointer arithmetic works with `field`s as well, returning pointers to arrays that share storage with the field. Thus, `f[0]` refers to the first element of the field `f`, but `(f+1)[0]` refers to the second element of `f`. As with PARALATION LISP, fields in PARALATION C are unshaped by default. No C-based shape facility has yet been defined, but it is expected that one that accommodates a more static description of shape than that of the LISP-based version will be created, in keeping with the static nature of C.

The familiar `make_paralation` function is available and returns the index field of a new paralation:

```
/* allocate a paralation, and print its index values */
field(int) p = make_paralation(10);
int i;
for(i = 0; i < 10; i++)
  printf("%d ", p[i]);
```

Of course, the index field of any field's paralation can be retrieved with the `index` function.

4.7.2   Elementwise Evaluation

As in PARALATION LISP, `elwise` begins with a number of variable names that specify the elementwise variables. However, because C is statement-oriented, the

---

[5]The syntax for PARALATION C was developed with the help of Sam Kendall.

elwise construct of PARALATION C is a statement, and therefore does not return a new field. The user of elwise can return parallel results only by side effecting an input field. A different means must therefore be provided for creating a new field in an old paralation. The function make_field_like returns a new field in the same paralation as its input field:

```
field(int) p = make_paralation(10);
field(int) x = make_field_like(p);
/* make x contain the values in p, with 1 added to each */
elwise(int p,x) /* within the body, p and x are integers */
  {
  x = p + 1;
  }
```

The full C declaration syntax is available for use in the declaration of the elementwise variables. For example, an elwise can use initializers:

```
elwise(int x = some_field;
       int y = index(some_field))
  {
  .....body.....
  }
```

4.7.3 Match

The match function in PARALATION C is the same as that of PARALATION LISP, except that it also accepts a type: the type of the elements of the fields being matched. match returns a mapping, which is a new type that has been added to the C base language:

```
mapping map = match(int)(x,y);
```

4.7.4 Move

The move function of PARALATION C also accepts a type, the type of the source field's elements. If the optional default field is supplied, it must have the same element type.

```
field(int) x, y, data_field, result;
.....
mapping map = match(int)(x,y);
result = move(int)(data_field, mapping, combiner, default_field);
```

4.7.5   Storage Allocation

In PARALATION C, the user is totally responsible for deallocating all static fields and
mappings with the functions `delete_field(f)` and `delete_mapping(m)`; automatic
(that is, dynamic or stack) objects are properly deallocated upon exit from their
lexical scope of definition. This matches the flavor of C, which has no built-in
garbage collector.

4.7.6   Sieve Programming Example

This section contains a translation of the PARALATION LISP sieve algorithm from
Section 2.8.1 into PARALATION C.

```
field(int) find_primes(n)
int n;
{
/* variable and storage allocation */
field(int) sieve = make_paralation(n);
field(int) candidate_p = make_field_like(sieve);
field(int) prime_p = make_field_like(sieve);
mapping map;
field(int) result;
int next_prime;

elwise(int sieve, candidate_p)
  {
  if (sieve > 1)
    candidate_p = 1
  else
    candidate_p = 0;
  }
elwise(int prime_p) prime_p = 0;
for(next_prime = 2;
    next_prime == NULL;
    next_prime = position(1,candidate_p))
  {
  prime_p[next_prime] = 1;
  elwise(int sieve, candidate_p)
    {
    if ((candidate_p == 1) && ((sieve % next_prime) == 0))
      candidate_p = 0;
    }
  }
map = choose(prime_p);
```

```
result = move(int)(sieve, map);
delete_mapping(map);
return(result);
}
```

The execution of this version of find_primes is almost identical to that of the
LISP version, except that more detail is paid to precisely how fields and mappings
are allocated and deallocated. The algorithm begins by allocating space for the field
containing the sieve, along with predicate fields that indicate whether each sieve
number is a candidate for primality or has been verified as a prime. Elementwise,
the two predicate fields are initialized (0 represents false or nil, 1 represents true).

The main loop consists of finding the next prime, checking it off as prime, and
killing off all of its (non-prime) multiples. Finally, the prime numbers are culled
with choose, the space for the choose mapping is deallocated, and the result is
returned.

The C notation described in this section has a number of shortcomings. Some
of these are due to a lack of experimentation with a full implementation of this
notation; others are due to the low-level flavor of C. The remaining chapters use
the high-level LISP notation exclusively.

Chapter 5

Ease of Use

5.1 Pragmatics

The *syntax* of a language describes the form in which its constructs appear. Since the paralation model adds only three new constructs to an already defined serial base language, it is easy to define the syntax of a paralation language. When a LISP is used as the base language, the task becomes almost trivial, since LISP constructs are almost always written as lists. The *semantics* of a language defines the underlying meaning of its constructs. Chapter 2 addresses this topic informally; Chapter 6 addresses it more formally. Everything that remains to be discussed can be grouped into *pragmatics*, which deals with the practical use of a language's constructs. Pragmatics covers nebulous but important issues, such as programming style. What is the purpose of a particular programming construct and how do most programmers use it? Why not use alternative constructs that can perform the same task? This chapter presents a number of programming examples in order to demonstrate the pragmatics of PARALATION LISP and to support the ease of use claim for the paralation model.

5.2 Prime Number Generators

Section 2.8.1 included a program that generated the prime numbers between 2 and n by using the sieve of Eratosthenes and $O(n)$ paralation sites. This section presents another algorithm for generating prime numbers that uses $n^2/2$ paralation sites, or processors, to do its work.

The algorithm, in Figure 5.1, works by recognizing that a prime number p is divisible by exactly two numbers in the range $1..p$. Therefore, a number can be

```
(defun find-primes-divisors (n)
  (let* ((p (make-paralation (1- n)))
         (possible-vals (elwise (p) (+ 2 p)))
         (num-divisors-equal-two-p
           (elwise (possible-vals)
             (= 2
                (count-num-divisors possible-vals)))))
    (<- possible-vals :by (choose num-divisors-equal-two-p))))

(defun count-num-divisors (x)
  (let ((my-possible-divisors (make-paralation x)))
    (vref (elwise (my-possible-divisors)
            (if (zerop (mod x (1+ my-possible-divisors)))
                1
                0))
          :with #'+)))
```

Figure 5.1: Divisor method for generating prime numbers

checked for primality by calling a procedure to count how many divisors it has and then checking if the count is equal to two. Of course, many candidate numbers can be checked for primality in parallel.

The second function, count-num-divisors, accepts a number x and returns a count of how many divisors it has. It begins by generating a field containing the numbers in $0..(x-1)$, which, of course, is the index field of a paralation x long. Elementwise, each of these numbers plus 1 (to shift the range to $1..x$) is tested as a divisor for x, resulting in a field that contains 1 for successful divisors and zero elsewhere. A vref is used to sum these, and the result is returned as the count. Thus, $O(n)$ paralation sites are used to count the divisors of a single number.

The first function begins by generating an index field, p, for a paralation $n-1$ long; the field therefore contains the numbers $0..(n-2)$. By adding 2 to each of these numbers, the function generates the list of prime candidates that are less than or equal to n: the numbers in $2..n$. Next, the count-num-divisors function is called elementwise for each prime candidate, and the result is compared to the number 2. The field num-divisors-equal-two-p contains the result (true or false) of this comparison. Finally, a choose is performed to select from the possible-vals the ones that are prime.

This prime number function makes use of the same kind of nested, modular parallelism as the A* algorithm of Section 4.2.2. Candidates are each separately tested for primality, in parallel. The test for primality is itself a function that uses parallelism. However, the prime number algorithm as a whole is performing unnecessary work: when an $O(n)$ site algorithm like the sieve of Eratosthenes is available, why bother with an $O(n^2)$ algorithm? One reason might be that a surplus of processors is available, and the extra processors should be used since the $O(n^2)$ algorithm is much faster than the $O(n)$ algorithm ($O(\log n)$ time instead of O(number of primes in $2..n$)). This type of tradeoff between space and speed is familiar in the serial world; paralation sites are simply active, rather than passive, memory spaces.

The paralation model is expressive in that it allows one to describe formally many possible algorithms for a particular task. It accommodates the expression of inefficient algorithms as well as efficient ones. For example, `count-num-divisors` is inefficient in that it tests all numbers in $1..x$ as possible divisors. If it only tested numbers below the $\sqrt{x}$ (that is, if the argument to `make-paralation` were changed to `(ceiling (sqrt x))`), the number of sites used by `find-primes-divisors` would drop from $n^2/2$ to approximately $2n \lceil \sqrt{n} \rceil /3$.

Because of its transparency, the paralation model keeps the programmer informed as to the order of complexity of an algorithm; the programmer is responsible for making use of that information. As is the case with serial languages, paralation languages do not take care of the problem of algorithm design; the model does not do the programmer's work for him. As a tool, however, it can make that work easier.

5.3 More Library Functions

This section presents a number of library functions; they are used to construct a parallel version of quicksort in the next section.

5.3.1 Library Function: Collapse

Like `choose`, `collapse` accepts a field and returns a mapping. While `choose` merely counts how many values in its input were true, `collapse` counts how many *different* kinds of values there are in a field, according to an equality predicate. It then creates a new paralation, with precisely that many sites, and returns a mapping connecting each site of the input to an appropriate site in the output. If two values in the field being collapsed are equal, they are mapped to the same site. Thus, `collapse` performs a histogram-like function. For example, suppose there are two fields in a paralation five elements long. One contains symbols, the other contains numbers. The following code sets up two such fields and then performs several moves according to a collapse mapping:

```
(setq p (make-paralation 5))
(setq name (elwise (p) (elt '(a a d a b) p)))
(setq value (elwise (p) (elt '(9 1 4 3 7) p)))
(setq map (collapse name))

(<- value :with #'+ :by map)          ;; Add up values for each name
  => #F(13 4 7)
(<- (elwise (value) 1)                ;; Take a histogram
    :with #'+ :by map)
  => #F(3 1 1)                        ;; 3 A's, 1 D, 1 B
(<- name :with #'arb :by map)         ;; Transfer names
  => #F(A D B)
(<- (elwise (value) (list value))     ;; Collect values into a list per name
    :with #'append :by map)
  => #F((9 1 3) (4) (7))
```

The first of the `<-`'s sums the numbers associated with each distinct letter. The second sums a 1 for each letter, thus creating a histogram describing the number of times each letter occurred. The third `<-` creates a field containing the letter that each site of the destination represents. The collapse mapping simply causes all keys K to rush toward the single site in charge of K's; the `#'arb` combining function, introduced in Section 2.4.1, simply chooses any one of the identical colliding keys. The fourth move appends all the values that arrive at a site into a list of numbers. Note that the values being sent (the contents of the source data field) are not numbers; they are singleton lists, created elementwise, and each contains a single number. The combining function appends these lists to collect the values.

To describe `collapse` more precisely, `collapse` returns a mapping that connects each site of its input field's paralation to the site of a new paralation that represents the same key value. The order of assignment is based on the index ordering of the input field. All sites of the paralation that contain the nth (zero-based) distinct value in the input are mapped to (collide at) the site of the newly created paralation whose index value is n. The purpose of `collapse` is to allow the user to easily obtain summary information about the contents of fields. Section 6.3.1 defines the semantics of `collapse` in terms of the paralation primitives.

5.3.2   Library Function: Collect

The fourth `<-` in the example above, the one that appended the arriving values into a list of numbers, turns out to be generally useful. Guy Blelloch has abstracted it into a library function called `collect`. Unlike the `<-` example, `collect` collects colliding values into a subfield of values rather than a sublist. It works just like `<-` of a group of singletons, with three differences. The first is that `collect` does not

```
(defun collect (field &key by)
  ;; set to-key to the mapping's destination key field:
  (let ((to-key (mapping-to-key by)))
    (<- (elwise (field)
          (make-sequence 'field 1 :initial-element field))
        :with #'field-append-2
        :by by
        :default (elwise (to-key) (make-paralation 0)))))))
```

Figure 5.2: An implementation of `collect`

accept a combining function, since it knows it must concatenate colliding values. The second is that `collect` automatically encapsulates the source data field's values in singleton `fields` during the transfer, so the user does not have to prepare a special field of singletons. The final difference is that `collect` does not accept a default value, for if no values arrive at a site, the result should be a collection of no values, a field in a paralation of length 0. Thus, `collect`'s only arguments are a field and a mapping. The following example applies `collect` to the `map` and `values` of the previous example.

```
(collect value :by map)
  ⇒ #F(#F(9 1 3) #F(4) #F(7))
```

The `collect` function can easily be implemented as is shown in Figure 5.2.

`make-sequence` is a built-in COMMON LISP function that can build sequences of any type and initialize them. A user who was not familiar with it might have replaced the call to `make-sequence` the following more verbose code:

```
(let ((singleton (make-paralation 1)))
  (elwise (singleton) field))
```

The code for `collect` makes use of a new combiner called `field-append-2`. It takes two fields and returns a new field that contains the contents of both concatenated together into a single field:

```
(field-append-2 (make-paralation 3) (make-paralation 2))
  ⇒ #F(0 1 2 0 1)
```

One simple way to define `field-append`, shown in Figure 5.3, would be to use COMMON LISP's built-in sequence concatenation function. (In the current implementation of PARALATION LISP, sequence functions run in parallel when their sequence arguments are all fields.)

```
(defun field-append-2 (field1 field2)
  (concatenate 'field field1 field2))
```

Figure 5.3: A simple implementation of `field-append-2`

A more verbose way to define `field-append-2` would do the work of copying and concatenating explicitly. The explicit method begins by measuring the length of the two input fields and creating a new paralation long enough to hold their concatenation:

```
(defun field-append-2 (field1 field2)
  (let* ((size1 (length field1))
         (total-size (+ size1 (length field2)))
         (p (make-paralation total-size))
         (no-data (elwise (p) (cons :no-data nil)))
         (from-field1 (<- field1 :default no-data
                          :by (match p (index field1))))
         (from-field2 (<- field2 :default no-data
                          :by (match (elwise (p)
                                       (- p size1))
                               (index field2)))))
    (elwise (from-field1 from-field2 no-data)
       (if (eql from-field1 no-data)
           from-field2
           from-field1))))
```

Data from the first, `field1`, is moved over into `from-field1` in the new para-lation; `field2` is moved over into `from-field2`. The mappings used to move the data assure that they arrive at the correct location (that is, `field1` data is left-justified; `field2` data is right-justified). A special flag, `no-data`, is used as filler in both cases. Finally, an elementwise calculation calculates a field that splices `from-field1` and `from-field2` together into the final, concatenated result.

5.3.3   Library Function: Expand

`expand` takes a field of subfields and returns a field containing the concatenation of the contents of the subfields. For example:

```
(expand '#F(#F(A B) #F(C) #F() #F(3 2 9 0)))
   ⇒ #F(A B C 3 2 9 0)
```

`expand` is defined in Figure 5.4.

```
(defun expand (field)
  (vref field :with #'field-append-2
               :else (make-paralation 0)))
```

Figure 5.4: An implementation of expand

5.3.4   Library Function: Fork

fork is a macro that takes a number of LISP expressions. It causes a new paralation
to be created, with one site for each of the expressions. Each of those sites computes
the value of the corresponding expression. Thus, fork is a syntactic sugar that
describes calculations that are traditionally thought of as MIMD in nature. It does
its work by using elwise in an appropriate manner. For example,

```
(fork
   (calculate-this 34 x y z)
   (calculate-that a b)
   (calculate-me))
```

might expand into the following code:

```
(let ((temp (make-paralation 3)))
  (elwise (temp)
    (case temp
      (0 (calculate-this 34 x y z))
      (1 (calculate-that a b))
      (2 (calculate-me)))))
```

Thus, in this case, fork returns a field in a three long paralation that contains
the results of executing the three forked expressions. fork is useful for expressing
the parallel execution of a number of tasks that do not share the same form (for
example, different function names, different numbers of arguments). Since fork
expands into an elwise, it shares the same barrier synchronization semantics.

5.4   Quicksort

Often a new approach to a problem can be stated in an inefficient but clearly correct
form which can then be optimized. Consider a quicksort. A concise description of
the algorithm might use a functional form, one that recursed on subsequences of
the original sequence, and then merge the sorted subsequences to create a sorted

```
(defun value-count (field)
  (length (<- field :with #'arb :by (collapse field))))

(defun qsort (data predicate)
  (if (> (value-count data) 1)
      (let* ((pivot-value (elt data (random (length data))))
             (side (elwise (data)
                      (if (funcall predicate data pivot-value)
                          0
                          1)))
             (sub-data
               (collect data :by (match (make-paralation 2) side))))
        (expand
          (elwise (sub-data)
            (qsort sub-data predicate))))
      data))
```

Figure 5.5: Functional paralation Quicksort

sequence. An alternative, less clear method would take as arguments boundary
pointers to a shared sequence and would sort it in place using side effects. This
section presents paralation versions of both approaches. The fact that the functional algorithm repeatedly copies subsequences (by using <-) is not as important
a problem as it would be on a serial machine, because copying n items is a constant
time operation with n processors.

5.4.1 Functional Approach

This particular quicksort was written by Guy Blelloch. The qsort code in Figure 5.5
begins by calling a function called value-count to count how many different values
there are in its input. If it turns out that there is only one (or zero) kind of value,
the sort is finished, since a field of identical values certainly is in sorted order! This
is the base case of the algorithm. value-count itself works by collapsing the key
values into a field and then checking the length of that field.

In the general case, not all values are equal, and value-count is larger than 1. A
pivot-value is picked; any element from data will do.[1] Elementwise, each element
of data determines which side of the pivot value it belongs on, according to the

---

[1]A random element is picked because randomizing results in better performance than simply
choosing the first element when the data happens to be in almost-sorted order (which occurs
disproportionately often in practice).

sorting `predicate`. The data is then partitioned, using `collect`, into a field in a paralation two elements long. The first element of that field is a subfield containing the values less than the pivot value; the second is a subfield containing the values greater than or equal to the pivot. Since `collect` obeys the index order of data when it appends it, this is a *stable* partitioning; it does not change the relative order of values that end up in the same partition. For example, if `qsort` was called on `#F(8 5 1 9 20 3 4)` with a `predicate` of `#'<`, and the pivot value was 5, the result of the `collect` would be `#F(#F(1 3 4) #F(8 5 9 20))`.

The partitioned data is stored in `sub-data`. Elementwise in `sub-data`, quicksort can then recursively sort the two subsequences in parallel. Finally, the subfields of `sub-data` must be concatenated together by `expand`, producing the final answer.

Of course, since in this case there are only two subfields to be appended, the general power of `expand` is not really necessary. A user who did not know about `expand` might have used something like the following verbose program fragment, which is based upon COMMON LISP's `concatenate` sequence function. (`concatenate` was used earlier in Section 5.3.2 in the implementation of `field-append-2`, which itself was used to implement `expand`.)

```
(let ((sorted-sub-data
       (elwise (sub-data) (qsort sub-data predicate))))
  (concatenate 'field
               (elt sorted-sub-data 0)
               (elt sorted-sub-data 1)))
```

The functional `qsort` algorithm recurses at most $\log n$ times. Thus, it uses $\Omega(n \log n)$ space, but only $O(n)$ sites are computing at any one time (n sites holding the numbers actively being sorted, plus $O(\log n)$ sites that control the recursion). Therefore, the average execution time is $O(\log^2 n)$ with n processors, compared to $O(n \log n)$ for standard quicksort on a serial machine.

Static versus Dynamic Nested Parallelism

Hierarchical parallelism and problem subdivision can be fixed, as it is when a subroutine calls several other subroutines to help solve a problem. (That was the type of nested parallelism that was exploited in the multiple levels of the A* algorithm.) Subdivision can also be dynamic, however, as it is when a recursive divide-and-conquer algorithm like `qsort` calls itself on a portion of the original problem.

5.4.2   In-Place Quicksort

An in-place sort requires a place to hold the sequence being sorted and a mechanism for exchanging two elements of the sequence. In this implementation, the sequence

```
(defvar *x*)

(defun swapper (p1 p2)
  (let ((swap-temp (elt *x* p1)))
    (setf (elt *x* p1) (elt *x* p2))
    (setf (elt *x* p2) swap-temp)))
```

Figure 5.6: In-place data structure and element swapper

is stored in the global variable `*x*`. Any type of sequence, such as field, list, or array, is an acceptable value for `*x*`. `swapper` is a function that takes two positions (cursors into `*x*`) and swaps their elements in-place. Figure 5.6 contains the code for these support functions.

The following quicksort algorithm, in Figure 5.7, is adapted from [AHU74, page 96]. It accepts as arguments two integers, `lower` and `upper`, which are cursors into `*x*`. They designate (inclusively) the subsequence to be sorted. Thus, if `*x*` were a sequence of length 10, the initial call to the algorithm would be (`qsort-in-place` 0 9).

The algorithm begins by checking to see if there is any work to be done, by checking if the sequence from `lower` to `upper` has a non-zero length. Assuming it does, a pivot value is selected from the subsequence, and, for convenience, it is placed at position `upper` using the `swapper`. Then, a `do` loop is entered in order to perform the work of partitioning. Initially, `i` and `j` point to the entire subsequence, but they are slowly swept inward by the loop, and the contents of `*x*` at `i` and `j` are exchanged when necessary. After a possible cleanup swap of `lower` and `upper`, the partitioning is complete. All `*x*` values in the subsequence `lower..(i-1)` are less than the pivot; those in `i..j` are equal to the pivot; those in `(j+1)..upper` are greater than the pivot.

All that remains to be done is to recursively call `qsort-in-place` on the two unsorted subsequences. Since the subsequences are independent, the two sorts can take place in parallel by performing an elementwise sort in a paralation that has a length of two.

This in-place sort certainly is more confusing than the functional sort. The functional sort was written in about five minutes without any reference materials, and it worked the first time it was run. The `in-place` sort was written with reference to a serial version of the algorithm written in Pascal and took approximately thirty minutes to get working due to a number of errors. Maintaining cursors into `*x*` is an activity that is quite prone to fencepost errors; the functional sort is able to automate that activity by allowing `elwise` to keep track of the length of the

```
(defun qsort-in-place (lower upper predicate)
  (when (> upper lower)
    (let* ((pivot-point
             (+ lower (random (1+ (- upper lower)))))
           (pivot-value (elt *x* pivot-point))
           (i lower)
           (j upper))
      (swapper pivot-point upper)
      (do () ((> i j))  ;; do until i > j
        (do () ((or (< j lower)
                    (funcall predicate
                             (elt *x* j)
                             pivot-value)))
          (decf j))  ;; decrement j
        (do () ((or (> i upper)
                    (not (funcall predicate
                                  (elt *x* i)
                                  pivot-value))))
          (incf i)) ;; increment i
        (when (< i j)
          (swapper i j)
          (incf i)
          (decf j)))
      (when (= i lower)
        (swapper lower upper)
        (incf i)
        (incf j))
      (fork
        (qsort-in-place lower (1- i) predicate)
        (qsort-in-place (1+ j) upper predicate)))))
```

Figure 5.7: In-place paralation quicksort

various subsequences. In addition, the in-place algorithm is harder to verify, at least intuitively. Perhaps the reader has already wondered if all of the bugs in the in-place algorithm have been removed. On the other hand, it seems clear that there are no bugs lurking in the simpler functional version.

`qsort-in-place` is able to find parallelism in the recursive call to itself, but it is not able to parallelize the process of partitioning. To parallelize partitioning, one must perform communication, which produces a new subsequence: it is equivalent to copying the data. Certainly, the program might then elementwise side effect the original sequence to contain the new sequence to maintain a semblance of being an in-place sort, but why bother? Conventional compiler technology can detect that the functional `qsort` no longer needs its original sequence after it has passed it to a recursive call and can perform the same optimization. Of course, the optimization is not strictly necessary for efficiency, since copying a sequence takes constant time. In any case, the paralation primitives permit one to express algorithms in either a functional or a side effecting style. The model, however, makes no promise to reduce the complexity that can arise in side effecting programs.

5.5   I/O: System Paralations

The paralation model can make effective use of parallel peripherals. The peripheral is simply represented by a special system paralation. A peripheral might present input to a program in the form of a field full of values. Thus, a frame grabber that digitizes pictures can return a field of pixel brightnesses.

```
(defun describe-picture ()
  (let ((current-picture (get-frame-grabber-data)))
    (if (= 0 (vref current-picture :with #'+))
        (print "the picture is all black")
        (print "the picture is not all black"))))
```

This would accommodate any degree of parallelism or bandwidth in the I/O device. For example, the frame grabber might be linked to the computer by a slow serial link, but that link could be upgraded to a link that quickly transfers all pixel values in parallel without changing the paralation programs that use it. The principle is the same one that allows paralation programs to run on computers with any number of processors: it is easier to serialize parallelism that is explicitly described than it is to detect parallelism in an inherently serial program.

Output to a paralation I/O device can take place in two ways. A device like a frame buffer can be represented as a field of values that a program can write into using elementwise side effects:

```
(defun blacken-the-screen ()
  (elwise (*special-frame-buffer-output-field*)
    (setq *special-frame-buffer-output-field* 0)))
```

Alternatively, a function can be provided that takes a point and a color to set it to. The function can be called `elementwise` in any paralation to modify points in parallel. This approach allows the user to ignore locality:

```
(defun blacken-the-screen ()
  (elwise ((i (make-paralation *num-pixels*)))
    (set-point i 0)))
```

On the other hand, a functional approach might be used in which one passes a field of output values to an output function. Of course, the field must be in the frame buffer's paralation:

```
(defun blacken-the-screen ()
  (let ((data (elwise (*frame-buffer-index-field*)
                0)))
    (frame-buffer-output-function data)))
```

As is often the case with functional data structures, it is difficult to change a small part of the screen without first copying the whole screen; side effecting methods for dealing with parallel I/O devices are normally more appropriate.

5.5.1   Line Drawing

One simple program that could make use of a parallel frame buffer would accept a field containing pairs of points and would then draw the lines (really line segments) defined by those points on a screen. Given a pair of line endpoints, there are many possible algorithms for selecting which screen pixels should be turned on. The algorithm used here, which is based upon code written by Guy Blelloch, is one of the simplest. It does not attempt to draw bushy, filled-in lines, to maintain constant density along the lines it draws, or to perform any kind of anti-aliasing. It simply turns on the pixels that lie on the line between two points.

The algorithm begins by finding out in which dimension a line is longest. Suppose the line is longest in the X dimension, so that it is more horizontal than vertical. Then, for each vertical column of pixels that hits the line, the line travels through either one or two pixels. If there are two, the algorithm picks, in each column, the one that contains the largest portion of the line segment. The appropriate pixel in each column is turned on. This results in a more filled-in line than if a nearly horizontal line were to be intersected with horizontal rows of pixels. Of

course, if the line is more vertical than horizontal, it should be intersected with
horizontal rows of pixels rather than with vertical columns.

The line-drawing program consists of three functions. The first is x-or-y-line-
length, which simply accepts a list of two endpoints and returns the length of the
corresponding line segment's longest dimension. Each endpoint is represented by
a list of two points. Note that this function does not use any of the paralation
operators.

```
(defun x-or-y-line-length (endpoints)
  (let ((p1 (first endpoints))
        (p2 (second endpoints)))
    (max (abs (- (first p1) (first p2)))
         (abs (- (second p1) (second p2))))))
```

The second function, point-location, takes a list of two endpoints and a number, fraction, between 0 and 1. It returns the coordinates of the point on the line
defined by the endpoints, fraction of the way from the first point to the second.

```
(defun point-location (endpoints fraction)
  (let ((p1 (first endpoints))
        (p2 (second endpoints)))
    (list (+ (first p1)
             (round (* fraction (- (first p2) (first p1)))))
          (+ (second p1)
             (round (* fraction (- (second p2) (second p1))))))))
```

line-draw is the main program. It accepts a field of line segment descriptors.
Each descriptor is a pair of endpoints. The function returns a field of points; the
pixel corresponding to each point should be turned on in order to display the line.
Since the function is written in an applicative, functional style, it is helpful to
explain it in two directions: working down toward successive line numbers and
working outward from inner function calls to surrounding code.

The first task is for each line segment to calculate elementwise its length along
its maximum dimension by calling x-or-y-line-length, and then to create a
subparalation 1 longer (fencepost) than that length. This is done in lines 3, 4, and
5 (line 5 uses elwise's binding shorthand). The various points on each line are
calculated by the sites of the line's subparalation.

```
0 (defun line-draw (endpoints)
1    (let ((points
2            (expand
3             (elwise (endpoints)
4               (let ((line-length (x-or-y-line-length endpoints)))
5                 (elwise ((point (make-paralation (1+ line-length))))
6                   (point-location endpoints
7                                   (/ point (float line-length)))))))))))
8      (<- points :with #'arb :by (collapse points :test #'equal)))))
```

After binding `point` to an index field, line 5 causes each line segment to begin elementwise execution in it (still nested within line 3's `elwise`). The index value and the `line-length` are used by each point to calculate a fraction, and `point-location` is then called to calculate the points along each line segment. The result that is returned by lines 3–7 is a field of lines. Each line is a field of points, and each point is a list of two coordinates. Line 2 uses `expand` to flatten this into a field of points. Line 8 applies `collapse` to this field simply to make sure that there are no duplicates.

Example of `line-draw` execution:

```
(line-draw '#F(((0 0) (5 5)) ((4 3) (2 7)) ((4 4) (6 4))))
  ⇒ #F((0 0) (1 1) (2 2) (3 3) (4 4) (5 5)
       (4 3) (3 5) (2 6) (2 7) (5 4) (6 4))
```

The purpose of `line-draw` is to calculate the X-Y coordinates of the points that have to be turned on. The next step in actually drawing lines would be to perform the I/O by turning on the appropriate points in a frame buffer. (This step is not shown here.) A row-major order calculation might be used to transform the X-Y coordinates into index form. Alternatively, the preexisting site-names of a grid-shaped paralation (see Chapter 8) might be used to simplify the transformation into a trivial call to `match`.

5.6 Shortest Path in a Graph

In order to illustrate the use of PARALATION LISP with problems based upon graphs, this section presents a function that calculates the length of the shortest sequence of vertices between two connected points in a graph.

The algorithm to find the shortest distance from A to B, from [Hil85, page 44], is:

1. Label all vertices with plus infinity.

2. Label vertex A with 0.

3. Re-label every vertex, except A, with 1 plus the minimum of its neighbor's
   labels. Repeat this step until the labels stabilize.

4. Terminate. The label of B is the answer.

5.6.1 Graph Representation

The graph is stored in an expanded form in two fields, `from-node` and `to-node`.
The fields are in the same paralation; each site of the paralation represents a single
directional edge of the underlying graph. In the following sample data, the shortest
path from A to D is of length 2, by way of C:

```
(setq graph-index (make-paralation 6))
(setq from-node (elwise (graph-index)
                   (elt '(a a b b c d) graph-index)))
  ⇒ #F(A A B B C D)
(setq to-node (elwise (graph-index)
                   (elt '(b c c a d a) graph-index)))
  ⇒ #F(B C C A D A)
```

This representation is different from that used by Hillis in [Hil85]. Hillis's representation was based on a parallel collection of nodes and their neighbors rather
than on a parallel collection of edges. A paralation representation equivalent to
Hillis's would consist of a paralation with two fields: `from-node` and `neighbors`.
The `neighbors` field would contain a subfield which listed all of the nodes that are
connected to a particular `from-node`. The graph data would then be represented
as follows:

```
(setq graph-index (make-paralation 4))
(setq from-node (elwise (graph-index)
                   (elt '(A B C D) graph-index)))
  ⇒ #F(A B C D)
(setq neighbors (elwise (graph-index)
                   (elt '(#F(b c) #F(c a) #F(d) #F(a)) graph-index)))
  ⇒ #F(#F(B C) #F(C A) #F(D) #F(A))
```

A multi-valued mathematical mapping between elements (that is, from an element to a set of elements) can be handled in these two styles in many parallel
programming models. For example, in SETL [DSSD86] one might have a multi-
valued map (expanded representation) similar to the following set:

```
GRAPH = {(x,y) : x,y are in the graph | x connects to y}
```

The designers of SETL mention in [DSSD86, pages 3–38] that they prefer the expanded representation above to the alternative set-valued map:

```
GRAPH = {(x,n) : x in the graph, n in the power set of graph
              | forall y in n | x connects to y}
```

5.6.2 Path-Length in Paralation Lisp

The paralation shortest-path algorithm presented here uses the expanded graph representation. When a numerical label is assigned to a paralation site, and therefore to an edge, the meaning is that the `from-node` is the labeled distance from the finish, according to the best path computed so far. Although a single graph vertex, such as A, may appear as the `from-node` of several edges, all of its labels will always be identical (move performs concurrent read).

```
(defconstant infinity 999999)

0 (defun path-length (from-node to-node start finish)
1    (let ((label (elwise (from-node)
2                   (if (eql from-node start)
3                       0
4                       infinity)))
5          (old-label (elwise (from-node) 0))
6          (infinities (elwise (from-node) infinity))
7          best-neighbors-label)
8      (let ((map (match from-node to-node)))
9        (do ()
10           ((vref (elwise (old-label label)
11                    (= old-label label))
12                  :with #'and-func))
13          (setq best-neighbors-label
14              (<- label
15                  :by map
16                  :with #'min
17                  :default infinities))
18          (elwise (old-label label best-neighbors-label)
19            (setq old-label label)
20            (setq label (min label
21                             (+ 1 best-neighbors-label))))))
22      (vref (<- label :by (choose (elwise (from-node)
23                                    (eql from-node finish))))
24            :with #'arb)))
```

Lines 1–4 implement steps 1 and 2 of the algorithm by labeling the vertices with the proper initial values. Since the algorithm terminates when labels stabilize, a place to store the labels from the previous iteration is allocated in line 5. Line 6 creates a field that contains `infinity` at each site, and line 7 creates the variable where a neighbor's label can later be stored. Finally, line 8 creates a mapping based on the interconnectivity of the graph. Thus, `path-length` creates a single mapping that captures the connectivity of the graph and then repeatedly reuses it in the label propagation loop.

Line 9 introduces a loop; the body of the loop is lines 13–21. The loop's end test, contained in lines 10–12, is satisfied when the previous iteration of the loop did not change any of the labels. The job of the loop body is to implement step 3 of the algorithm by updating the vertex labels. This begins when the labels are propagated from vertices to their neighbors by lines 13–17. Collisions are resolved with the `min` function. The result is that each vertex receives the minimum value of the labels of the vertices that are connected to it.

Elementwise, each vertex then updates itself: Line 19 saves the current `label` in `old-label` for the loop's end-test (stabilization of the labels). Finally, lines 20–21 calculate the new value of each label according to step 3 of the algorithm. After the labels stabilize and the loop terminates, lines 22–24 calculate the answer by returning the label of `from-node`.

`path-length` can be tested on the sample data presented earlier:

```
(path-length from-node to-node 'a 'd)
  ⇒ 2
```

The successive values of `best-neighbors-label` and `label` that occur during this calculation are as follows (* represents infinity):

```
from-node  #F(A A B B C D)
to-node    #F(B C C A D A)
label      #F(0 0 * * * *)     ;; Start node = A, distance from start = 0

best       #F(* * 0 0 0 *)     ;; B and C are direct neighbors
label      #F(0 0 1 1 1 *)     ;; B and C are now up to date

best       #F(1 1 0 0 0 1)     ;; D is a neighbor of C
label      #F(0 0 1 1 1 2)     ;; D is up to date

best       #F(1 1 0 0 0 1)
label      #F(0 0 1 1 1 2)     ;; labels are stable, terminate
```

If there were no path from A to D, the algorithm would have returned `infinity`.

5.6.3 Possible Mappings

Since `match` is the only function that can actually create a mapping (library functions such as `collapse` and `choose` are built on top of `match`) and the arguments to `match` are simply fields containing keys, only patterns that can arise from an equality-based correspondence between keys can ever be computed. This implies a kind of transitive closure on the arrows in a mapping. For any sites S1 and S2 in a source paralation, and D1 and D2 in a destination paralation, if a mapping connects site S1 to D1, S1 to D2, and S2 to D1, it *must* connect S2 to D2. The reason, of course, is that since both S1 and S2 connect to D1, S1, S2, and D1 must all have the same key K. If S1 connects to D2, D2 must also have key K. Since S2 also has key K, S2 must connect to D2. Because of this transitivity there are far fewer possible mappings than possible arrow patterns.

The example in Section 5.6.1 represented and manipulated a fully general graph, so the transitivity of mappings is not a limitation of the paralation model. There is no concept of an "Illegal Mapping." Rather, `match` is based upon a correspondence between keys, and only certain types of mappings can arise in that context. The idea of arrows between paralation sites was a metaphor that was convenient when discussing the contents of a mapping; to discuss patterns of arrows that do not correspond to paralation mappings is to fracture the metaphor.

Chapter 6

Paralation Semantics: A Formal Description

6.1 Why Formal Semantics?

The semantics of a computer language relate the form of a construct, such as a procedure or a variable name, to its meaning, what is denoted by the presence of the construct in a program. Semantics can be described in many ways. The earliest computer languages were described in paragraphs of informal English, but this approach has several shortcomings. First of all, it is difficult to ascertain that all of the possible ways of using a construct have been covered when a description is simply a collection of paragraphs. Perhaps there is some program that can be formed out of the constructs of the language which produces interactions between constructs whose meaning the informal semantics does not describe. Alternatively, the paragraphs of the semantics may even contradict themselves.

Certainly, it is possible to describe language semantics using English or any other natural language. The definition of Algol 60 serves as a paragon of brevity and clarity. The point is that natural language tends to hinder the attempt to produce precise, all-encompassing, "correct" semantics and that a formal mathematical language is more appropriate for the task. A formal definition of semantics has the additional advantage that, through its rigor, it can help to reveal structural irregularities or deficiencies in a language. Of course, semantics in natural language are invaluable for imparting an intuitive understanding to a language user. Often such understanding is an invaluable aid in the attempt to digest the esoteric notation of a mathematical semantics!

6.1.1   Types of Semantics

Formal semantics consists of assigning a meaning to each construct of a language. Of course, the description of a meaning itself must be written in some language, so semantics can be thought of as a description of how to translate the constructs of a language into the constructs of a target language, such as mathematical notation. It is assumed that the semantics of the target language are fixed and already understood. The differences between the various approaches used for defining semantics involve the target language that is selected and the means used to relate language constructs to their definition in the target language.

One simple type of semantics is called operational semantics. It defines the meaning of a construct by describing precisely what the construct does. In effect, one takes an implementation of a language and indicates that the way that implementation works precisely describes the semantics of the language. Thus, the text of the compiler or interpreter defines the semantics of the input language. The size and language of an operational definition can vary. One can take a huge compiler, written in assembly language, for a new language, and call it an operational semantics. On the other hand, an author can handcraft a small interpreter for a new language, and write the interpreter in a high-level language like LISP or Prolog.

It is easy to understand how operational semantics works. To determine what a certain construct means, one simply types it into a computer and sees what it does! This certainly is more precise than an informal natural language description of semantics. The operational approach can be rather opaque in that it does not necessarily describe how the semantics are arrived at, and it is not necessarily amenable to mathematical proofs about the language or its programs. The reader of an operational definition may have difficulty extracting an abstract, intuitive "meaning" from the definition of language constructs.

In some ways, operational semantics is similar to a behaviorist view of a computer as opposed to a cognitive view: one makes use of the input and output of the semantics without attempting to describe its inner workings. A semantic definition that is small, one whose inner workings necessarily accommodate inspection, would be preferable. Finally, an operational approach illustrates one way that a construct might behave, but it does not illustrate other ways that are also possible and legal (non-determinism), and it does not explicitly illustrate behavior that should not occur.

The denotational approach to semantics works by creating a precise correspondence between language constructs and their meaning. Denotational semantics maps a computer language onto mathematical objects such as sets and functional mappings. Because of the richness of the history behind the target formalism (one could safely say that the structure of mathematical objects has been well-investigated), denotational semantics is both precise *and* amenable to proofs. This is most unlike the operational approach, which allows one to describe semantics using machinery, such as goto statements, that is cumbersome to theorists attempting to prove theorems about programs.

6.1.2 Form of Paralation Lisp Semantics

The semantics for PARALATION LISP are presented via a small operational definition written in COMMON LISP. Because of the ties between LISP and the lambda calculus, one can think of this definition as drawing a correspondence between the kernel constructs of PARALATION LISP and the concepts of lambda calculus [Lan65]. This approach has several advantages. When read along with the accompanying text, the LISP code of the definition is understandable to a large community of application programmers and language implementors. In addition, the definition is runnable on any implementation of COMMON LISP: anyone can experiment with PARALATION LISP simply by typing the definition into a computer. Finally, Chapter 7, which discusses the parallel implementation of the paralation constructs, is able to build upon the functions presented in this chapter.

The main disadvantage of presenting an operational semantics for PARALATION LISP is that some of the features of the language (for example, the associative grouping to be used during reduction and the degree of synchronization during `elwise` execution) are not fully specified by the abstract language definition. For these features, implementations are free to choose any convenient implementation method. But an operational semantics must specify a particular implementation of these features. Therefore, the flexibility available to the implementor is not captured in the code of the operational semantics but only in the English text that surrounds the code.

The portion of the definition that describes `elwise` is a rewrite rule, a kind of compiler, which translates an invocation of `elwise` into pure COMMON LISP. On the other hand, the other portions of the definition are simply COMMON LISP interpreters for various constructs. In effect, the semantics form a compiler and runtime library that implement PARALATION LISP on a degenerate parallel computer that happens to have only one processor.

In order to be useful to human beings, the definition must be kept small. As a result, the definition is not a full definition of PARALATION LISP; instead it is a definition of a kind of TINY PARALATION LISP. TINY PARALATION LISP is simpler than the full PARALATION LISP implementation because it performs absolutely no error or type checking; it does not attempt to provide convenience features (such as user specifiable `match` equality predicates, among other things); and it is not meant to be efficient.

Because the definition must be complete enough to run on an actual computer, a certain amount of linguistic machinery and notation is unavoidable. Although the

```
(defstruct (paralation-internal)
  length
  index)
```

Figure 6.1: Internal paralation data structure

specificity of such notation makes the definition quite precise, it can also obscure its meaning for readers who are not familiar with the notation, which is simply COMMON LISP. The text that surrounds the paralation function definitions explains what the functions are supposed to do, rather than attempting to explain the meaning of the notation in detail, a task that is properly in the domain of a COMMON LISP tutorial.

One final note: Since efficiency is an important part of the paralation model, in some cases it can be difficult to describe its semantics without referring to one or more implementation models. Although one could describe paralations, fields, `elwise`, `match`, and `<-` without referring to an implementation model, such a description would be incomplete. The use of an implementation model as a framework allows one to point out where the opportunities for efficiency and optimization lie, and the existence of these points is an important part of the paralation model.

6.2   Operational Semantics for Tiny Paralation Lisp

6.2.1   Data Structures

COMMON LISP contains a `defstruct` primitive that is used for defining record structures. Fields and paralations are both represented as structures. To begin with, Figure 6.1 presents the definition of a `paralation-internal`.

A paralation is represented by a structure with two slots. The first slot, named `paralation-internal-length`, contains an integer indicating the length of the paralation. The second slot, `paralation-internal-index`, contains the index field of the paralation. A field is defined by the `defstruct` in Figure 6.2.

The `pvector` slot of a `field` contains a vector that contains the actual contents of the field: its values at each conceptual paralation site. The second slot contains the field's paralation, which is a `paralation-internal` object. The presence of `:print-function` in the `defstruct` causes the function `print-field` to be called whenever an object of type `field` must be printed out; `print-field` prints fields using the `#F` notation. A definition of `print-field` is presented in Appendix A.

```
(defstruct (field (:print-function print-field))
  pvector
  paralation)
```

Figure 6.2: Field data structure

```
(defun make-paralation (length)
  (let ((index-pvector (make-array length))
        (paralation (make-paralation-internal :length length)))
    (dotimes (i length)
      (setf (elt index-pvector i) i))
    (let ((result-field (make-field :paralation paralation
                                    :pvector index-pvector)))
      (setf (paralation-internal-index paralation) result-field)
      result-field)))
```

Figure 6.3: An implementation of `make-paralation`

Clearly, these two structures are mutually recursive: A field points to a paralation, and a paralation points to an index field. But that is not a problem, as the definition of `make-paralation` in Figure 6.3 shows.

`make-paralation` begins by creating an array of the specified length; it will serve as the pvector of the index field. In addition, a paralation is created, and although its length is initialized, its `paralation-internal-index` slot is left empty. A `dotimes` loop then initializes the pvector so that it represents an index field, in which the ith element contains the value i.

Now that the pvector for the index field exists, the field itself can be created and its two slots can be filled in. Before this `result-field` can be returned to the caller of `make-paralation`, however, one task remains: the `paralation-internal-index` slot of the paralation must be filled in. This is easily done now, since the value that should go into that slot is simply `result-field`. Figure 6.4 shows the `field` and `paralation-internal` data structures that might be created by a call to `make-paralation` with a `length` argument of 4, and illustrates the circular nature of the data structures. The `paralation-internal` data structure on the left is, of course, internal. `make-paralation` returns the data structure on the right, the index field, as its result.

The remaining data structure in TINY PARALATION LISP is the mapping, defined in Figure 6.5. A mapping is represented as a structure containing fields that

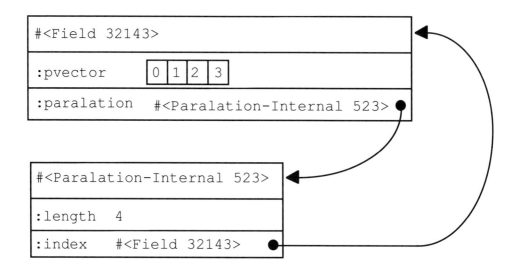

Figure 6.4: Representation of a 4-site paralation and its index field

```
(defstruct (mapping)
  to-key
  from-key)
```

Figure 6.5: Mapping data structure

encapsulates the equality relationship between the two arguments of the `match` function: the key fields.

6.2.2 Access Functions

The functions in Figure 6.6 allow the user to access the paralation data structures. (The various slot accessors provided by `defstruct`, such as `paralation-internal-length`, are not at user-level; they are meant for use by the paralation implementor only.) `index` allows a program to retrieve the index field of any field's paralation. `elt-f` allows serial access to the elements of fields, even though such access could have been implemented by using `elwise` in a convoluted way. In ordinary PARALATION LISP, this task is performed by the COMMON LISP sequence

```
(defun index (field)
   (paralation-internal-index (field-paralation field)))

(defun elt-f (field position)
   (aref (field-pvector field) position))
```

Figure 6.6: User access functions

```
(defmacro elwise (sym-list &body body)
   '(elwise-s ,sym-list ,.body))
```

Figure 6.7: A macro for elwise

function elt. elt is modified so that it acts just like elt-f when its sequence
argument is of type field. Of course, when its sequence argument is a list or an
array, elt must still take appropriate action. Appendix A describes how this type
of modification can be made.

6.2.3   elwise

In Appendix A, a different version of elwise is presented that builds upon this one.
In order to accommodate that future expansion, elwise here is simply defined by
making use of elwise-s, which stands for elwise-simplified.

In LISP, a macro is a kind of rewrite rule. The macro in Figure 6.7 simply
indicates that all calls to elwise should be rewritten into a call to elwise-s on
the same arguments.

elwise-s, presented in Figure 6.8, is also a macro. It actually performs the
work of compilation. The strategy is to turn a call to elwise into a loop that
contains the same body as the elwise. Each iteration of the loop performs the
calculations required for one particular paralation site. This takes place because
at the start of each iteration, each elwise variable is rebound to its field value
at the appropriate paralation site. After each iteration, the values of the elwise
variables are copied back into the fields where they came from, in order to preserve
any elementwise side effects that the body might have made in them. In addition,
the value returned by this iteration of the body is stored away. After the loop has
finished simulating all of the paralation sites, a field containing all of these results
is to be returned.

With this algorithm, site i of a paralation completely finishes running the body

```
(defmacro elwise-s (sym-list &body body)
  (let ((paralation (make-symbol "paralation"))
        (length (make-symbol "length"))
        (result-pvector (make-symbol "result-pvector"))
        (each-site (make-symbol "each-site"))
        (new-sym-values (make-symbol "new-sym-values")))
    '(let* ((,paralation
              (get-paralation-of-fields ,@sym-list))
            (,length (paralation-internal-length ,paralation))
            (,result-pvector (make-array ,length))
            (,new-sym-values nil))
       (dotimes (,each-site ,length)
         (let ,(field-var-and-element-value-pairs sym-list
                                                  each-site)
           (setf (aref ,result-pvector ,each-site)
                 (progn ,.body))
           (setq ,new-sym-values (list ,@sym-list)))
         ,@(update-sym-for-body-side-effects sym-list
                                             new-sym-values
                                             each-site))
       (make-field :pvector ,result-pvector
                   :paralation ,paralation))))
```

Figure 6.8: A macro for `elwise-s`

code before site $i + 1$ even begins. This extreme desynchronization is convenient in a serial simulator but is not a part of the semantics of the paralation model; a parallel implementation can overlap and synchronize site execution of the `elwise` body to any degree desired.

The series of calls to `make-symbol` is a protective measure to prevent conflicts between variables in the user's program and variables used by the compiler and run-time support package. The template for the output code therefore contains symbols produced by `make-symbol` that are guaranteed not to conflict with any user variables. These symbols are printed in this chapter as the input name surrounded by the following distinguished punctuation: `#:|variable-name|`.

The output code template begins with a call to `get-paralation-of-fields`, which is shown in Figure 6.9. The `elwise` symbols on `sym-list` must be bound to fields that are in the same paralation, and the `get-paralation` function returns that paralation. This sparse semantic definition simply returns the paralation of the first field on `sym-list`. No error checking is performed to make sure that the

```
(defun get-paralation-of-fields (&rest fields)
  (field-paralation (car fields)))
```

Figure 6.9: Find the paralation from the elementwise fields

remaining fields are in that same paralation.

The output code template produced by `elwise-s` simply binds the variable `paralation` to that paralation. Next, the length of the paralation is stored in `length`, and the pvector for `elwise`'s result field is created and saved. Finally, a variable named `new-sym-values` is created; it will be used to preserve side effects to the elementwise variables.

The main body of the template is a `do-times` loop that iterates the variable `each-site` from 0 to the number of sites in `paralation`. The body of the loop consists of binding the `elwise` variables to their values at site `each-site`, executing the body code, and saving away the result of that evaluation, as well as any side effect it might have had on the `elwise` variables. After the loop has terminated, the template calls `make-field` to encapsulate the pvector of results, and returns it as the result of the `elwise`.

The `elwise` variables are bound to particular values at the beginning of the loop with the help of a compile-time call to `field-var-and-element-value-pairs`, which is presented in Figure 6.10. Given a list of symbols, a list of fields, and a site number, this function returns a binding list that can be spliced into a `let`.

The execution of `field-var-and-element-value-pairs` can best be illustrated with an example.

```
(elwise (a b) body)
```

causes the following compile-time call:

```
(field-var-and-element-value-pairs '(a b) (list a b) each-site)
```

which returns the list

```
((a (aref (field-pvector a) #:|each-site|))
 (b (aref (field-pvector b) #:|each-site|)))
```

which is precisely what is required for the `let` in the `dotimes` loop, which binds `elwise` variables to their site values.

Now that the elementwise variables have been rebound to the appropriate site's field values, the execution of the list of `body` statements can be invoked by including the `body` code, wrapped in a `progn` block construct, in the output template. The

```
(defun field-var-and-element-value-pairs (symbols site)
  (mapcar #'(lambda (symbol)
              '(,symbol (aref (field-pvector ,symbol) ,site)))
          symbols))
```

Figure 6.10: Compile code to bind `elwise` symbols to their site values

result of executing the body at a particular site (the result returned by the `progn`) is then saved away in the `result-pvector` by a call to `setf`. All that remains is to explain the purpose of the variable `new-sym-values`, as well as the mysterious call to `update-sym-for-body-side-effects`.

The variable and function simply cooperate to preserve any change that the `body` may make in the `elwise` variables. This extra complication is necessary because COMMON LISP does not support space sharing by variables (locatives).[1] Although during body execution an elementwise variable contains the same value as a field at a particular site, if the `body` modifies the elementwise variable with a side effect, the value at the paralation site is not automatically changed as well. The propagation of the side effect must be orchestrated explicitly by `update-sym-for-body-side-effects`.

After the `body` has been executed at a particular site, a list is created that contains all of the final values of the elementwise variables. This list is stored in `new-sym-values`. After the `let` that had rebound the elementwise variables has been exited, `update-sym-for-body-side-effects` is called to store the values in the list into the elementwise fields. Figure 6.11 contains this update code.

As with `field-var-and-element-value-pairs`, the execution of `update-sym-for-body-side-effects` can best be illustrated with an example.

```
(elwise (a b)
  (setq a nil)
  (setq b t))
```

causes the following compile-time call:

```
(update-sym-for-body-side-effects '(a b) new-sym-values '#:|each-site|)
;; new-sym-values contains a list like this: '(nil t)
```

---

[1] Alternatively, one could say that the complication is necessary because `elwise` binds its variables in a very unCOMMON LISP–like manner.

```
(defun update-sym-for-body-side-effects (symbols values-list site)
  (mapcar #'(lambda (sym) '(setf (aref (field-pvector ,sym) ,site)
                                 (pop ,values-list)))
          symbols))
```

Figure 6.11: Transfer the possibly side effected values of the elementwise symbols from the list back to the paralation site

The call to `update-sym-for-body-side-effects` returns the list:

```
((setf (aref (field-pvector a) #:|each-site|) (pop #:|new-sym-values|))
;; the first pop returns nil
 (setf (aref (field-pvector b) #:|each-site|) (pop #:|new-sym-values|)))
;; the second pop returns t
```

which is precisely what is required to update the field values and therefore preserve the values of possibly side effected elementwise variables.

`elwise` Summary

The following illustrates the actual code that is output by the `elwise` macro for a simple call to `elwise`:

```
(elwise (x) (+ x 1))
```

becomes

```
(LET*
  ((#:|paralation| (GET-PARALATION-OF-FIELDS X))
   (#:|length| (PARALATION-INTERNAL-LENGTH #:|paralation|))
   (#:|result-pvector| (MAKE-ARRAY #:|length|))
   (#:|new-sym-values| NIL))
  (DOTIMES
    (#:|each-site| #:|length|)
    (LET ((X (AREF (FIELD-PVECTOR X) #:|each-site|)))
      (SETF (AREF #:|result-pvector| #:|each-site|) (PROGN (+ X 1)))
      (SETQ #:|new-sym-values| (LIST X)))
    (SETF (AREF (FIELD-PVECTOR X) #:|each-site|)
          (POP #:|new-sym-values|)))
  (MAKE-FIELD :PVECTOR #:|result-pvector| :PARALATION #:|paralation|))
```

The output code begins by calculating what paralation is involved and its length, and it then creates a pvector of that length. The result of the `elwise` is a field

```
(defun match (to from)
  (make-mapping :to-key (elwise (to) to)
                :from-key (elwise (from) from)))
```

Figure 6.12: An inefficient implementation of `match`

containing this pvector. A `dotimes` loop is executed that rebinds the elementwise field variables to their field values at the various sites of the paralation, executes the body, and then preserves any changes to the variables. Finally, the pvector of results is encapsulated in a `field` and is returned.

6.2.4   Match

In the implementation in Figure 6.12, `match` is a simple function. It simply stashes the two key fields away in a mapping object, and then returns that mapping. The purpose of each `elwise` is simply to create a copy of the values in each key field. The copy, rather than the original, is stored in the mapping. The reason is that if the user later modifies one of the fields that was used as a key, the pattern of arrows represented by the mapping must not change—it is frozen at the time of `match` execution.[2] Similarly, when one adds two variables and saves the result, the result should not change if one of the two variables is changed after the addition takes place.

A more efficient implementation is described in Chapter 7, which actually performs work at mapping creation time to identify which keys are equal to each other. That is a more efficient implementation because `<-` might be called several times on a single mapping, and it is most efficient to factor out work that can be precalculated once rather than perform it anew for each call to `<-`. In effect, the inefficient implementation forces `<-` to perform communication from the `to-key` back to the `from-key`, to indicate which data items are needed, and *then* performs the transfer from `from-key` to `to-key`. The efficient implementation performs the backward communication at `match` time, allowing `<-` to perform only forward communication.

Mapping Access Functions

Often, it is convenient to retrieve key fields, or their canonicalized equivalents, from a mapping. That is the purpose of the code presented in Figure 6.13.

---

[2]LISP programmers may wonder why a deep, tree-walking copy is not necessary. The top-level copying is sufficient since `match` in TINY PARALATION LISP always uses `eql` as its equality predicate, unlike full PARALATION LISP, which supplies several equality predicates. Full PARALATION LISP uses a canonicalized mapping, which is described in Section 7.4.

```
(defun to-key-field (mapping)
  (let ((result (mapping-to-key mapping)))
    (elwise (result) result)))

(defun from-key-field (mapping)
  (let ((result (mapping-from-key mapping)))
    (elwise (result) result)))
```

Figure 6.13: Mapping access functions

Each of these functions accepts a mapping and returns one of its key fields. More precisely, the user is given a copy of the key field that is actually stored in the mapping, rather than the actual key fields themselves. Thus, even if the user modifies the fields returned by the access functions, the mapping remains unchanged. The functions return equivalent fields of keys.[3]

6.2.5   <- (Move)

The version of <- that is described here first performs calculations that depend only upon the key fields. Then it performs a transfer of the contents of the source data field into a field in the destination paralation according to the mapping, combining function, and default field. In Chapter 7, a different, simpler version of <- is presented. In order to accommodate that later version, <- here is initially defined as a simple macro that expands into a call to a function, match-move-internal, which performs the actual work of data movement at run-time. In addition, that simpler version of <- includes a number of convenience features. For example, it makes the combining function and the default field arguments optional because it provides appropriate defaults.

The serial algorithm presented here makes extensive use of table lookup. It begins by sequentially storing each item in the source field that is being moved under its corresponding key in a table. As each item is being entered, a check is made to see if the table already contains an entry with the same key. If not, the new value and key are stored in the table. Otherwise, the value to be entered is combined with the previously stored value, using the user-specified combining function. The result returned by the combining function then replaces the old value indexed by the key.

Next, the algorithm creates a field in the paralation of the destination key of

---

[3](match (to-key-field mapping) (from-key-field mapping)) is equivalent to mapping with respect to <- , but they are not eql.

```
(defmacro <- (field &key by with default)
  '(match-move-internal ,field ,with ,default ,by))

(defun match-move-internal (field combiner default map)
  (let* ((no-value (cons :a-unique-cons nil))
         (key-hash-table (initialize-needed-keys
                            (mapping-to-key map) no-value)))
    (enter-source-data-into-table key-hash-table
                                  (mapping-from-key map)
                                  field combiner no-value)
    (make-field :paralation
                (field-paralation (mapping-to-key map))
                :pvector
                (table-to-pvector key-hash-table
                                  (mapping-to-key map)
                                  default
                                  no-value)))))
```

Figure 6.14: An inefficient implementation of <-

the <-'s mapping. Then, the algorithm sequentially goes through the keys of the mapping's destination key field. Each key is looked up in the previously created table, and the result of the lookup is stored at the corresponding site of the result field. If a key is not found in the table, the corresponding user-specified default value is used.

The serial implementation of match-move-internal is contained in Figure 6.14. It centers around the use of a hash table. The call to initialize-needed-keys returns a hash table that, when given any value that occurs in the to-key field of the mapping, returns a special, unique item. That item is (:a-unique-cons), which is stored in the variable no-value. It is used to detect which keys should receive default values. Thus, initialize-needed-keys conservatively assumes that all keys require default values.

The next function to be called is enter-source-data-into-table, shown in Figure 6.16. It loops through the values of the mapping's from-key, loading the corresponding source data into the table. If the old value was no-value, the new value is simply inserted into the table. If, however, a value had already been inserted (that is, if this is not the first time the corresponding key was encountered in the from-keys), the new value is combined with the old value, using the user-specified combining function. The combined value is then inserted into the table. Of course, this algorithm uses a particular associative pairing for colliding values, a serialized

```
(defun initialize-needed-keys (key-field no-value)
  (let ((result (make-hash-table)))
    (dotimes (i (paralation-internal-length
                   (field-paralation key-field)))
      (setf (gethash (elt-f key-field i) result) no-value))
    result))
```

Figure 6.15: Initially, all `to-key` values return `no-value`

```
(defun enter-source-data-into-table (table key-field
                                        data-field combiner
                                        no-value)
  (dotimes (i (paralation-internal-length
                 (field-paralation key-field)))
    (let ((key (elt-f key-field i)))
      (multiple-value-bind (current-value in-table-p)
          (gethash key table)
        (when in-table-p
          (setf (gethash key table)
                (if (eql current-value no-value)
                    (elt-f data-field i)
                    (funcall combiner
                             current-value
                             (elt-f data-field i)))))))))
```

Figure 6.16: Load source data into the hash table based upon `from-key`

left-associative pairing. A parallel implementation is free to use a different pairing, but not a different left-to-right ordering.

When `enter-source-data-into-table` exits, each key in the hash table maps one of two things: `no-value` (if the key was not found in the source keys) or some other value (if the key was found in the source keys, and the value is computed based upon the contents of the source data field). It is now evident why `no-value` must be a unique value, one that cannot possibly occur in any of the user's `fields`: It is an internal flag that indicates no user data item was found. If the source-field had contained it, this implementation would become quite confused!

Most of the work of `<-` is now complete. All that remains to be done is to transfer the values in the hash table into a field, which is what `<-` must return. Of course, any time a `no-value` is encountered in the hash table, the field

```
(defun table-to-pvector (table key-field default no-value)
  (let* ((to-size (paralation-internal-length
                    (field-paralation key-field)))
         (result-pv (make-array to-size)))
  (dotimes (i to-size)
    (let ((val (gethash (elt-f key-field i) table)))
      (if (eql val no-value)
          (setf (aref result-pv i) (elt-f default i))
          (setf (aref result-pv i) val))))
  result-pv))
```

Figure 6.17: Turn the hash table into a field pvector

should instead contain a default value. The production of this result field is a
two-step process: `table-to-pvector` converts the hash table into a pvector, and
`match-move-internal` creates and returns a field that includes that pvector.

`table-to-pvector` begins by creating a pvector, `result-pv`, of an appropriate
size, as shown in Figure 6.17. It then proceeds to loop through the various `to-keys`
and retrieves their corresponding value in the hash table. If that value is not
`no-value`, it is inserted into the pvector. Otherwise, the appropriate default value
is inserted. Finally, the function returns the pvector.

6.3   Semantics for Convenience Features

What has been presented to this point is everything that is essential to the paralation model. There are many non-essential features, however, that can add convenience to a language. Different features and library functions facilitate different
programming styles. This section implements several new features. Some of them,
such as `choose`, might be desirable in any paralation language. Other features, such
as the way that built-in base language sequence functions operate on fields, or the
availability of convenient field-reading and field-printing user-interface functions,
are not directly related to the paralation model. However, they illustrate how the
model can be made to match the flavor of a particular base language, LISP.

6.3.1   Library Functions

In previous chapters, implementations for library functions such as `vref`, `expand`,
and `collect` were presented. This section presents implementations for `choose`
and `collapse`.

```
0 (defun choose (field)
1    (let ((point-back
2          (expand
3             (let ((i (index field)))
4                (elwise (field i)
5                   (if field
6                      (make-sequence 'field 1
7                                  :initial-element i)
8                      (make-paralation 0)))))))))
9       (match point-back (index field)))))
```

Figure 6.18: An implementation of choose

Implementation of choose

Figure 2.11 illustrated the type of mapping the choose returns. It must connect the true sites of a source paralation to the sites of a new paralation. The implementation in Figure 6.18 does this by using expand to create the new paralation.

Lines 4–8 cause each element of choose's input, a boolean field, to calculate a value. If the boolean was true, the value is a singleton field containing the site's index value; otherwise it is a field in a paralation with 0 elements. Line 3 uses expand to concatenate all of these values together. Finally, match is used to create the final mapping. For example:

```
(choose '#F(t t nil nil t))
  after elwise ⇒ #F(#F(0) #F(1) #F() #F() #F(4))
  after expand ⇒ #F(0 1 4)
  match is called on: (match '#F(0 1 4) '#F(0 1 2 3 4))
```

Implementation of collapse

collapse must return a mapping that condenses values that are equivalent into single value. One way to do this begins by selecting one from each group of values as special; the others are deemed to be copies. choose is used to create a field in a new paralation that contains only the special values. This is the approach used in the implementation in Figure 6.19, where the special value in a group of values is simply the one with the lowest index.

Lines 2–3 cause each site of field's paralation to retrieve the index of the site holding the special version of its field value. Line 4 causes each site to elementwise determine if it itself is the special site. This creates a boolean. choose can then be used to create a field containing the special values (and thus containing one of

```
0 (defun collapse (field)
1    (let* ((i (index field))
2          (min-holder
3             (<- i :with #'min :by (match field field)))
4          (min-holder-p (elwise (min-holder i)
5                            (= min-holder i)))
6          (distinct-vals (<- field :by (choose min-holder-p))))
7      (match distinct-vals field)))
```

Figure 6.19: An implementation of collapse

each type of value). This almost completes the task of collapse. All that remains is to create a mapping based upon the information, by matching from the input, with its duplicate values, to the new field of distinct values. For example:

```
(collapse '#F(a b a a b c))
  min-holder ⇒ #F(0 1 0 0 1 5)
  min-holder-p ⇒ #F(t t nil nil nil t)
  distinct-vals ⇒ #F(a b c)
  match is called on: (match '#F(a b c) '#F(a b a a b c))
```

6.3.2   Combining Functions

Many of COMMON LISP's built-in functions, such as +, *, max, and cons, are useful as combining functions. This section introduces several new functions that the programmer may find convenient.[4] Simply being aware of the existence of these functions and their applicability to data reduction can help a programmer in formulating an approach to a problem.

The Error Function

@ is the standard, default combining function. It ignores its arguments and signals an error when called. <- uses it as a combining function if a collision occurs and the user did not specify a combining function:

```
(defun @ (x y)
  (error "unexpected collision between data values ~s and ~s;
          no combiner was specified"
         x y))
```

---

[4]The names of a number of these functions, in particular @, arg1, arg2, arb, and cfun, come from CONNECTION MACHINE LISP [Con87].

Selector Functions

arg1 is a simple combining function; it always returns x, its first argument:

```
(defun arg1 (x y)
  (declare (ignore y))
  x)
```

Thus, a <- with arg1 takes any number of colliding data items and returns the very first one (according to the index order in the source paralation, of course). The combining function arg2 is identical to arg1 except that it returns y, the second argument; a <- with arg2 reduces a group of items into the last item.

The arb combining function was mentioned earlier. It returns either its first argument or its second, whichever is convenient. The choice is arbitrary. It may return x one call and y the next. arb is used as a combining function when it does not matter exactly which value of a collection of values is returned. arb is obviously useful when all the values in a group are identical, but there are other more subtle cases arising in various algorithms where arb can be useful when applied to non-homogeneous collections of values.

Although a perfectly legal implementation of arb could always return its first argument (that is, arb could simply call arg1), the programmer should use the more general arb where it is applicable, rather than arg1 or arg2. The reason is that this provides an accurate portrayal of the requirements of the algorithm both to humans reading the program and to compilers that must execute it. Certain kinds of parallel hardware may be able to better cope with congested communications paths and overloaded routing switches when arb is used, rather than a more restrictive combining function like arg1.

Logical Functions

and-func ANDs its two arguments together, returning the first if it is non-nil, returning the second if the first was nil. It could be defined with the following:[5]

```
(defun and-func (x y) (and x y))
```

COMMON LISP's and cannot be directly used as a combining function because it is not actually a function: and is a macro. and-func is useful with <- when it is necessary to determine whether or not all items in a group are true. If they are all true, a reduction of the group with and-func returns a single, true value (the very last object in the collection), otherwise the group is reduced to a nil.

---

[5]Of course, actual implementations are free to perform optimizations when particular built-in combining functions are used. For example, a serial implementation might use short-circuit evaluation when and-funcing together a large number of booleans.

`or-func` is a similar combining function that checks to see if *any* objects in a group are true (non-`nil`). A reduction of a group according to `or-func` returns the first true object, or `nil` if there are no true objects in the group.

```
(defun or-func (x y) (or x y))
```

A Function Generator

`cfun` itself is not a combining function; it is a function that creates and returns combining functions. `cfun` accepts a single value as its argument. It returns a combining function that, when applied to two colliding values, ignores those two values and simply returns the value that the user specified to `cfun`. It might be defined as follows:

```
(defun cfun (value)
  #'(lambda (x y)
      (declare (ignore x y))
      value))
```

The purpose of `cfun` is to allow non-colliding messages to pass through to their destinations unhindered, while transforming any colliding messages into a constant `value`, such as `'ouch`:

```
(setq f '#F(a a b c))
(<- f :by (collapse f) :with #'arb)
   ⇒ #F(A B C)
(<- f :by (collapse f) :with (cfun 'ouch))
   ⇒ #F(OUCH B C)
```

Concatenation Functions

Earlier in Section 5.3.1, the utility of `append` was demonstrated as a combiner for collecting colliding lists; `field-append-2` was then introduced and used to define such useful functions as `collect` and `expand`. In general, concatenation of data is a useful paradigm for combining, since it can preserve any desired information. For example, one can even preserve the arbitrary combining tree chosen by the PARALATION LISP implementation simply by using `cons` as a combining function. Of course, there is no guarantee that it will be the same twice!

```
(vref '#F(A B C D E) :with #'cons)
   ⇒ ((A . B) . ((C . D) . E))
(vref '#F(A B C D E) :with #'cons)
   ⇒ (A . ((B . C) . (D . E)))
```

Chapter 7

Implementation Strategies

7.1 Overview

This chapter describes how the paralation base operators can be implemented using various kinds of parallel hardware directly. Several different compilation strategies, for several different kinds of hardware [Sab87c], are discussed in a style that assumes familiarity with conventional compiler technology. In addition, optimizations that are applicable on serial implementations of paralation languages are presented. Some LISP code fragments are presented in order to illustrate points, but, unlike the code in Chapter 6, this code is not meant to form a complete and executable system.

7.1.1 Why Describe Implementations?

One of the two main goals of the paralation model is to be easy to compile for a variety of target architectures. The model has been implemented in prototype form on only one parallel architecture to date (the Connection Machine® Computer), so a discussion of theoretical implementation techniques is the only means available for measuring success against this goal.

Compilers and interpreters both serve to remove programming abstractions and transform them into more concrete, lower-level concepts. Thus, compilers are useful because they output code that is easier to implement than their input. A compiler serves the additional purpose of taking advantage of constants via precomputation. For example, program code often remains constant at run-time.

A PARALATION LISP compiler must perform several important transformations. The input program can make use of a dynamically sized set of independent, dynamic objects (fields) that can be nested hierarchically; the output code should be targeted for a fixed number of addressable objects (that is, processors) that do not necessarily have a hierarchical organization. Input programs can make use of a kind of abstract communication that is based on symbolic key values; output programs must use numerical addresses (that is, processor or memory addresses) to describe communication. The compiler automatically coerces serial data and serial programs to parallel as necessary (when they are used elementwise). Thus, the target machine is free to use different instruction sets for serial and parallel execution, as is the case with SIMD architectures. The compiler must transform elementwise evaluation, which can be applied to atomic data, expressions, LISP forms, and entire programs, into parallel calls to a limited set of basic functions.

7.1.2   Which Base Language?

The choice of base language obviously has an effect on the implementation of a paralation language. All of the constructs of the base language and all of the paralation constructs must be implemented, along with all possible combinations and nestings of the two. Base languages that are easy to compile serially lead to paralation languages that are easy to compile. In particular, purely functional base languages can be especially easy to compile, since they do not require the proper implementation of elementwise side effects. In addition, interference between `elwise` bodies can never occur, since there is no way to write an illegally side effecting `elwise` body. If interfering `elwise` bodies are to be detected with a base language that permits side effects, some error checking will usually have to take place at run-time. However, it is possible to have a side effecting base language, with certain key restrictions, in which interference can always be detected syntactically [Rey78]. In any case, this chapter addresses issues at a level that applies to any type of base language.

7.1.3   How Many Processors?

The discussion assumes that the target machine has n processors, where n is as large as the largest paralation being manipulated. This is a general approach, since the simulation of n virtual processors with k physical processors is a problem that is for the most part orthogonal to the paralation model. Wherever the discussion refers to processors, simply substitute virtual processors.

A virtual processor facility is analogous in purpose to a virtual memory facility. A physical processor is assigned the role of performing the duties of some number of virtual processors. The physical processor partitions its available memory, assigning different portions of it to represent the memories of different virtual processors. Thus, the number of virtual processors is not directly coupled to the number of available physical processors. The virtual-to-physical mapping might not even be fixed. This would free the implementation to perform dynamic load balancing.

Even obvious implementations of virtual processors can be efficient; the simulator in Chapter 6 represents the logical extreme of a simple round-robin approach to virtual processors. More complex approaches might use some sort of lazy evaluation, or might attempt to factor out duplications in effort among the simulated processors. Because the use of virtual processors means that data from several paralations might be represented within the same processor, virtual processing strategies can have interesting and complex implications for the exploitation of locality. In any case, given that a simple and efficient technique exists, it becomes clear how a coarse-grained machine with, say, 64 processors can make use of a paralation implementation strategy that presents n (much larger than 64) independent tasks that must be done.

At appropriate points in the discussion, certain optimizations relating to the implementation of the paralation model on a computer with virtual processors are presented. For example, a serial machine (an extreme case of virtual processing) can use short-circuit evaluation during a `vref` with `and-func` rather than attempt to simulate a parallel machine and examine all of the involved booleans. Similarly, during the execution of the same `vref` on a parallel machine, the work of many sites may be mapped onto a smaller number of physical processors. Physical processors that handle the work of more than one paralation site can make use of the same short-circuit optimization. Thus, optimizations that are useful in serial implementations of the paralation model may also be useful in parallel implementations.

7.2 Data Structures

In any problem, the choice of data structure interacts with the algorithm to be used with it. Clearly, different compiler techniques may require different representations of paralation data structures. In all cases, however, the basic idea is to spread the data values of a field among many processors and to make use of the locality properties of fields and paralations. At this level of generality, the description of paralation data structures can be given in the form of a few small changes to the data structures of the implementation presented in Chapter 6.

The pvector of a field, which holds its element's values, are represented as a *slice*. A slice is a cross section through the local memories of a group of processors. For example, a field containing small integers (say, representable in 16 bits) in a ten-element paralation might be stored in word 1000 of the local memories of processors 100 to 109. Thus, a slice contains the data values of a field packaged in a form in which processors can easily operate on them in parallel. The slices that represent fields in the same paralation are aligned; their values are spread among the same set of processors.

More precisely, the internal structure of a paralation is augmented with a field that indicates what processor its slices begin in:

```
(defstruct (paralation-internal)
  length
  index
  first-processor)
```

In addition, the field data structure's pvector slot now holds a memory address that is valid in all of its paralation's processors.

```
(defstruct (field (:print-function print-field))
  pvector-address
  paralation)
```

This type of data structure accurately implements elementwise locality, but it can be a bit restrictive of the storage allocator. A more general field data structure would allow for the possibility that its pvector data is stored in a different set of processors than its paralation indicates. Thus, the user's locality advice could be ignored where it conflicts with the problems of storage allocation or virtual memory management. One way to provide this freedom for non-alignment would be move the `first-processor` slot from the `defstruct` for `paralation-internal` into the `defstruct` for `field`. Another way in which this representation complicates the task of the storage allocator is by its insistence that the processors used by a slice be contiguous. Storage allocation might be simplified if holes could exist within a slice. Implementation of such a strategy would involve replacing the `first-processor` and `length` fields with an explicit representation of which processors are used by a slice.

Many other optimizations of the field data structure are possible, some of which depend upon the base language and target architecture. For example, in a SIMD implementation that uses a dynamically typed base language like LISP, fields should have slots for caching type information in summarized form. Mathematical operations might then execute faster on fields that dynamically contain only integers and no floating point numbers than they would on fields that mix the two data types, even without a static type declaration.

7.2.1 Fields Within Fields

The simple, contiguous, aligned field representation described above is sufficient for the implementation of fields within fields. A field contains values, and those values may happen to be instances of data type `field`, as defined by the `field` defstruct.

However, this pointer-based strategy can be inefficient for a SIMD target computer. The problem is that the easiest way to implement fields on SIMD computers is to store the pvector on the SIMD processors and the `field` data structure itself on the host machine. Whenever a field contains another field as an element, its pvector contains a pointer to the subfield's descriptor on the host. Therefore, parallel operations on fields of fields are serialized because each SIMD processor needs to access the host in order to follow its subfield pointer. Note that this is not a problem with SIMD architectures, but arises from the decision to store important information on a serial host. Of course, a SIMD architecture is perfectly capable of storing field descriptors in its SIMD processors, and if it did so it could efficiently implement nested `elwise`.

A second field representation is possible; it is based upon the concept of a segment and can be used with both SIMD and MIMD architectures [Ble87]. Segments can be thought of as a kind of field descriptor, which means this second field representation is quite similar to the first. Guy Blelloch is developing a compiler for a subset of PARALATION LISP; it uses the segment-based field data structure. As a result, it can compile nested `elwise`s into efficient code.

In a segmented representation, the pointers to subfields are represented implicitly by position; instead of including a pointer, one includes the entire subfield. Thus, this new implementation makes a special case out of fields within fields, storing them by concatenating their contents and having an auxiliary slice to flag the segment boundaries. For example, the following nested field:

```
nested-index = #F(0 1 2)
nested       = #F(#F(1 2 3) #F(A B) #F(33 22 90 38))
```

could be represented with the following internal data structures:

```
index    = [0 1 2] : parent is nil
data     = [1 2 3 A B 33 22 90 38] : parent is index
indirect = [0 3 5] : parent is nil
segment  = [1 0 0 1 0 1 0 0 0] : parent is index
```

The `index` is simply a pvector containing the index field of the top-level paralation; `data` is a longer pvector containing the data of the subfield. Either `indirect` or `segment` can be used to manipulate the `data` in a segmented fashion, depending on what computations are to be performed. (There are many interchangeable ways to implicitly or explicitly represent the segment boundaries.) Guy Blelloch's compiler uses the `indirect` field to send information to the header of the subfield when it must be combined with data from the parent field. For example, suppose the following were to be compiled:

```
(elwise (nested-index nested)
  (elwise (nested)
    (+ nested-index nested)))
```

The compiled code would have to send the appropriate `nested-index` to the segment headers. A segmented parallel prefix could then propagate that information to the other members of the segment (see Section 7.4.1). Finally, the + would be executed in parallel on `nested` and the propagated `nested-index` values.

In general, all nested fields can be implemented in a segment-based way, but it is possible to mix the pointer and segment-based representations. For example, after some depth of field nesting has been exceeded (perhaps when all processors have been used), one might want to switch from using segments to using pointers.

7.2.2 Inherited Locality

The combination of elementwise locality and the storage of fields within fields can make the task of the storage allocator quite difficult. For example, consider the representation of the following three fields:

```
(setq f1 (make-paralation 4))
(setq f2 (elwise (f1) 0))
(setq nested (elwise (f1) (make-paralation 2)))
```

In the programmer's locality model, each site of `f1`'s paralation contains three values in close proximity:

```
f1     = #F( 0        1        2        3)
f2     = #F( 0        0        0        0)
nested = #F( #F(0 1)  #F(0 1)  #F(0 1)  #F(0 1) )
```

However, since a field in a paralation of length two probably takes up more memory space (as well as typographical space) than an integer, a space-efficient storage strategy can seem to violate the contagious spirit of inherited elementwise locality mentioned in Section 4.2.4. For example, in the simple pointer-based strategy, `nested` would be represented by a field containing `field` descriptors, but the values of those fields would be in some other processors. Of course, the allocator might ensure that those other processors are near the `field` descriptor that points to them, properly implementing inherited locality.

The segment-based strategy has an even more difficult problem: Either it must violate elementwise locality, or it must leave large holes in fields in order to keep them aligned (the holes are analogous to the large amounts of white space that were between the elements of `f1` and `f2` above). The space-efficient, locality-violating strategy might represent the field's pvectors as follows:

```
f1       = [0 1 2 3] : parent is nil
f2       = [0 0 0 0] : parent is nil
nested   = [0 1 0 1 0 1 0 1] : parent is f1
indirect = [0 2 4 6] : parent is nil
segment  = [1 0 1 0 1 0 1 0] : parent is f1
```

The segment-based representation simplifies the task of a nested elwise. However, as with the pointer representation, communication can still be required to bring the information in a subfield together with a parent field when a computation must use information from both of them (see the addition example in Section 7.2.1). Therefore, this representation ignores some kinds of locality information in order to simplify the compilation of elwise. Of course, information does not always have to be distributed from parent to child when elwise is nested; the following nested elwise can be implemented without any communication. It simply adds 1 to every item in the pvector of nested:

```
(elwise (nested)
  (elwise (nested)
    (+ 1 nested)))
```

7.2.3 Mapping Representation

In the interpreter presented in Chapter 6, mappings were represented as a structure that contained two fields: copies of the key fields that were given to the match function. A more efficient parallel implementation of mappings would save canonicalized (that is, simplified and standardized) versions of the key fields. Additional slots might have to be added to the mapping defstruct in order to describe more accurately the contents of the canonicalized keys. The exact nature of that canonicalization and its new slots is presented in Section 7.4.

7.2.4 Nature of Optimizations

The MIMD notation for parallel execution used in the next section, pardo (for "parallel do"), can contain any arbitrary body code. Therefore, this particular MIMD notation glosses over important issues of synchronization and load balancing. As a result, this chapter presents more optimizations for SIMD architectures than for MIMD architectures. Another reason for this may be that the author has had more experience with SIMD architectures than with MIMD architectures.

7.3   Elementwise Evaluation

It is relatively easy to take a large number of processors, mount them in a box, and call the box a parallel computer. It is more difficult to create a communications network that permits a large number of processors to communicate in a useful way. Similarly, it is quite easy to implement `elwise`, at least in a naive way that uses the simple `field` representations discussed above and does not attempt to optimize for efficiency. For example, a naive implementation would not attempt to factor out duplications in effort among sites.

When the linguistic details are stripped away, the serial implementation of `elwise` used by the interpreter takes an `elwise` body and wraps an iterative loop around it. Parallel implementations of `elwise` simply turn that serial loop into an appropriate kind of parallel loop.

7.3.1   SIMD `elwise`

Parallel SIMD code can be thought of as having an implicit loop. Its iterations are defined by the particular processors that are selected and are listening to the code being broadcast by the serial host. Therefore, instead of wrapping a loop around the `elwise` body, a SIMD implementation of `elwise` must compile the contents of the body and turn its contents, and everything that it calls, into appropriate synchronized SIMD code. For example, consider the following sample code:

```
(setq x (make-paralation 10))
(defun complex-thing (z)
  (* z 2))

;; top-level call
(elwise (x) (+ 1 (complex-thing x)))
```

That code simply takes the numbers 0..9 and returns a field containing the numbers times 2, with 1 added. A SIMD compiler might turn that code into the following:

```
(setq x (make-paralation 10))
(defun parallel-complex-thing (z)
  (parallel-* z (parallel-coerce 2)))

(select-processors-representing-paralation x
  (parallel-+ (parallel-coerce 1) (parallel-complex-thing x)))
```

`parallel-coerce` simply returns a field containing its argument in all the selected processors. `parallel-`*function*, for any *function*, causes all of the SIMD processors to execute `function` on their own local data. Certain parallel functions are predefined: those in the instruction set of the SIMD processors. All other parallel functions, such as `parallel-complex-thing`, must be defined in the code output by the SIMD compiler.

7.3.2 MIMD `elwise`

Because the notations commonly used to describe MIMD programs are so powerful, the MIMD implementation of `elwise` is almost trivial. The serial `dotimes` loop is simply changed into a parallel `pardo` loop, which conceptually assigns a separate MIMD processor to each of the 10 paralation sites, and `complex-thing` is left unchanged:

```
(setq x (make-paralation 10))
(defun complex-thing (z)
  (* z 2))

(pardo (i 10)
  (+ 1 (complex-thing (elt x i))))
```

There are many other more complex strategies that a MIMD computer could use to implement `elwise`; a few of them are described below. They exploit a MIMD machine's ability to perform different tasks in different places at the same time. Because of the universality of both SIMD and MIMD computers (see Chapter 9), a SIMD computer could also use these same strategies.

7.3.3 Message-Passing Implementation

One strategy that a MIMD machine might use is to simulate a SIMD machine. A single processor, or even a group of processors, would be designated as the host and would be responsible for broadcasting instructions to the remaining processors. Each of these receiving processors represents a site in a paralation in which an `elwise` is taking place. ("Broadcast" is used in a figurative sense; it may or may not be implemented by a hardware broadcasting fan-out tree.) The other processors would be treated exactly like SIMD processors; that is, only a selected subset actually listens to the host and performs the broadcast instruction on their local data. This seems to waste the ability of MIMD processors to perform different tasks at the same time in different processors. A more MIMD-like version of this strategy can be created simply by explicitly decoupling the execution of an instruction from the time of its broadcast by the host.

Each processor would run at least two processes. One process, `RECEIVE`, listens to instruction-messages broadcast from a processor (or group of processors) designated as the host and records them in local memory. Another process, `DO-IT`, executes instructions in local memory. This second process blocks if an instruction is necessary but has not been received, or if an instruction needs data that is not yet available (perhaps due to the overlapping of the execution of a communication instruction with successive computation instructions). Communication (match and move) is implemented by a special class of broadcast instruction which happens to control the physical communications ports in each processor. These instructions have more stringent synchronization requirements than instructions that do not require cooperation between processors. The implementor might choose to exaggerate these requirements in order to simplify the implementation of `elwise`. For example, perhaps no communication can take place until all processors confirm that their instruction queues are empty.

The powerful host in this suggested implementation can broadcast instructions describing, for example, a conditional, its `then` clause, which might contain a loop, and its `else` clause, which might consist of a long straightline segment of code. Thus, it can broadcast the `then` clause without waiting for make sure that the processors are keeping up with it. As soon as a processor finishes executing its conditional, it instantly has the proper clause (`then` or `else`) available; no processors are forced to idle. Many MIMD machines are organized into some sort of hierarchy of successively less powerful processors, such as the M/SIMD PASM [SKS81, SSKI87], and DADO and NON-VON [Tra85]. Like pure SIMD machines, such architectures seem to have built-in hardware support for the concept of a host. Unlike the one-level SIMD hierarchy, however, a multilevel hierarchy provides *direct* hardware support for nested `elwise`: the compiler matches the hierarchy of processors to the hierarchy of `elwises` in a program.

At some point, because the instructions that were just broadcast require the results of a `send` that has not yet terminated, the host might wait to allow the processors to catch up and synchronize. Alternatively, it might continue to broadcast other instructions, perhaps generated by other users of a time-shared parallel machine. Multiple `DO-IT` processes can run in each processor, one for each user program running in the host. The distribution of instructions can be decoupled from their execution because `elwise` places no limitation on synchronization.

If the instructions from the host are stored in a small queue at each processor, rather than in a large local memory, there is a possibility that an instruction queue might fill up. (Of course, it is unlikely that a MIMD computer with large amounts of local memory would be forced to allocate only a small amount of memory to store broadcast instructions.) The host can be notified of a queue-full condition through the communications network. Assuming that all processors are acting in accord with a single instruction stream (that is, a single user running a single `elwise`), when the queue of a single processor is full, the host must cease broadcasting to all processors. This is not a catastrophic occurrence. A queue-full condition causes the host to be idle, not the parallel processors. The fact that queues are full means that some of the parallel processors currently have more than enough to do.

It is possible that a small number of processors can have full instruction queues at the same time that many others have empty queues; this means that a majority of the processors can be idle. This is unlikely to be a problem because the way in which `elwise` is used in most applications naturally balances the load between paralation sites. In any case, such an occurrence would only affect the single `elwise` that caused it, not other nested or nesting `elwise`s or other timesharing users. This same problem is encountered by *any* implementation that equates a paralation site with a fixed processor and does not allow load balancing process migration to take place during an `elwise`. Finally, if the local program memory only has room for one instruction-message at a time, this desynchronized machine would degenerate into a traditional synchronized SIMD architecture.

7.3.4 Shared Memory Implementation

A shared memory MIMD implementation might be centered around a list or queue of "task" objects [GLR83]. An invocation of `elwise` would combine a pointer to the body code with pointers to the various sites of the involved paralation, thus creating many tasks. These tasks are then appended to a list of "things-to-do." The operating system causes free processors to constantly forage over the list of tasks looking for things to do. Communication operations simply spawn a special kind of task that requires cooperation between processors.

This queue-based implementation has excellent load balancing properties but totally ignores the locality properties of paralations and fields. However, this is inherent in the idea of shared memory hardware, which hides the cost of communication.

7.3.5 Interference Between Sites

As was mentioned in Chapter 2, it is an error if the various sites in a paralation interfere with each other during an `elwise`. If such interference does occur, `elwise` is free to take any action that it chooses. This section discusses several possible classes of actions.

Non-Portable `elwise` Interference Actions

One action to take in response to `elwise` interference is simply to obey the underlying nature of the hardware. In a shared memory multiprocessor, one might allow the various interfering side effects to take place in whatever order happens to be convenient. There are no guarantees on atomicity. The side effect produced by a site might immediately be clobbered by another site—that is the very essence of interference.

On the other hand, one might imagine an implementation that gave each processor and associated paralation site a copy of the entire global state. A site is perfectly free to modify any variable that it wants to, but its modifications are not visible to other sites. At the end of the `elwise`, the various modified copies of the global state would be merged in any convenient way. Perhaps a modicum of error checking would be performed at this merge stage: if two sites have changed a certain variable in two different ways, signal an interference error. Of course, this does not detect all interference errors, because a processor might modify a variable and then change it back to its original value before the `elwise` terminates.

`elwise` Interference Detection

Perhaps the best action to take in response to `elwise` interference is to notify the programmer of the error. However, in order to do this, error checking may have to take place at run-time. Detection of `elwise` interference at compile-time is a difficult problem; it is equivalent to the problem of automatic unwinding of serial loops into parallel loops. Loop unwinding translates a certain class of loops (those with non-interfering iterations) into a kind of `elwise`.

In conventional side effecting languages such as Pascal and Fortran, current compiler technology can divide loop bodies into three classes: parallelizable (no interference), non-parallelizable (interference), and "can't tell" [KKP*81, LKK85]. In loop unwinding, "can't tell" means that the loop is not unwound. However, an `elwise` body is always executed in parallel. In order to signal an error reliably when interference occurs, run-time checking is necessary in that third "can't tell" case. In the future, the third case might be eliminated by improvements in compiler technology or by the use of a language in which interference is detectable syntactically [Rey78].

One method for detecting interference at run-time is based on time-stamping. Whenever a site reads or writes data, it stamps the location as read or written at a certain time, by a specific dynamic invocation of `elwise`, and includes the site's index. Therefore, whenever a site reads from a location that is stamped as modified by another site since the beginning of the `elwise`, an error is signalled. Also, whenever a site attempts to modify a location that has been read by another site since the beginning of the `elwise`, an error is signalled.

7.4 Match

The version of `match` presented in Section 6.2.4 does not actually do any work to create a mapping; it postpones all calculations until it is time to use a mapping.

In any actual implementation that attempts to be efficient, however, match should perform a number of calculations, described below, in order to canonicalize the mapping. For example, the following two mappings:

```
(match '#F(a b c d b) '#F(b a a z a))
```

```
(match '#F(alpha beta gamma delta beta) '#F(beta alpha alpha zeta alpha))
```

might both be represented by the canonicalized form:

```
(mapping :to-key #F(0 1 NIL NIL 1)
         :from-key #F(1 0 0 NIL 0))
```

A canonicalized mapping can be described as follows. Suppose the key fields are K1 and K2 (it does not matter which is source or destination). Each key K in K1 is labeled with the *index* of its first occurrence in K2, or nil if it is not needed because it was not found in K2 (a key is needed only if it occurs at least once in *both* K1 and K2). Next, each key K in K2 is labeled with its *label* in K1, or nil if it is not found there. The labels of K1 and K2 represent the canonicalized mapping.

The requirements satisfied by the canonicalized key format can be described combinatorially. The labels are all integers from 0..length(K2) or nil. The labels of the first occurrence of each needed key in K1 are monotonically increasing, and the non-needed keys are nil. The labels of all other occurrences of needed keys in both K1 and K2 are equal to the label of the first occurrence in K1; non-needed keys are nil.

Canonicalization can be implemented with the use of table lookup. The most appropriate form of lookup depends upon the type and size of the key fields, the match predicate involved, and, of course, upon the target architecture. For example, the serial simulator for PARALATION LISP can choose to use hash tables, linked lists, or arrays to canonicalize a particular mapping.

The PARALATION LISP simulator optimizes the user-specified equality predicate of match. It changes weak and inefficient LISP equality predicates, like equal, into a stronger and more efficient ones, like eql, if it can prove (at compile-time or run-time) that they will return the same results given the contents of the key fields. For example, the compiler knows that equal and eql return identical results when their arguments are of type fixnum.

A simple, non-optimizing, canonicalizing match is contained in Section B.1. That particular serial implementation is not efficient because it *always* makes use of hash tables, rather than attempting to use a faster, if more limited, lookup algorithm when appropriate. For example, if the keys are all small integers, an array could be used instead of a full hash table. If the fields involved are small (say, 30 long), an association list is usually faster than a hash table. The full PARALATION LISP simulator performs this type of optimization.

The canonicalized mapping format is useful because it allows <- to be implemented with less expensive forms of communication. In a serial implementation, <- would be able to use array lookup rather than hash table lookup. In a parallel implementation for the Connection Machine, a `send` to numerical processor addresses could be used instead of a sort. The canonicalized integers explicitly describe locations that can be used for the rendezvous of <-; the original key fields had described the same rendezvous locations encoded in a less accessible, implicit manner.

7.4.1   Parallel Table Lookup

The serial implementations of `match` described above can be converted into parallel implementations by replacing the core, serial table lookup, with parallel table lookup. Just as the `dotimes` loop serial implementation of `elwise` suggested several simple parallel implementations, the table lookup version of `match` can lead to several different parallel algorithms. Basically, the idea is to create a parallel table lookup routine that allows each element of a key field to get information from another key field. For example, each key might receive the index of the very first equal key in the other field. In a sense, the hash table–based procedure `match-move-internal` presented in Section 6.2.4 is almost a canonicalizing implementation of `match`. (As is shown below, <- itself has no need of hash tables if it has access to a canonicalized key.)

The precise implementation of parallel table lookup varies from architecture to architecture. A MIMD message passing or shared memory machine might cause the various key values to rendezvous in parallel at a hashed memory location in the table. This implementation is close in spirit to the serial, hash table–based <-.

Alternatively, both SIMD and MIMD machines might sort the keys to bring similar keys near each other, and then use a logarithmic spreading operation like parallel prefix to cause them to communicate.

Parallel Prefix

Parallel prefix is an extremely useful operation. It takes a problem that at first glance seems to require linear time and solves it in logarithmic time. (Blelloch argues that it can be considered a unit time operation [Ble87].) Given a list of numbers X1 to Xn and an associative two-argument operator *, parallel prefix (like the scan operation of APL) computes Y1 to Yn as follows:

```
Y(1) = X(1)

Y(i) = Y(i-1) * X(i)
     = X1 * X2 * x3 * ... * Xi
```

Put another way, a parallel prefix algorithm takes an associative function that is just like a combining function[1], call it F, and quickly applies it to data field values in successive processors of:

```
a       b           c               d                       e
```

resulting in output fields in the same processors with the values:

```
a     F(a, b)   F(F(a, b), c)   F(F(F(a, b), c), d)   F(F(F(F(a, b), c), d), e)
```

The key point is that, since F is associative, parallel prefix can be implemented so that it performs its task in a logarithmic number of applications of F and of communication operations, on a variety of processor interconnection topologies [LG87, KRS85, KRS86]. Thus, 16 applications of F and 16 **send** operations are sufficient to scan F across the 65,536 processors of a Connection Machine.[2]

One implementation of parallel prefix that is easy to understand involves pointer doubling [Ble87]. Each processor has a pointer to the next location. Each processor sends the current value through that pointer to its destination. The processors then apply F to the received value and the current local value. Then, each processor takes the pointer of the processor that it points to, thus doubling the length of its pointer. This cycle continues until all pointers point past the last processor, indicating that the parallel prefix has terminated. The intermediate stages might look like this:

```
a       b           c               d                       e
a     F(a, b)   F(b, c)         F(c, d)               F(d, e)
a     F(a, b)   F(a, F(b, c))   F(F(a, b), F(c, d))   F(F(b, c), F(d, e))
a     F(a, b)   F(a, F(b, c))   F(F(a, b), F(c, d))   F(a, F(F(b, c), F(d, e)))

≡       ;; Since F is associative
a     F(a, b)   F(F(a, b), c)   F(F(F(a, b), c), d)   F(F(F(F(a, b), c), d), e)
```

Section B.2 contains a PARALATION LISP implementation of this pointer doubling algorithm.

If the F function supplied to parallel prefix is the **arg1** function, which simply returns its first argument, the effect of the prefix calculation is to spread the first value of a collection to all of the successive values. In the above example, the result is a row of all a's.

---

[1] Combining can be thought of as an unsynchronized, and therefore more flexible and machine-independent, version of parallel prefix [KRS86].

[2] Because of the distribution of overhead costs between on-chip and off-chip communication, on the Connection Machine, with its current size and speed parameters, parallel prefix takes about the same amount of time as a single global routing cycle (not counting the time to repeatedly apply the F function) and grows *less* than linearly with the number of virtual processors per physical processor.

With a few more complications, a segmented version of parallel prefix can be created, one that performs separate prefix calculations in separate segments of a sequence. A segmented prefix of `arg1` spreads data from the first processor of each separate segment to the remaining processors in its segment. Therefore, table lookup can be implemented by appending the sequence of keys being looked up to the sequence of keys that make up the table, and then sorting the resulting collection. After the sort, each table key will immediately precede a contiguous group of identical keys that are trying to perform a lookup. A segmented prefix of `arg1` propagates the necessary table data from each table key to the lookup keys. Finally, a communication operation is used to send the looked-up keys and table data back to their original locations [Sab86].

7.5   Move

7.5.1   Efficient Serial Move with Canonicalized Mappings

Unlike the `match-move-internal` function presented earlier, the `move-internal` in Figure 7.1 centers around the use of an array rather than a hash table. Other than this, the algorithm used is identical: move data from a source field into a table indexed by the source key and then create a destination field by looking up the destination keys in the table. Of course, the job of `move-internal` is simpler because keys that are not found in both source and destination are always `nil` (precomputed at `match` time) and also because the non-`nil` key values are guaranteed to be small integers that are less than `key-limit` (since they are index values). This guarantee enables the use of an array to implement the table instead of a comparatively expensive hash table.

The function `source-data-to-table` in Figure 7.2 is used to produce an array, `key-table`. It maps small integers into their combined data values. The small integers, of course, are the canonicalized keys. The function is analogous in purpose to the `enter-source-data-into-table`. The function loops through the indices of `key-field`'s paralation, combining the corresponding `data-field` values into the array location indicated by the canonicalized `key-field` value. A function comparable to `initialize-needed-keys` is not needed here because it is clear which keys are needed: the non-`nil` ones.

The new `array-table-to-pvector` function in Figure 7.3, like the `table-to-pvector` which it replaces, produces a pvector from a table of combined keys. In this case, however, the table is an array. The function loops through the `key-field` of the destination and fetches the corresponding combined value from the `table` with a simple array reference. If the value is available, it is inserted into the result. If there is `no-value`, the corresponding `default` is used.

```
(defmacro <- (field &key by with default)
  '(move-internal ,field ,with ,default ,by))

(defun move-internal (field combiner default map)
  (let* ((to-key (mapping-to-key map))
         (from-key (mapping-from-key map))
         (key-limit (max (paralation-internal-length
                           (field-paralation to-key))
                         (paralation-internal-length
                           (field-paralation from-key))))
         (key-table (source-data-to-table from-key key-limit
                                           field combiner)))
    (make-field :paralation (field-paralation to-key)
                :pvector (array-table-to-pvector key-table
                                                 to-key
                                                 default))))
```

Figure 7.1: An efficient implementation of <- using canonicalized keys

```
(defun source-data-to-table (key-field key-limit
                             data-field combiner)
  (let* ((no-value (cons :no-value nil))
         (table (make-array key-limit :initial-element no-value))
         (data-vector (field-pvector data-field))
         (key-vector (field-pvector key-field)))
    (dotimes (i (paralation-internal-length
                  (field-paralation key-field)))
      (let ((key (aref key-vector i)))
        (when key
          (let* ((current-value (aref table key))
                 (in-table-p (not (eql current-value no-value))))
            (setf (aref table key)
                  (if in-table-p
                      (funcall combiner
                               current-value
                               (aref data-vector i))
                      (aref data-vector i)))))))
    table))
```

Figure 7.2: Load source into an array based upon canonicalized from-key

```
(defun array-table-to-pvector (table key-field default)
  (let* ((to-size (paralation-internal-length
                    (field-paralation key-field)))
         (key-vector (field-pvector key-field))
         (default-vector (if default
                             (field-pvector default)
                             nil))
         (result-pv (make-array to-size)))
    (dotimes (i to-size)
      (let ((key (aref key-vector i)))
        (if key
            (setf (aref result-pv i) (aref table key))
            (setf (aref result-pv i) (aref default-vector i)))))
    result-pv))
```

Figure 7.3: Turn the array table into a field pvector

7.5.2 Parallel Move

A parallel version of move can also use the two-step process of combining values into a table and then converting the table into a pvector. `source-data-to-table` can be parallelized simply by using a combining `send`, since the key values are small integers that can be treated as addresses of rendezvous processors. Thus, the table is distributed among a range of processors. A combining `send` can be implemented by a combining network, one in which the communication nodes themselves perform the computation necessary to combine colliding data. Alternatively, if such a network is not available, or not able to execute a particular combining function, a sort and parallel prefix algorithm can be used. These implementation techniques for `source-data-to-table` work for both MIMD and SIMD machines, as well as for local and shared memory machines.

The `array-table-to-pvector` function becomes a concurrently reading `get` from the combined data table, performed by the destination paralation. A shared memory machine might implement this directly. A local memory machine might use sort and parallel prefix.

7.5.3 Efficiency on Parallel Hardware

Depending upon the nature of a computer's communications network, other kinds of information might be stored in a mapping in order to accelerate its use. This information can be updated each time a `<-` uses the mapping. For example, a mapping might contain information that captures the states of various hardware switches in the nodes of the communications network. This would be especially useful on a machine that calculates message routing patterns off-line.

A mapping can also contain type information, either explicitly declared by the user or calculated at compile or run-time, indicating whether the mapping requires concurrent read or combining. Type information about mappings can be used to accelerate the execution of `<-` for simple special cases like permutations and local communications. Although, in general, the implementation of `<-` on a local memory machine without combining can seem expensive (for example, it can require a sort, a parallel prefix of the combining function, a sort followed by a parallel prefix to implement concurrent read, and a `send`), this overhead can be reduced considerably with appropriate use of type information.

For example, if it is known that a mapping does not require combining (for example, the source key might be an index field or some other field that contains no duplications, or the user might explicitly declare that a mapping has no collisions, perhaps by not supplying a combining function), `source-data-to-table` can be simplified. Although, in general, it might require a sort and a parallel prefix, a simple `send` is all that is required in this special non-combining case. Similarly, if it is known that a mapping does not require concurrent read, `array-table-to-pvector` can also be simplified: instead of a sort, parallel prefix, and `send`, all that is required is a single `send`. In the especially simple permutation case in which neither concurrent read nor combining is required, the entire `match-move-internal` process can be implemented with a single `send`.

Shape is an extension of the paralation model that gives the user greater control over communication locality *within* a paralation. Chapter 8 covers shape and its implications for the efficient implementation of `<-` on certain local mappings, such as "northwest" within paralation sites that represent the points of a two-dimensional grid.

7.6 Library Functions

The implementation of various library functions, such as `vref` and `collapse`, in terms of the paralation primitives, has already been presented. However, the library functions can also be implemented at a lower level, perhaps directly on the hardware of a target machine. This can produce a faster implementation.

For example, the `choose` function might be implemented on a SIMD machine by selecting the processors of the `choose`'s boolean field, subselecting the ones that contain true, enumerating them, and then matching from the enumeration values to a new paralation of appropriate size. On the other hand, a serial implementation can perform the enumeration by a serial loop, as in Figure 7.4.

Another library function is `vref`, which combines the information in a field

```
(defun choose (field)
  (let ((count 0)
        (from-field (elwise (field) nil)))
    (dotimes (i (length field))
      (when (elt field i)
        (setf (elt from-field i) count)
        (incf count)))
    (match (make-paralation count) from-field)))
```

Figure 7.4: A serial implementation of `choose`

into a single value. For many simple combining functions, the Connection Machine can implement `vref` by using its GLOBAL-OR line. This line is a special piece of hardware that can logically OR together 1 bit from all of the processors in the machine and return the result to the host. `vref` with `logior` is easy to implement with this line. With a bit more work, simple logical and mathematical combining functions, such as `logand`, `max`, and `min`, can also be implemented. Of course, this method is efficient only for a single call to `vref` at a time (that is, it does not work as described here for a `vref` nested inside an `elwise`), since there is only a single GLOBAL-OR line. Nested invocations of `vref` are most efficiently implemented on the Connection Machine by using a segmented parallel prefix.

7.6.1   Idiom Extraction

Idioms are common patterns of language usage [PR79]. The paralation library functions are idioms that have been given names. However, idioms that do not as yet have names may still be worth optimizing. For example, communication according to certain combining functions might be checked for by move's compiler and implemented as a special case. `<-` according to `field-append-2` might have an especially efficient implementation that takes advantage of a machine's representation of the `field` data structure.

7.7   Partial Implementations

It certainly is possible to implement a subset of the paralation model in parallel and still have a useful language. This might be desirable as an intermediate step on the way to a full implementation or as a way of evaluating a paralation language. The compiler for such a subset produces serial (simulator) code for certain paralation constructs and parallel code for others. It is helpful to notify the user when serial code has been produced. However, in order to be useful, a paralation language subset should be chosen so that a programmer can tell easily whether a particular construct leads to parallel or serial code.

An initial implementation of a paralation language might limit the code that can appear in the body of an `elwise`, or in the code called from that body, to a small set of functions, such as mathematical and logical operations. Attempts to call more complex functions in parallel, such as `make-hash-table`, `elwise`, or `match`, would result in serialization.

Compared to the full paralation model and its goals, a language subset seems ugly and grotesque. However, the fact is that new machines need new compilers. Given a choice between taking a year to implement a well-defined, already existing language and taking a month to create and implement a tiny, ugly language that is tied directly to the hardware, machine designers usually choose the latter. Perhaps a paralation subset can provide a third option, one that can be as easy to implement as one tied to hardware (because it only parallelizes the constructs that are easy on your hardware), while simultaneously providing a growth path to a more general language.

7.8 The Ideal Target Machine

What is an ideal computer for a particular high-level language? It might be a computer that runs programs written in the language fastest for a given price, or it might be a computer whose assembly language most closely resembles the constructs of the high-level language. In the serial world, microcoded general register machines and RISC machines with simple, sparse instruction sets compete in the same domain. Similarly, there is no easy way to tell what an ideal architecture for the paralation model is. It is likely that the constructs of the model will not appear to map nicely onto the ideal architecture, just as the constructs of conventional languages do not trivially map onto the hardware of RISC machines or VLIW machines (Very Long Instruction Word [Ell86]). As in any optimization process, the first step in creating an ideal target would be to measure and analyze the usage of the paralation constructs in a variety of programs. The next step is to concentrate effort on improving architectural features that accelerate the most frequently used constructs and idioms.

That said, that there is no way to describe intuitively an ideal architecture from a programming model alone, I now present one (and only one) intuition: the ideal paralation target is a low-level machine that does *not* attempt to address the high-level issues that are addressed by the model itself. On this basis, a crossbar-based shared memory machine is not an ideal target, because it obscures an important issue by smothering it with hardware. A paralation implementation might not be able to execute an inherently simple program faster than a more complex program because complexity is hidden within the basic cycle of the machine and thus cannot be avoided. Of course, the RISC/CISC debate applies to the parallel domain, and my intuitions about an ideal paralation target can be viewed as a preference for relatively simple parallel architectures.

7.9   Current Implementations

There is currently one complete compiler for PARALATION LISP that produces code for the Connection Machine. It uses an implementation of CONNECTION MACHINE LISP as its back end [WS87]. The strategy of compiling from a paralation language into an already implemented parallel language greatly simplifies the compiler. For example, it eliminates the need to write a new parallel storage allocator, garbage collector, and Connection Machine code generator and optimizer.

For efficiency, the PARALATION LISP compiler depends upon certain internal details of the CONNECTION MACHINE LISP implementation. For example, it knows how to force CONNECTION MACHINE LISP xectors (used to implement fields) to stay aligned within processors when appropriate (when fields are in the same paralation). A user-level CONNECTION MACHINE LISP program cannot exercise this degree of control over the storage allocator; the compiled PARALATION LISP code contains direct calls to internal functions of the CONNECTION MACHINE LISP implementation.

The locality information provided by the operators and data structures of the paralation model is so rich that the compiler actually ignores much of it; the compiler is not yet sophisticated enough to take advantage of it (for example, fields within fields and nested parallelism are not yet implemented efficiently).

In addition to the Connection Machine–based compiler, a complete simulator for PARALATION LISP exists; it runs under any implementation of COMMON LISP. Finally, a second stand-alone compiler for an abstract parallel target machine is currently under development by Guy Blelloch (see Section 7.2.1). This compiler does implement nested parallelism efficiently.

Chapter 8

Shape

8.1 What is Shape?

This chapter discusses an important addition to the paralation model, a facility for accommodating shape. Shape is useful when a paralation is modeling a problem in which locality between data values is important. The shape information can be used by the compiler to produce better code and data-to-processor layouts, since an architecture may support certain shapes more efficiently than others. My idea for a generalized shape facility was stimulated by discussions with Guy Blelloch. Blelloch needed to perform nearest-neighbor (local) communications within the paralation model without sacrificing efficiency.

Many low-level vision algorithms assume a two-dimensional grid shape for the data and perform operations on all localized squares of 9 or 16 grid cells. If this shape information is accessible to the compiler, it can easily map the sites of the corresponding paralations onto processors that are interconnected in a grid format. Alternatively, in a hypercube-based machine, a grid can be laid out on the hypercube using Gray coding. Similarly, a wind tunnel simulator might make use of a three-dimensional grid. Sorting algorithms and FFT's make use of shapes such as butterflies. Cellular automata algorithms center around the use of various tessellated shapes, such as hexagonal arrays. Even linear locality (between an element of a linear structure and the element to its left and right) is a special, albeit simple, kind of shape.

Shape is also valuable from an ease of use standpoint. Shapes make it easy to perform shape-based communications and access. Thus, grid-shaped paralations make it easy to shift (with move) the values in a field one site to the "north," or to access a certain field value given its multidimensional cartesian coordinates. The shape facility also provides a way for the user to control the way a paralation's

0	1	2	3	4	5	6	7	8	9	10	11	12	13	14	15

Figure 8.1: Index field of a length 16 paralation, arranged linearly

0	1	2	3
4	5	6	7
8	9	10	11
12	13	14	15

Figure 8.2: Index field of a length 16 paralation, arranged as a 4 x 4 grid

fields are accessed. For example, it allows the user to specify explicitly the function that should be used to print a paralation's fields.

Because a user-defined shape is basically a new language construct, it is easiest to define a general shape extension facility in an extensible language like LISP. Paralation languages with a less extensible base language may find it difficult to provide a reasonable user interface to the shape facility. On the other hand, an object-oriented base language might have a much easier time than LISP of defining shapes because it could more easily exploit the commonality between new and old shapes.

This chapter presents a method of shape locality description that is very dynamic and more in keeping with the dynamic flavor of LISP than the static constructs of languages like Fortran. It is expected that most paralation languages will provide a library of predefined, efficient shapes. Perhaps a static base language would supply a large library of shapes but not allow the user to describe new shapes. Alternatively, a static language might allow the user to describe new shapes at compile-time by using some sort of static shape description facility.

Other than a brief reference to sites and noodles floating in a soup in Section 2.2, Chapter 2 did not specify precisely how the sites of a paralation were arranged. Due to the similarities between fields and arrays and the presence of an index field, the reader might have imagined the sites as being arranged linearly, as in Figure 8.1.

Of course, if a field were being used to model a two-dimensional problem, the sites might be visualized in a 4 by 4 grid formation, as in Figure 8.2. This layout is based upon row-major order.

The shape facility supports new paralation shapes in two ways. The first part of shape is *shape locality*.

0	1	2	3
4	5	6	7
8	9	10	11
12	13	14	15

⇓

Via move according to left shift mapping

⇓

1	2	3	**
5	6	7	**
9	10	11	**
13	14	15	**

Figure 8.3: Local communication in a grid

8.1.1 Shape Locality

Shape locality allows the user to describe the types of communication that should be inexpensive in a given shape, such as nearest neighbor communication. For example, in the above grid, a mapping that transfers data one position to the left should be inexpensive and should execute in constant time, independent of the size of the paralation. Figure 8.3 illustrates the result using such a mapping. Note that default values, represented by "**", are needed for the right edge; if the shape were a torus, the right edge would have taken its data from the toroidally connected left edge.

Similarly, in a paralation of linear shape (a one-dimensional grid), the nth site should be near the $n + 1$st and the $n - 1$st site. In a paralation of pyramid shape, the apex is near the sites directly underneath it, while a point in the middle of the pyramid is surrounded by neighbors. Thus, shape allows the user to describe precisely any desired intersite locality.

8.1.2 Shape Access

The second part of shape is *shape access*, which deals with how the various parts of a shape are named and manipulated. Until this point in the book, the only name a site could have was the index of the site. But in many shapes one would prefer a different system. For example, in a paralation with a three-dimensional grid shape, coordinates of the form (x y z) should be available; these might map onto index numbers by row-major ordering.

The shape facility allows one to assign any names to the sites of a paralation. This is accomplished by attaching a field that contains the site names to a paralation. Just as any site can access its index number, any site can access its site name. COMMON LISP's sequence function `elt` was sufficient for accessing field values according to their index value; a new function called `fref` is added that allows one to access sites according to their user-specified site-names.

Another part of access concerns how a shaped field[1] prints out; usually it should be printed in a distinctive style that is reminiscent of its shape. For example, one might want multidimensional grid-shaped fields to print out in a manner reminiscent of multidimensional arrays in the base language. For COMMON LISP, this would mean prefacing the field with a number indicating the rank of the field (number of dimensions), followed by appropriately parenthesized contents:

```
(make-grid '(4 4))
  ⇒ #2F((0  1  2  3)
        (4  5  6  7)
        (8  9 10 11)
        (12 13 14 15))
```

The remainder of this chapter covers the key points of shape by describing the highlights of PARALATION LISP's shape facility. The full details are covered by [Sab87d].

8.2   Shape in Paralation Lisp

The PARALATION LISP shape facility contains a number of standard functions, five of which are described in this section. Shape locality is handled by `make-shaped-paralation` and `shape-map`. Shape access is handled by `define-shape-access`, `fref`, and `site-names`. PARALATION LISP also contains a library of useful shapes; this section describes some of the library functions that make up the shape `grid`.

8.2.1   Shape Locality in Paralation Lisp

Shaped paralations are created by `make-shaped-paralation`. The user describes the locality properties of the new paralation by supplying a list of maps to this function. A single paralation must serve as the source and destination paralation of all of the mappings in the list of maps; that is, all of the sources and destination key fields of all of the mappings are in the same paralation. The result of `make-shaped-paralation` is the index field of a new paralation with a length identical to the paralation used by the mappings in the list of maps.

---

[1]A shaped field is simply a field in a shaped paralation; a field in a grid-shaped paralation is called a grid-shaped field.

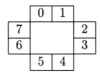

Figure 8.4: Index of a ring-shaped paralation

A <- involving this result paralation may execute more quickly when certain new mappings are used.[2] These new mappings are based upon the older mappings in the list of maps. They have been transported into the new paralation based upon the index numbers of the sites they connected. Thus, if the first old map connected site 10 to site 20 of the old paralation, the first new map connects site 10 to site 20 of the new paralation. Because the paralation created by make-shaped-paralation has a shape, the arrows of the new mappings may be "shorter" (but never longer) than the arrows of the old mappings—the sites are rearranged to be near each other according to the mappings. In addition, new mappings created in this paralation will transitively be able to take advantage of this shape rearrangement.

The code below creates a ring-shaped paralation that contains n sites and returns its index field:

```
(defun make-ring-internal (n)
  (let* ((p-old (make-paralation n))
         (p-next (elwise (p-old)
                   (if (= p-old (1- n)) 0 (+ p-old 1))))
         (old-forward (match p-next p-old))
         (old-backward (match p-old p-next)))
    (make-shaped-paralation
      (list old-forward old-backward)))))
```

Figure 8.4 illustrates the result of calling make-ring-internal with n equal to 7. Not shown are the two new fast mappings that are built into the ring's paralation. The first allows <- to rotate the contents of a field one position clockwise; the second works counterclockwise. The new, fast mappings are not returned by make-shaped-paralation. Instead, they are accessed using the shape-map function.

shape-map takes two arguments: a field and an integer, zero-based subscript. shape-map returns a fast mapping equivalent to the subscriptth mapping in the list of mappings originally supplied to make-shaped-paralation when it created

---

[2]Whether communication within a shaped paralation actually has the desired running time depends upon the ability of the underlying architecture to support the shape of the paralation by an appropriate embedding and upon the skill of the programmer who implements the shape facility.

`field`'s paralation. Thus, if `shape-map` is given a field in a ring-shaped paralation along with a subscript of 0, it returns the clockwise mapping. The following program creates a field that averages each value in its ring input with its clockwise and counterclockwise neighbors:

```
(defun shaped-avg (f)
  (let ((f-forward (<- f :by (shape-map f 0)))
        (f-backward (<- f :by (shape-map f 1))))
    (elwise (f f-right f-left)
      (/ (+ f f-right f-left) 3))))
```

Like any field, a ring-shaped field can be passed to `<-` with any mapping at all. The shaped mappings simply exist for convenience and efficiency.

8.2.2 Shape Access in PARALATION LISP

Shape access is controlled by `define-shape-access`. It allows the user to attach various pieces of information to any field's paralation that define how those fields behave. For example, the user can attach a new print function. An attempt to print a field is then passed off to the user function:

```
(defun make-ring (n)
  (define-shape-access (make-ring-internal n)
    :print-function #'ring-printer))

;; print the ring out any way you want to
;; this function uses a #R format, and lets lisp's built-in
;; list formatter worry about pretty printing large fields
(defun ring-printer (field stream depth)
  (declare (ignore depth))
  (format stream "#R~s" (coerce field 'list))
  field)
```

Like all of the shape access functions, `define-shape-access` can be called on fields of any paralation, including the unshaped paralations created by `make-paralation` (see Section 8.3).

The user can use `define-shape-access` to attach a field full of `:site-names` to a paralation. The `site-names` function allows one to retrieve these names at a later time. For example, a grid-shaped paralation would have cartesian site-names; each field element would be a list of the two coordinates of its site:

```
(setq a (make-grid '(2 3)))
   ⇒ #2F((0 1 2) (3 4 5))
(site-names a)
   ⇒ #2F(((0 0) (0 1) (0 2)) ((1 0) (1 1) (1 2)))
```

COMMON LISP's sequence function `elt` was used to reference field elements according to the index number of their site. A new function, `fref`, can be used to access field elements according to their site's names. For example:

```
(fref a 1 0)
  ⇒ 3
```

`fref` has no direct, hard-wired connection to `site-names`. `define-shape-access` can be used to attach any function to a paralation, and that function is then called when any field in that paralation is to be `fref`ed; the function is responsible for taking the arguments passed to `fref` and processing them in any way it sees fit. In the case of a grid, it might be more efficient to perform multiplications and additions (row-major) upon the cartesian coordinates in order to calculate a target index (in preparation for calling `elt`), rather than to perform an associative `vref` lookup in `site-names` to find the corresponding target index.

8.2.3 Shape Library: Grid Example

For each shape in a shape library, there are several types of functions that should be supplied. First of all, a way must be provided for making objects of the new shape. The way should be reminiscent of `make-paralation`. Thus, it should return the index field of the new paralation rather than its site-names. `make-grid` is an example of such a function. Although a shape may provide new access functions, the standard shape access functions like `site-names`, `fref`, and of course the print function, should work in an appropriate manner.

The grid shape library supplies a more convenient way to access the fast maps of a grid than `shape-map`. It is called `grid-map`. When thinking of movement in a grid, one normally picks a particular axis or dimension to shift along and then the direction in which to shift. `grid-map` takes a field in a grid-shaped paralation, an integer indicating a particular dimension, and an integer (plus or minus 1) indicating the direction of movement along that axis; it returns the appropriate map.[3] More specialized maps, such as north, east, and so on, in a two-dimensional grid, can easily be defined on top of this:

```
(defun north (field)
  (grid-map field 0 +1))
(defun south (field)
  (grid-map field 0 -1))
```

---

[3]One might want `grid-map` to take an argument indicating whether the mapping should wrap around the edges, thus rotating instead of shifting. However, a grid that wraps around really is a different shape from one that does not, and the user should have to note this distinction at the time of grid creation, perhaps with a `wrap` keyword argument to `make-grid`.

```
(defun east (field)
  (grid-map field 1 +1))
(defun west (field)
  (grid-map field 1 -1))
```

On a machine that has a network on which a multidimensional grid can be directly embedded, a move according to a **grid-map** can be implemented most efficiently by a direct call to the appropriate nearest-neighbor communication primitive. However, even if shape maps are no more efficient than ordinary general maps, the shape facility can be exceedingly useful simply from a user-interface point of view. For example, much of the experience and many of the operators and algorithms of the APL community can be transferred directly to the manipulation of grid-shaped fields. In addition, the shape facility can be viewed as a tool that enables the user to describe points for future optimization: the paralation programmer describes various shapes; later, some of them can be added to a shape-library that is optimized for a particular architecture, thus speeding up programs that use the shapes. This is useful because relatively little progress has been made on the automatic embedding of shaped data structures on parallel processors.

Grid-Shaped Fields versus Fields Of Fields

Consider the relationship in a serial language between a two-dimensional array of data and a vector (one-dimensional array) whose elements are themselves vectors containing data. Depending upon the base language, these two different structures may be represented differently. The two-dimensional array structure is often represented internally as a one-dimensional vector of data stored in row-major order. A pair of X-Y coordinates can be converted to serve as an index into the vector by performing a simple calculation (a multiplication and an addition). On the other hand, the second, vector-based, array structure consists of a single main vector whose contents are pointers to the other subvectors. Accessing an element uses the X coordinate to get a pointer to the proper subvector and then uses the Y coordinate to access the proper data element. Thus, two pointer-following operations are required for this structure, whereas only one is required for the row-major structure. Depending upon the relative costs of multiplication and pointer-following, one or the other representation may be preferable. However, from the serial user's point of view, the two structures are almost identical. Given an X-Y pair, one can access any array element in unit time.

In the paralation model, the difference between a field of fields (all unshaped) and a two-dimensional grid-shaped field is more significant, both in terms of efficiency and user interface. From the efficiency point of view, the locality relationship between the data is quite different in a grid than in a field of fields. An element of a grid field has four close neighbors, north, south, east, and west. On the other hand, an element in a field of fields is near all the elements in its subfield (since they are all floating in the same soup bowl). Each such subfield corresponds to a single row (assuming row-major order)[4] of data in a grid, so a data element is equally near all the data in its row. Finally, all rows are near each other since the top-level field is a field of rows, each of which is represented by a field.

From the user-interface viewpoint, a grid-shaped paralation makes it easy to perform grid-based communication, such as shifts, by using the built-in `grid-maps`. `fref` makes it easy to access data elements in one step simply by naming their coordinates. On the other hand, a field of fields has no built-in mappings and no built-in `site-names` to simplify the creation of new grid-based maps. Access to elements of a field of fields must occur in two stages (just two serial pointer-following operations in the vector of vectors), using two calls to `elt`: the first call picks the correct subfield, the second picks a particular data element.

Paralations have a third alternative to grids and fields of fields: One can create something that is just like a grid from a shape access point of view but without its cartesian locality properties. Internally, `make-unshaped-grid` might operate just like `make-grid` except that there is no need for it to arrange paralation sites to accommodate grid-communication efficiently (see Section 8.3.1).

8.3 Other Views of Parallelism

The shape facility allows new language paradigms to be built on top of the one provided by the kernel paralation constructs. A new shape, like a grid, can make use of special shape maps to be even more specific about the locality of parallel data than the base paralation model. On the other hand, one can imagine a model with the grid's user interface that is less specific than the paralation model about locality. Such a model would be very much like APL. It could be built simply by using `define-shape-access`, without ever using `make-shaped-paralation`.

8.3.1 A Grid-based Prime Number Algorithm

This section presents yet another prime number algorithm. The first algorithm used the sieve of Eratosthenes; the second algorithm was more wasteful and used $O(n^2)$ space. This algorithm is also uses $O(n^2)$ space. It is based upon the observation that any number that occurs in the body of the multiplication table is not prime since it is the product of two factors. Therefore, the primes can be operationally defined as the numbers that are not in the multiplication table! This APL-like algorithm uses the grid shape facility to control access to the multiplication table,

---

[4]There is an asymmetry here—what if both rows and columns are important in a problem? A field of fields must choose one or the other as primary; a grid-shaped paralation does not have to.

```
(defun find-primes-mult-table (n)
  (let* ((table (make-grid (list (1- n) (1- n)))) ;;0..n-2
         (self (site-names table))
         (row (elwise (self) (first self)))
         (col (elwise (self) (second self)))
         (table-vals
           (elwise (row col)
             (* (+ 2 row) (+ 2 col))))        ;2..n
         (possible-vals (elwise ((p (make-paralation (1- n))))
                          (+ 2 p))))           ;2..n
    (set-difference possible-vals table-vals)))
```

Figure 8.5: Multiplication table method for generating prime numbers

which is two-dimensional. It does not, however, make special use of the grid's cartesian locality.

The algorithm in Figure 8.5 begins by creating a two-dimensional grid paralation that is just large enough to hold a multiplication table covering the numbers 2 through n (0 and 1 do not appear in the multiplication table).[5] self is a field that contains a list of the cartesian coordinates of each site; these are appropriately parsed into row and column numbers. The table-values are then calculated; 2 is added to both row and col to skip over the unnecessary multiplications that involve 0 and 1.

All that remains at this point is to find out what numbers are *not* in the multiplication table. This can be done by generating a list of candidate possible-vals, the numbers from 2..n, and set-subtracting the table-vals from the possible-vals. (The implementation of set-difference is discussed in Section 2.8.2.)

8.3.2 Unstructured Data Collections

One can imagine a model based upon a data structure with a less complicated geometry than the paralation data structures. It might be based upon parallel sets (unordered) of ordered pairs. Each pair associates an object from a domain (the site-names) to a range (a field of values). A version of elwise, x-elwise, might be constructed that could work with fields from several paralations at once, because it would intersect the site names of its inputs:

---

[5]The algorithm is inefficient in that it generates the entire multiplication table through n. Only the portion of the multiplication table from $2..n/2$, which requires one quarter of the space of the full table, is absolutely necessary.

```
(setq field1 '{joe→20 george→11 dave→9})
;; Note: This is a special print format for a field containing
;; #F(20 11 9) with site names #F(joe george dave)

(setq field2 '{dave→8 ralph→93 joe→43 george→19})
(x-elwise (field1 field2)
  (+ field1 field2))
  ⇒ {dave→17 george→30 joe→63}
```

This model would be very much like CONNECTION MACHINE LISP [SH86, WS87, Con87]. Each main data structure, called a xapping, is represented by the contents of two fields: a range field and a field of domain elements (the site-names). The user can combine xappings without worrying about which paralations they come from; the `x-elwise` operator automatically performs communication to align the xappings according to their site names. The one-argument β operator of CONNECTION MACHINE LISP is simply a `vref`; the two-argument β operator is simply a `<-` according to a mapping created by `collapse`. The paralation match operator can be productively and efficiently used with fields of xapping shape, even though `match` has no equivalent in CONNECTION MACHINE LISP. Thus, although it is very precise about locality, a paralation language can be used as a tool for defining less precise, but perhaps more concise, languages. Due to the specificity of the paralation model, such a definition can also serve as an efficient implementation.

Chapter 9

The Power of Paralations

9.1 Equivalent Models

In one sense, all parallel programming models are equivalent to all serial models, since they all can be simulated by a serial Turing machine. A more pragmatic equivalence would take into account the speed difference between a serial machine and a parallel machine. Parallel models are more powerful than serial models because they seem to make more efficient use of the basic "stuff" out of which computers are made: active switching devices.

9.2 Universality

The PRAM (Parallel Random Access Machine) is a universal parallel machine. Anything that a machine with n processors (or the corresponding metric, such as paralation sites, gates, and so on) can do, a PRAM with n processors can do, within a polylogarithmic factor of the same speed. For example, PRAMs, vector machines, and uniform VLSI are all *similar* in their use of space and time [Hon86, Hon84, DC80]. The paralation model is also a universal model; one can write a PRAM simulation program in a paralation language. When that simulation program is run on any n-parallel universally powerful machine, the resources used by the simulator, space and parallel time (reversal), are bounded by a polynomial of the corresponding resource being simulated. Thus, the simulator transparently applies the power of the underlying paralation implementation to the simulation of the PRAM without adding an unreasonably large cost of its own.

9.2.1   Emulation of PRAM

The functions below illustrate how a PRAM simulator can be written using the paralation primitives. The particular PRAM below is a CREW (concurrent read, exclusive write) PRAM. The simulation program does not make use of combining; all it needs is `elwise`, `match`, and `<-` without any combining function. Combining, which mixes computation with communication, can be implemented using these restricted primitives by employing the techniques discussed in Section 7.5.2, which showed how to implement combining on a non-combining communications network.

The PRAM simulator has two main data structures: a paralation of **processors** and a paralation of **memory** cells. Each site of the **processors** paralation represents a processor and its state; each site of the **memory** paralation represents a single memory location. The instructions and data for the processors are stored in the **memory**. The basic cycle of a PRAM consists of the processors fetching an instruction from memory, executing it, and then repeating the cycle. The paralation simulator mirrors this cycle with a basic loop that causes each **paralation** site to fetch (with a `<-`) an instruction from **memory**, execute it based upon local **register** contents, and then write the results back to the **memory**.

Each simulated PRAM processor has its own program counter, **pc**, and a single **register**. The variable **processors** simply contains the index field that enumerates the sites of its paralation, thus numbering the processors of the PRAM. Each simulated **memory** location holds a single **value**, either an instruction or a piece of data (**memory** itself is an index field; **value** holds the actual memory data). A PRAM instruction contains fields with the following values: opcode type, memory address of input argument, and memory address where the result should be written. Thus, every instruction writes out a result to some location. Instructions that produce no useful result merely write the value to a nonexistent address such as −1, or ***BIT-BUCKET***. In addition, every instruction fetches an operand from some location in memory—there is no such thing as immediate data. (If an instruction, such as complement a register, needs no operand, the fetched value is simply ignored.) Clearly, this is a very limited PRAM, but it illustrates the point that the essentials of an efficient PRAM simulator can be expressed with the paralation operators.

The processors and the memory bank are created and initialized in lines 0–6 of the program. Line 7 is the main loop; it repeatedly calls **step-pram**.

```
0   (defun pram ()
1     (let* ((processors (make-paralation *num-processors*))
2            (memory (make-paralation *memory-size*))
3            (pc (elwise (processors) 0))
4            (register (elwise (processors) 0))
5            (value (elwise (memory) 0)))
```

```
6       (load-data pc register value)
7       (loop (step-pram pc register value))))
8
9  (defun step-pram (pc register value)
10   (let* ((instruction (<- value :by (match pc (index value))))
11          (result-address (elwise (instruction)
12                                   (parse-dest-addr instruction)))
13          (data-address (elwise (instruction)
14                                 (parse-data-addr instruction)))
15          (data-value (<- value :by (match data-address (index value))))
16          (result
17            (elwise (pc register data-value)
18              (setq pc (+ 1 pc))
19              (let ((function (get-function instruction)))
20                (funcall function pc register data-value))))
21          (mem-result
22            (<- result
23                :by (match (index value) result-address)
24                :default (elwise (value) nil))))
25     (elwise (mem-result value)
26       (when mem-result (setf value mem-result))))))
```

Each time `step-pram` is called, it causes each PRAM processor to fetch and execute a single instruction. Line 10 fetches the instructions by performing a `<-` according to each processor's `pc`. Lines 11–12 cause each processor to find out where the result of executing the current instruction should be written by parsing it from the appropriate `instruction` field. Similarly, lines 13-14 parse out the location where the instruction's data is located. Line 15 actually fetches that data.

At this point, the processors have fetched all of the data that they need to execute their instructions. First, the `pc` is incremented. Then, `get-function` parses the opcode field out of the instruction and returns a LISP function that implements it.

`get-function` is simply a lookup table that is called in an elementwise fashion. For example, if a particular processor had fetched the instruction "GOTO ADDR", `get-function` might return `#'goto`, defined by the following function:

```
(defun goto (pc register data)
  (setq pc data))
```

Line 20 applies the function returned by `get-function` in parallel, producing parallel results that are stored in the variable `result`. Lines 21–24 move those results from the processors to a field in the memory's paralation. A default value of `nil` is produced if there is no value to be written; an error occurs if there are any collisions.[1] Finally, lines 25–26 side effect the memory, thus saving the results.

9.2.2 Efficiency of PRAM Simulation

It is normally assumed that a PRAM takes unit time to perform a shared memory access. Given such an implementation engine, `match` and `<-` both become unit time operations (see Section 7.5.2). Therefore, the inner loop of the paralation PRAM simulator takes constant time per iteration, plus the time taken for the longest instruction to execute. The types of instruction executed by PRAMs, like those in the instruction sets of real CPUs, normally take unit time. Therefore, the paralation simulator takes constant time to simulate the basic PRAM fetch-and-execute cycle.

9.3 Irreducibility

The question of universality naturally leads to the interesting question of irreducibility. What is a minimum set of operators that is sufficient for universality, one that spans the set of expressible algorithms? Is the paralation model irreducible? In one sense, it is. None of the basic operators can be removed without losing universality by producing a model that cannot both compute and communicate in parallel.

For example, if the match operator is removed (leaving move, elementwise computation, and the field data structure), the model has no way to create a mapping. The model would not be able to perform parallel communications. If, instead, move is removed, the result is the same—the user can create mappings, but there is no way to use them. Finally, if elementwise evaluation is removed, no parallel computation can be performed. The user in such a model is limited to creating index fields, matching between them, and moving according to the mappings produced by match. Matching between index fields will never be able to create a mapping with a collision, since index fields contain no duplicates. As a result, move will simply produce fields that are copies of index fields, and will never need to call a combining function. Therefore, parallel computation cannot be accomplished indirectly through the use of combining functions.[2]

---

[1]To change this CREW PRAM simulation into a particular type of concurrent write (CRCW) PRAM, one would use the appropriate combining function in place of the @ error function. For example, one such function would check that both of its arguments are identical and then return one of them, or signal an error if they were different. This would implement a PRAM in which concurrent write is legal when all values written to a location are identical. Alternatively, data values could be tagged with the index of the processor writing them, and then one could write a combining function that allows only the highest numbered processor attempting to write to a location to succeed (this is a useful strategy for a number of PRAM algorithms).

[2]Of course, the user could cause a combining function to be called in parallel by first *serially* modifying the elements of a field so that move can produce a mapping containing a collision. This should not be thought of as a way to accomplish parallel computation without using element-

In another sense, the paralation model is not irreducible: One can replace the
<- operator with a simpler one, one that does not perform combining, and still have
a universal model. The PRAM program demonstrates that elementwise evaluation,
match, and <- *without* combining are functionally complete and universal.

Similarly, one could remove both the match and move operators from the model
and replace them with a single "match-and-move" operator. This new operator
would accept two key fields, a source field, a default field, and a combiner as arguments and return a new field in the destination paralation. Thus, match-and-move
accepts simultaneously all of the arguments of match and move and then returns the
result that a move according to the corresponding mapping would have produced.
Thus, two of the paralation operators can be reduced into a single operator. However, the mapping is not a user-visible data structure if `match` has been removed
from the model, which makes it difficult to create library functions like choose and
collapse.

Both of these changes produce paralation models that are harder to use than the
original, thereby violating the ease of use goal of the model. It is useful, however,
to consider making changes to the paralation model that are in accordance with its
goals.

9.4   Alternative Paralation Models

The power of the paralation model comes from its providing mechanisms that describe and manipulate issues that are important in parallel programming. However,
the only thing that is really new about parallel computers is parallel communication.
Parallel data structures, locality, and elementwise evaluation, are not very different
from serial data structures, locality, and loops with independent iterations. The
equivalent of parallel communication is rarely written as a loop with independent
iterations, since time and space can be saved by making use of serial shortcuts. As
a result, even though the data structures of the paralation model and its elementwise evaluation operator are relatively simple, the <- communication operator is
complicated. In fact, its complications can seem arbitrary. One explanation for
that would be that the choice to include the <- operator in the model, instead of
some other high-level operator, is indeed arbitrary!

Although it is convenient for pedagogical purposes to supply a single communication function, <- itself is not distinguished from the many useful library operators
that can be built from it. APL is an example that illustrates that many different
communication operators can be built and are useful as a group. By focusing on a
small set, I had hoped to make the paralation model easier to understand, easier

---

wise evaluation, since to perform $O(n)$ computations one must first perform $O(n)$ serial setup
operations.

to see how it fulfills its twin goals of ease of use and ease of compilability. But any particular implementation can provide many possible library functions. The compiler can have special knowledge about how to compile optimally each and every library function, or the library can be defined in terms of some smaller set of directly (efficiently) implemented core functions.

`<-` is one way of expressing communication in the paralation model. It abstracts the idea of sending and receiving to and from symbolic processor addresses; it introduces combining as a powerful way of dealing with communications collisions. However, one can imagine other communication operators that differ from `<-`, and yet are also universal. By substituting such operators for `<-`, or merely supplementing the paralation model with them, one produces new versions of the paralation model. The choice of which communications operators are the most convenient, or the most basic, is a matter of taste. In fact, the choice is not critical, so long as the user is able to build new, but still efficient, communication operators on top of those supplied by the model (communications must be extensible).

This section explores other possible choices for the core communication operators and idioms of the paralation model. Particular attention is paid to the paralation ease of use goal. In part, ease of use depends upon the peculiarities of a particular operator. For example, important questions to ask include: How well does an operator match the communication required by real-world problems? How many and what kinds of programming errors can arise when using an operator? Even a mundane question, such as how many arguments an operator takes, can uncover important ramifications for ease of use. However, concentrating only on the advantages and disadvantages of particular operators in isolation can lead to a language that has a large number of useful operators which, as a *group*, are confusing to the programmer.

9.4.1   One Alternative

Guy Blelloch believes that in addition to the field data structure, `elwise`, and `match`, the paralation model should simply contain the functions `vref`, `collect`, and `merge`. In his model, `<-` is not a primitive. `vref` is already familiar to us; it takes a collection of values and reduces it to a single value. `collect`, which was introduced in Section 5.3.2, is simply a kind of `<-` that collects colliding data into subfields.

`collect` performs communication and resolves collisions by saving all colliding data. `<-` also performs communication, but if a combining function is supplied it resolves collisions according to the function, thus mixing computation with communication. Therefore, Blelloch's paralation model can be said to draw a sharper distinction between communication and computation because they are always invoked by different names. Reduction is simply a computation that can be performed elementwise on a field of fields. For example, in order to perform a `<-` with `#'+`, Blelloch would use the following:

```
(elwise ((data (collect data :by mapping)))
  (vref data :with #'+))
```

rather than the form I would use:

```
(<- data :by mapping :with #'+)
```

The expectation in this particular case is that the compiler can detect that the user simply applies a `vref` to the collected data and does not make any further use of the collections. Therefore, the collections themselves do not actually have to be created; the `collect` and the successive elementwise `vref` could be transformed (internally, by the compiler) into an operation equivalent to a combining `<-`. A paralation model based on `collect` could therefore make just as efficient use of a combining network as the `<-` model, given a bit more work by the compiler. Along with `elwise` and a reduction operation like `vref`, `collect` can do everything that a combining `<-` can do. Blelloch believes that it is easier to use. One nice feature of `collect` is that it takes only two arguments, a data field and a mapping; no optional default field or combining function is needed.

Blelloch's `merge` function is the inverse of his `collect` function. It takes a field of fields and runs it backward through a mapping, producing a field. That field, if run through the mapping with `collect`, would produce a field with the same contents as the original input to `merge`. For example, consider this:

```
(setq d '#F(a a b b))
(setq i (index d))
   ⇒ #F(0 1 2 3)

(setq save (collect i :by (collapse d)))
   ⇒ #F(#F(0 1) #F(2 3))
(setq newdata (elwise (save) (- save)))
   ⇒ #F(#F(0 -1) #F(-2 -3))
(merge newdata :by (collapse d))
   ⇒ #F(0 -1 -2 -3)   ;; in the same paralation as i
```

Blelloch was able to add a few macros to PARALATION LISP that efficiently compile his new constructs; he then could immediately begin to experiment with his new version of the paralation model. While I share his enthusiasm for `collect`, `merge` seems to be a bit too low-level for my taste. It is unclear, from an ease of use viewpoint, what should happen when `merge`'s input is not "formatted" properly. That is, what should happen if the subfields are not of the proper length, according to the mapping? A single site might be connected to 5 sites in the destination, each of which wants its own value, and yet the single site might have a subfield of length 4 or 6. Despite my misgivings, given the combination of `collect` and `merge`, Blelloch has been able to define easily a large number of other communication operations, including an interesting variant of the `fetch-and-op` operator popularized by the Ultracomputer project ([GGK*83],[GLR83]).

Clearly further work is needed to investigate the properties of various communication operators. Just as clearly, the basic paralation model can serve as a useful and stable semantic staging point for this type of research, as well as providing a path to fast language implementation via the extensibility of PARALATION LISP.

Chapter 10

Comparison With Other Models

10.1 Language Comparison

The purpose of this chapter is to compare the paralation model to several other programming models and languages, using the goals of the paralation model as a success metric. Of course, certain language concepts are more relevant to some languages than to others, so the text in the various subsections does not cover the same topics in a parallel fashion. However, charts are presented at the end of the chapter which measure many of the languages against the core language concepts that are discussed. This chapter assumes that the reader has some familiarity with each of the languages involved and therefore makes no attempt to explain the details of some of the language features that are discussed.

10.2 APL: An Early Explicitly Parallel Model

Interestingly, some of the most abstract, machine independent, explicitly parallel languages in existence were not created with parallelism as their focus. These languages were created as concise notations for general problem solving. Most problems are inherently parallel in nature and good problem models naturally reflect that. What these languages have in common is that their programming model permits the manipulation of multiple large groups of data objects as a single unit. The progenitor of many such languages is APL [Ive62, GR76]. Its modern descendants, such as Sharp APL [Ive87], APL2 [APL84], Q'Nial [JJ85, Mor79], and

SETL [DSSD86], permit groups of objects to be nested within other groups, thus addressing the hierarchical nature of parallelism.

10.2.1   APL

APL is a concise and compact serial programming language. The elegant underlying paradigm of APL, the application of mathematical operators to large arrays, is easily mapped onto collections of communicating parallel processors—a parallel computer [GS87]. Some APL operations perform elementwise operations, such as multiplying the corresponding elements of two arrays. Operators of this type can make use of conditional execution and local pointer indirection. Other APL operations, like scan, reduce, and dyadic index, can invoke communications. For example, one can determine the largest number stored in an array by reducing the array with the maximum function.

APL is neither a SIMD model nor a MIMD model; it is a concise language with abstract parallel features. Unfortunately, APL has many unique characteristics, some of which have become less attractive with age. APL lacks the block-structuring primitives of modern languages. Some minor language features imply a serial implementation model (for example, the guaranteed right-to-left associativity of the scan operator). Data structuring is limited to specifying the dimensions of arrays (no record-like structure is provided). The APL character set can be confusing to the uninitiated, and APL programs can be so concise that they become impenetrable. One explanation for this problem is the relative cost of idiom encapsulation in APL. Rather than encapsulate a useful idiom as a function, such as `delete-duplicates-from-array`, APL programmers will often retype what would have been the function body. Although the body might consist of several function calls, in APL each built-in function call is a single character from APL's large character set. On the other hand, functions written by the user must have alphanumeric names, which makes them inherently more verbose than built-in functions. Therefore, it is often more concise to copy idiomatic code than to use library functions that encapsulate idioms. In addition, the fact that APL functions can take at most two arguments can make it cumbersome to write library functions that operate on more than two objects. The designers of APL's descendants have attempted to address some of these problems.

A major difference between APL and a paralation language is the type of automatic parallel compatibility coercions that are available. For example, the paralation model requires the user explicitly to use the elementwise evaluation operator to invoke parallel execution, and elementwise evaluation can be applied only to fields in the same paralation. APL will automatically execute any scalar operator in parallel when it is supplied with arrays as arguments; the arrays merely have to be of compatible shape.

This difference has an impact both on run-time efficiency and on ease of use. A parallel implementation of APL may be required to perform implicit communication to align parallel arrays that were originally allocated in different parts of the machine. Some might feel that because this frees the programmer from having to worry about what "paralation" an array is in, it makes APL easier to use. However, the problem has simply changed form. The APL user must worry about which arrays are of compatible sizes. In addition, because APL executes in parallel based on the dynamic content of variables, rather than by an explicit syntactic marker, the user cannot tell by a simple examination whether a particular piece of code will be executed once or many times.

Another kind of coercion is from serial to parallel by replication. Paralation languages detect serial data lexically: anything in the body of an elementwise operation that is not the name of an elementwise field is serial and is automatically coerced to parallel. On the other hand, APL performs this type of coercion dynamically: when two variables, one a scalar and one an array, are combined with a scalar operation, APL coerces the scalar data to an array of appropriate type. Again, one cannot tell by inspection whether scalar or parallel execution will occur; one must have knowledge of the dynamic, run-time types of variables.

Unlike elementwise evaluation, APL's type-based mechanism for invoking parallel execution does not support a hierarchical view of parallelism, one that contains parallel collections within other parallel collections. APL parallelism is invasive and dives directly down for the basic scalar elements of an array. The problem is that the array is the only structure type in basic APL, and APL's parallelism strips away all array structure. (`elwise` only parallelizes a single layer of field structure.) More modern APLs add facilities for setting up barriers to this invasive parallelism. One such extension consists of adding a second type of structure, built with the *enclose* operator. A different extension is based on the ö (rank) operator. ö is applied to a function and numerical arguments; the numbers describe the shape and depth of the parallelism at which the function should be applied. If the argument has a deeper, compatible shape, nested parallel execution occurs.

In terms of the goals of the paralation model, APL has another problem. APL consists of a large set of useful functions.[1] Introductions to APL normally do not attempt to classify the functions as being part of a small, necessary kernel or as part of a library (although some of APL's descendants attempt to correct this presentational problem [Mor79]). This makes it difficult to reason about the efficiency of the APL programming model on parallel machines. The library functions mix communication with computation; no distinction is drawn between the two. As a consequence, there is no attention paid to the issue of locality. For example, all

---

[1]Large is a relative term; APL is a small language when compared with the hundreds of functions of COMMON LISP; it is only large when contrasted with the three operators of the paralation model.

array elements are equally near each other—there is no concept corresponding to
that of a paralation or to elementwise locality. In addition, APL has a user interface
based on an array shape, but no corresponding array-based locality.

What is admirable about APL is the way that it allows a program to operate on
collections of objects as units *without* its high-level semantics being closely tied to a
particular hardware implementation (there are some minor, correctable ties to serial
hardware; for example, scan should be redefined as parallel prefix). Important and
useful primitives, such as tree building, data reduction, communication, parallel
allocation, and parallel execution, are elegantly integrated into the model. Finally,
APL recognizes and wholeheartedly supports an applicative programming style.

10.3   The PRAM/MIMD Programming Model

The PRAM consists of a large number of von Neumann–style processors that access
and modify a shared memory. In general, each processor executes its own program
and operates asynchronously from the other processors. Various strategies are used
to resolve concurrent reads and writes to locations in memory.

As was mentioned in Section 9.2, given the same number of processors as any
other model, a PRAM can efficiently (that is, with polylogarithmic resources) simulate any other model [Hon86, Hon84, DC80]. Unfortunately, there is no inherent
structure organizing the PRAM's processors, communication between them, or the
control flow of their programs; there is only a flat expanse of processors that together theoretically have a large amount of processing power. The PRAM empha-
sizes the separation of concurrent tasks, but it ignores the more difficult problem
of controlling cooperation between tasks.

10.3.1   Shortcomings of the PRAM Model

The unadorned PRAM model provides its MIMD power in an unstructured, non-
hierarchical format; there is nothing to distinguish any one processor from the
other equally powerful processors. Such a model is confusing and hard to program.
The reason is that it is difficult for programmers to keep n asynchronous tasks
in mind simultaneously when they are not organized into a hierarchical structure.
PRAM power is overwhelming, much like horizontal microcode for a computer
with an extraordinarily wide instruction word. However, the meaning of a field in a
microword is normally fixed by simple hardware such as registers or adders. The n
instruction "fields" of each PRAM instruction are even more overwhelming because
they are executed by a fully general processor and can contain any von Neumann
instruction, such as a `goto`.

One way that programmers deal with the MIMD power of the PRAM is to organize it into a queue structure based on the operating systems notion of a *ready-list* of tasks ready to be performed. This adds a primitive kind of virtual processor facility to the PRAM model: there can be more, or fewer, tasks on the queue than physical processors in the system. Implicitly, this approach actually proposes a new programming model. The new model is built around a basic unit called the task. The model allows programs to expand and contract to match the parallelism required during different phases of an application. The PRAM is proposed as an efficient implementation engine. The drawback of this task-based model is that its ready-list, like a PRAM, has no hierarchical structure.

Another way that programmers deal with the power of the PRAM is by writing SIMD style programs for it. For example, many parallel graph theoretic programs are of the SIMD form: "All nodes in the graph look at a neighbor, and ..." *All* of the parallel algorithms in the proceedings of the ACM Symposia on Theory of Computing (STOC) that I examined (1984–86, approximately forty algorithms per year) were of this data parallel form [ACM84, ACM85, ACM86].

A final problem arises from the shared memory of the PRAM, which does not allow a programmer to take advantage of locality. For example, a shared memory may not allow a program to note that a particular image processing problem is two-dimensional. The shared memory paradigm encourages a programmer to ignore the nature of the communication patterns inherent in a problem, just as a uniprocessor paradigm encourages a programmer to ignore parallelism.

A programming model should help the programmer to examine a problem closely rather than foster a style that ignores important problem features. Programs written specifically for such models are tied to expensive hardware, even though the original task was not. That is, once a program has been embedded in a concrete notation that does not express locality, it seems as if the program requires n processors with dense interconnections to a shared memory. The problem is that compilers for other architectures probably would not be able to infer locality patterns that may have been obvious to the original programmer. One cannot easily determine whether or not a PRAM program truly needs the generality of a shared memory because the notation does not explicitly separate general communication from elementwise computation.

10.4 SIMD Programming Models

Another solution to the problem of organizing the active components of a parallel computer into a coherent model is to view the computer as an active array or smart memory, the result of a cross between a vector computer and a communications network. That is, there are n processors with local memories, interconnected into some sort of communications network. The processors all perform the same operation on their own private data. The active array approach closely matches the nature of the SIMD hardware architecture. SIMD models and hardware have inspired several languages, including Parallel Pascal and *Lisp. In addition, APL, although not developed as a parallel language, shares many characteristics with SIMD languages, such as a focus on data (as opposed to control) parallelism.

Parallel Pascal [Ree84, RB87, Pot85, BR83] and *Lisp [Thi86b, Thi86c] are fairly representative of many other SIMD languages, such as DAP Fortran [Red73, F*77] or Pascal/L [Fer82]. Aside from the base language, the important differences among most SIMD languages arise from the availability of communication functions and from the types of serial-to-parallel coercions that are performed automatically. Communication functions in SIMD languages are usually based upon (but preferably hide) particular types of communications hardware, such as grids, pyramids, highways, or packet switched networks.

The topology of an interconnection network that might be used to implement the communication operations (implicit or explicit) permitted by a model is not important. What is important for generality is that the model permits global communication in addition to more efficient, but less powerful, local forms of communication such as shifts. If a model only permits communication between nearest neighbors in a given topology, it is applicable only to problems that naturally fit that topology. Of course, the topology of an interconnection network dictates its asymptotic speed when used to implement global communication—a grid interconnect can take $\sqrt{n}$ time, whereas a hypercube would take $\log n$ time. However, for a given machine size and technology, a "slower" topology might outperform a more densely interconnected topology.

A fine-grained, active array parallel programming model is adequate for the expression of efficient algorithms for a large class of interesting application problems. Any problem that can be solved by performing identical operations on a sea of homogeneous data is a good match. Examples of such problems include cellular automata models, real world simulations (VLSI simulation, weather simulation, low-level computer vision, wind tunnel simulation), finite element analysis, graphics rendering algorithms, and most scientific computing.

The rapid progress of the MPP working group [Fis86] and of users of the Connection Machine [Thi86c, HS86] in a variety of diverse application areas, such as plasma physics and document retrieval, empirically demonstrates the programmability of SIMD languages. This sort of programmability is crucial to any useful programming model.

SIMD models have an advantage over MIMD models in that their *obvious* implementation consists of inexpensive processors and an inexpensive communications network (it is reasonable, although not obvious, to implement a SIMD model using expensive MIMD hardware). SIMD processors are inexpensive because common parts, such as stack pointers and microengines, are factored out into a single host processor. The network can be inexpensive because it is used only when the problem itself requires communication, not every time an instruction must be fetched. Since SIMD models make relatively parsimonious use of communications, a well-balanced SIMD machine can be built with a relatively low-capacity communications network.

10.4.1 Shortcomings of SIMD

SIMD models and hardware are sufficient for a broad class of problems. Unfortunately, SIMD hardware seems to lack the power to implement efficiently certain important applications that require real-time responses to individual data items, such as operating systems and transaction processing systems. The underlying explanation for this is that the SIMD implementation of such applications contains deeply nested conditionals (or very wide multiway branches). When conditionals are implemented by processor selection, such conditionals are necessarily inefficient on SIMD hardware. This is a shortcoming of SIMD hardware and of an implementation strategy that equates conditional branches with processor selection, not a shortcoming of SIMD programming models. It is not necessarily true that SIMD systems become less efficient as conditionals are nested more deeply.

One could create a SIMD program to simulate a MIMD machine as follows: All SIMD processors fetch, from their local memories, their next MIMD instruction to execute. Then, the host or front end computer loops through the MIMD instruction set, broadcasting a brief, equivalent, SIMD routine for each possible MIMD instruction. The host broadcasts these routines to the appropriate selected subsets of the SIMD processors.

This looping algorithm allows a SIMD machine to simulate a MIMD machine with a constant (related to the fixed size of the MIMD machine's instruction set) slowdown, no matter what MIMD program is to be executed (that is, independent of the depth of conditional nesting). It is unclear how large this constant will turn out to be in actual practice. The relevant factors include the number of instructions in the MIMD instruction set, the relative execution speeds of the MIMD and SIMD processors for each of the simulated instructions, the number of processors involved, and the nature of the instruction mix to be simulated.

A machine design that is a constant factor slower than an alternative design can be viable if it has sufficient offsetting benefits. One case where this is currently true is in processor design, where flexible microcoded designs have been quite successful despite their inherent speed disadvantage relative to hardwired designs [Kuc78, pages 304–306]. The main offsetting benefit of a SIMD hardware design over a MIMD design is the relatively inexpensive and simple nature (in terms of synchronization) of SIMD hardware.

If all other things were equal, MIMD processors would be preferable to SIMD processors. However, SIMD processors can be built from less silicon than MIMD processors, so that a SIMD computer will have more processors than a MIMD computer made with the same raw materials. In a MIMD machine, every processor requires its own instruction register, instruction decoding, microcode engine, program counter, stack pointer, and so on. In a SIMD machine, these common elements are factored out of the replicated processors and are built only once, in the front end (host) computer. Because the front end only has to be built once, it can use expensive, fast technology. The replicated SIMD processors themselves basically consist of an ALU, a communications port, and a few registers.

The detailed evaluation of the tradeoffs between MIMD and SIMD designs for parallel computers is an open area for research. Perhaps some hybrid between full MIMD and full SIMD will turn out to be optimal in terms of raw power, ease of programming, and ease and cost of construction [Yan87].

SIMD Models and One-Level Parallelism

Difficulties can be encountered even when a SIMD model is applied to application areas with a suitably flat (one-level) data parallel nature, one that does not require deeply nested conditionals or the emulation of a MIMD machine. Most of these difficulties arise from the semantics of the *selection* primitive. Selection is the hardware mechanism used to choose which processors will be affected by a particular global instruction. Languages that avoid this problem, such as C*, distinguish between the hardware concept of SIMD processor selection and the conditional selection of data objects, such as the elements of a C* domain. Because languages that avoid the problem are not inherently one-level in nature, one should hesitate before classifying them as SIMD languages, despite the fact that they may be intended for use on SIMD hardware. For this reason, C* and CONNECTION MACHINE LISP are discussed in later, separate sections.

Problems Resulting from SIMD Selection

Most current implementations of SIMD models do not distinguish between the selection of data objects (for example, select graph nodes that have exactly 3 neighbors) and the hardware selection of active processors. That is, high-level language conditional branches and hardware selection are explicitly equated. The result is a confusing interaction when the program attempts to manipulate data stored in more than one basic "type" of processor, as most programs do. For example, a course-scheduling program might use a group of processors to represent people needing to be scheduled, other processors to represent constraints, and still other processors to represent courses. The programmer has to explicitly keep the different types of objects separate, since an attempt to apply a single (SIMD) instruction to more than one type of object would just generate garbage. Similarly, a graphics program would need to keep the group of data structures representing shaded surfaces separate from the group representing nodes of polygons.

The SIMD machine appears to the programmer as a *single* active array, rather than as a dynamic source of many active arrays. The situation is analogous to programming in machine language and viewing all of memory as a single array (which must be carefully partitioned by the programmer), instead of programming in a high-level language that allows one to easily allocate and deallocate variables and arrays (for example, compare the let of COMMON LISP to the .BLKW (BLock of Words) allocation command of MACRO-11 [Lew81]).

Apparently, the SIMD programming model breaks down when many different operations must be performed on many different classes of objects concurrently. In addition, as it has been implemented to date, the model also breaks down when a problem merely requires many different classes of objects to coexist. The reason is that the programmer is responsible for explicitly selecting and deselecting processors and their associated data objects in ways that prevent the various classes from interfering with each other. Selection affects all processors; thus, selection implicitly influences all parallel data structures. The application programmer must maintain any semblance of a separation.

The direct result of this can be seen in the types of applications that have been most successfully implemented on SIMD machines to date. Most require only one or two object types to coexist and communicate with each other at a time. For example, in natural language processing, the first phase may convert a group of characters (one character per processor) into a group of words; the second phase may convert the words into parsed sentences. This approach is sufficient for pass-oriented programs such as seed document search (also known as query by example, see [Thi86c]). It does not, however, accommodate heterarchical programs that operate in a mixed fashion on multiple forms of data, such as polygons, splines, and pixels in a graphics program.

Another problem arising from selection is that SIMD models must create arbitrary policies to deal with the strange way that processor-based selection can interact with data-based communication. For example, what should happen when a selected processor sends data to, or requests data or services (such as expression evaluation) from, an unselected processor?

Often, SIMD programmers rely on features that happen to be present in a simple implementation on SIMD hardware of their SIMD model, but which are inherently crippling to any future MIMD implementation.[2] For example, *Lisp programmers rely on the fact that the various branches of a parallel condition are

---

[2]This is analogous to a PRAM programmer writing a shared memory program that ignores the locality inherent in a problem, thus crippling any future local memory implementation.

executed in the order they occur in the program text, which is an artifact of its current implementation on the Connection Machine. Thus, programmers insert serial LISP code within the branches of a parallel *Lisp conditional and expect it to be executed serially before the succeeding parallel branches are broadcast to processors.

In addition to making a MIMD implementation more difficult, this reliance on ordering actually makes the task of optimizing the SIMD implementation of the language more difficult. The serial host now must step through all of the branches of a parallel conditional, even if it can be determined (at either compile or run time) that no parallel processors are selected or could possibly execute the code. The problem is that serial code with side effects might be present in any one of the branches.

Failing to distinguish between parallel conditional branching and its SIMD implementation (selection) is a conceptual problem that can be solved in the design of a particular programming language. However, it points out the pitfalls inherent in basing a software model directly on a hardware model. Perhaps because SIMD hardware is relatively simple, it is easy (and therefore tempting) for a language designer to equate the semantics of what should be an abstract model with the behavior of the hardware. In one extreme case, a machine designer suggested that if an application problem did not naturally fit into his 32 x 32 grid of SIMD processors, the original approach to the problem should be rethought [Par86]. The concept of using the machine to simulate a virtual machine of larger or smaller size was rejected on the basis of its "inefficiency."

10.5   Implicitly Parallel Models

Implicitly parallel models, such as dataflow [Den80, AI83], are based on the premise that it is best to write programs in a serial form and then allow a compile-time or run-time analysis to extract all available parallelism. Normally, this is thought of as a MIMD model, but since the loops that are being unwound contain a single body that is executed for different data, it can also be thought of as a SIMD model.

Implicitly parallel systems can only discover parallelism that is inherent in the precise code and algorithm being used; they cannot discover parallelism in the underlying application. The reason is that the text of most serial programs does not reflect the inherent parallelism of the problem domain. For example, consider the mask convolution algorithm presented in Section 1.5.3, which smoothed noise out of an array of samples, or even Horner's rule for evaluating a polynomial at a point. Good serial programmers attempt to reuse results rather than recalculate them. Thus, good serial programmers intentionally insert dependencies; they intentionally remove parallelism.

Some dataflow models attempt to recover parallelism at run-time rather than at compile-time, but the same problem occurs: the run-time dynamics of a program do not necessarily reflect the problem the program is solving. In addition, it is impossible to unwind parallelism at run-time with infinite speed. Thus, the need to unwind slows down execution unnecessarily. Token passing dataflow models also impose an extra cost in the form of communications and matching overhead; the basic execution cycle of a tagged token dataflow machine makes use of global communication. Finally, no notion of locality is available to a programmer who wants to write a program with a low communications overhead.

One can compare the strategy of `elwise` with that of attempting to unwind loops whose iterations are independent. The implicitly parallel strategy of unwinding attempts to prove independence and defaults to serial execution if no proof can be found (either because no proof exists or because the theorem prover is not powerful enough to find one). The explicitly parallel `elwise` performs no deduction since, by definition, the execution of `elwise` body code at each paralation site is independent.

I believe that the premise of implicitly parallel models, that serial style programs are the best way to solve parallel problems, is incorrect; it is based upon years of experience with serial languages and relatively little experience with massively parallel machines or languages. Adherence to this premise causes implicit models to block a programmer's intuitions about parallel algorithms. Implicit models give the programmer little ability to specify parallelism explicitly, yet they promise that any inherent parallelism will be discovered automatically. Such models do not help the programmer to discover and think about application-based parallelism, even though it is the original source of any implicit parallelism.

In addition to locating data parallelism by unwinding loops, implicit models may promise to extract a kind of *control* parallelism. For example, several adjacent lines of code may be executed simultaneously, as long as they contain no dependencies. This type of parallelism only offers a small, constant amount of speedup, because the size of the program is fixed. Data parallelism offers greater benefits than control flow analysis because the amount of speedup can track the size of the problem's data, which often dwarfs the size of the program. For example, consider problem domains such as circuit simulation (small program, many transistors to be simulated), finite element analysis, database systems, program compilation, and state-space search.

Even if the benefits of control parallelism were worth the complications (for example, the flow of execution can no longer be localized to a single point in the program text), the same benefits could be gained by performing the control flow analysis on data parallel programs. For example, a compiler could apply sophisticated techniques to find parallelism within `elwise` body code. If the compiler determines that two successive lines in the body might be executed at the same time, it might use two processors to implement each site that will execute that code. At best, this would lead to a constant (based upon program size) factor increase in execution speed for that section of the program. The point is that a paralation compiler can make efficient use of parallel hardware without such techniques and that paralation parallelism arises from the number of data objects to be operated on, rather than from the number of independent lines in the program.

Since implicit models usually do not allow the specification of locality, they ignore an important feature of real parallelism [LM86]. For example, a discrete simulation of a wind tunnel that notes that adjacent samples are somehow three-dimensionally "near" to each other in terms of expected communication patterns is preferable to one that ignores this spatial property. A machine with a grid-like network can make good use of this locality information; a compiler for a shared memory machine can ignore the extraneous locality information.

A programmer who manages to penetrate the obfuscation introduced by an implicit model and attempts to implement a parallel algorithm is forced into an interesting coding style: a loopless data parallel algorithm is specified by making use of ordinary serial loops in such a way that the language compiler or the dataflow system can then unwind the loops [KKP*81, LKK85]! For example, in the mask convolution algorithm, the programmer would have to calculate the new value of each data point without making use of an intermediate result from the previous loop iteration. The programmer must know that the algorithm cannot be based upon sliding a mask around an array; the mask should be applied to each data point and its neighborhood in isolation if the loops are to be unwound (see Section 1.5.3).

Just as an explicit description of parallelism can be more efficient than an implicit loop unwinding strategy, an explicit description of shape can be more efficient than an implicit strategy that asks an implementation to discover shape automatically in the data structures of an unfolding computation. In some specific cases, it might be feasible to extract shape automatically from a program's data structures and map data structures onto processors in an efficient manner without an explicit description of shape. For example, some actor-based programming languages hypothesize that an implementation might cause actors which often communicate with each other to dynamically migrate to nearby processors [YT87b, Luc87]. In general, however, shape locality must be described and cannot be easily deduced by a compiler. In addition, from an ease of use point of view, if shape is an important characteristic of a problem, the user should be given a tool that can describe shape. The fact that the paralation programmer either must explicitly describe and manipulate the various characteristics of shape or must forego the benefits of shape is in keeping with the precise flavor of the paralation model: the programmer receives a precise tool and the compiler receives useful information.

Of course, automatic shape extraction techniques can be applied to paralation programs; the paralation model simply supplies more information to the compiler than an implicit model. For example, an implementation might take a paralation and deduce detailed information about its shape according to usage patterns (either static or dynamic), thus reducing the cost of future moves within it.

There is one more problem with implicit models that should be emphasized: implicit models lack transparency. In order to calculate how fast an implicitly parallel program will run, one has to simulate many of the details of the execution of the compiler in order to determine exactly which loops will be unwound and how expensive interprocessor communication will be. Interestingly, this process of determining how much parallelism there is in an algorithm by hand-annotating its unwindable loops works because it forces a programmer to reexpress key parts of the algorithm in an explicitly parallel language!

10.5.1   Specificity, Cost Feedback, and Transparency

One way to view the limitations of implicit models is to recognize that they do not allow the programmer to describe the specific nature of parallelism of a particular problem in sufficient detail. In addition, they do not give adequate feedback on how expensive (in terms of time, space, or processors) a particular computation will be.

The characteristics of specificity and transparency are important to any programming model that is intended to run efficiently on physically feasible hardware. A model should supply scalable tools to allow a programmer to describe precisely what needs to be computed, rather than promising to determine how to perform a computation given only a semantic description (in the form of a serial program) of what is to be computed.

For example, consider the wind tunnel example mentioned above. A simple wind tunnel simulation algorithm can run efficiently on hardware with a three-dimensional grid interconnect system. But suppose this algorithm is encoded in an implicitly parallel language, or even in an explicitly parallel language that has been designed specifically for shared memory hardware. It is unlikely that the three-dimensional shape of the communication can be extracted from the program because the programming language provides no means for noting it. In this case, the wind tunnel program would run best on a machine with a relatively expensive (and far more general) log-degree interconnection network, whereas the original wind tunnel problem could run equally well on a less expensive three-dimensional grid network. Models that do not allow one to specify locality restrictions (such as the PRAM) or the precise parallelism required (such as implicitly parallel models) are *profligate* models.

One simple way of annotating locality in a parallel model based upon arrays is to indicate that array locations with nearby array indices (Manhattan distance metric) are near each other (that is, the full generality of the paralation model's shape facility is not necessarily required). Simply by keeping this grid locality in mind when allocating data structures, a programmer can painlessly describe the locality of a problem to a compiler. If the target parallel hardware cannot support this kind of locality for a particular array used in a program (say, an eight-dimensional array), the compiler simply ignores the extraneous information. This behavior is transparent because a programmer will know how many dimensions a parallel computer supports in hardware, just as programmers currently know how many bits of floating point precision a serial computer efficiently supports.

Specificity is important for the programmer. Better, more specific tools encourage a programmer to examine problems from a sharper, closer perspective. This results in a better understanding of the problem and its inherent parallelism. The implicitly parallel models supply no such tools. Such models discourage the direct understanding of parallelism by offering a single, overly powerful, monolithic tool.

On the other hand, specificity is important for machine independence. The compiler for any kind of hardware can produce better code from more detailed specifications. It is easy to ignore information and compile upward for more powerful and expensive hardware. It is quite difficult to compile in the other direction. A good model permits powerful operations but does not encourage (or force) their indiscriminate use.

10.6   Object-Oriented Languages

Some object-oriented languages permit many objects to perform computations in parallel [YT87b, YT87a, Luc87]. However, they do not facilitate the manipulation of *groups* of objects as a unit. This is a severe limitation because it hinders the creation of hierarchically structured parallel objects (groups that contain recursively nested groups).

The programming model that object-oriented languages seem to imply acts much like an abstract, architecture-independent PRAM. First, the unstructured "actors" that make up an object-oriented program can be viewed as an abstract version of the processors of a PRAM. Like the processors of a PRAM, objects are not organized into a structure; computational power is only available in the form of a flat expanse of equally powerful objects. Second, message-based communication and synchronization can be thought of as an abstraction of the more machine-dependent shared memory paradigm of the PRAM.

Because each actor can have its own private (local) instance variables, object-oriented languages allow a programmer to specify one kind of locality. Object-oriented languages draw a separation between computation on local variables and computation based upon communication messages from other objects. However, the programmer cannot explicitly specify that certain actors will often communicate and should, therefore, be stored "near" to each other. The result is that there is no programmer-visible separation between global communications and local communications. This can be inefficient on many kinds of target hardware. It also leads to less precise problem descriptions.

In an attempt to gain communications efficiency, some implementations of object-oriented languages propose to use implicit actor migration [YT87b]. The idea is to analyze run-time communication patterns and to relocate actors, periodically and automatically, so that they are clustered according to the exhibited locality patterns. Thus, these object-oriented languages incongruously ask the programmer to specify parallelism (computation and synchronization) explicitly, while preventing the programmer from describing locality (an important part of communication) explicitly. Of course, it is possible to ask the user to describe locality and make use of automatic actor migration as well [Luc87].

10.7 C*

C* [RS87, Thi86a] is an object-oriented parallel language; it shares many concepts with the C++ [Str86] language. Its main goals are to support a data parallel style of programming and to be compatible, semantically and culturally, with the C base language. In most ways, C* has an even more static view of parallelism than the paralation model. For example, the user must declare at compile-time precisely what types of *domain* structures will exist. This is equivalent to requiring a paralation user to declare in advance how many paralations will be needed by a program and what fields will exist in those paralations, except that automatic parallel variables (stack) can be used freely. These static declarations pave the way for C* to be more dynamic in the types of allocation it allows. In particular, the user can create new objects of a predeclared domain type at any time during execution. This is equivalent to allowing a user to add sites onto a paralation, which the paralation model does not allow (the paralation user must create a new paralation of an appropriate size).

Like the paralation model, C* attempts to extend its base language in a minimal fashion. C* adds a new data type (the domain), a new statement type (for parallel execution in domains), and a number of library functions. The new statement type is called a selection statement, but it selects the members of a domain, not processors. This abstraction eliminates the difficulties that SIMD languages such as *Lisp have with keeping classes of data separate, because there is no way to select elements from two different domains simultaneously. Of course, this may turn out to be an overly restrictive abstraction because one might indeed want to select two different domain types simultaneously.

The code that C* domains can execute in parallel is basically standard C code, not the full C* language with its parallel execution statement. Although C* permits nested parallel data structures, since a domain element can contain a pointer to a domain, it does not accommodate nested parallel execution: one cannot write parallel code and then call it in parallel.

C* extends the meaning of standard C operations and type coercions so that they perform useful tasks when applied to domain data. For example, consider the way that C* programs perform communication between domain elements. General communication is viewed simply as a parallel execution of ordinary C pointer-following mechanisms, which is both elegant and compatible with the base language. Reduction is viewed as an extension of C's family of += operations: when the right-hand side is parallel and the left-hand side is serial, a reduction occurs.[3] The same reduction mechanism is used to handle collisions during parallel pointer-following. Thus, reduction can be accomplished according to a small set of simple arithmetic and logical operators. More general reductions, however, can be accomplished only through library functions (that is, the language does not include a primitive that permits reduction according to any two-argument function). The reason is that C*, like C, contains no primitive functionals.

In extending the C base language's concept of a single uniform address space to a parallel uniform address space, C* takes notice of the concept of locality. When an array of domain structures is allocated, the elements are guaranteed to be near each other. In fact, they are adjacent, and can be addressed as if they were an ordinary array of structures (for example, a pointer to a domain element can be incremented to point to the next element). This is analogous to a grid-based intersite locality. Domain elements that are not in the same array are far from each other, a kind of interparalation lack of locality. The data stored in a single domain element is packaged into a record, resulting in a kind of elementwise locality.

The abstract processors that implement domain elements in C* execute their parallel programs in a synchronous mode, based on the idea of a host broadcasting a program at slaved processors. For example, the host might ask a domain to execute an addition; each domain would then perform an addition on its own local data at the same time. If a conditional statement is broadcast, first the condition is executed by all domains, then certain domain elements execute the **then** code, and, *after* they are finished, the remaining domain elements execute the **else** code. This is reminiscent of the behavior of a SIMD architecture.[4] However, C* can perform MIMD-like function calling by making use of pointers to functions, since the pointers can be dereferenced in parallel.

A completely synchronous model has an advantage in that it is deterministic

---

[3]Actually, the left-hand side is replicated as a target, and a simple "As if serial rule" is followed—the result must be *as if* the various right-hand side increments were added in serially, although the implementation is free to sum them in parallel.

[4]One could imagine a smart compiler for a MIMD target executing both branches of a conditional in parallel if it could prove that they would not interfere with each other. However, the C* language does not allow the user to explicitly help the compiler in this proof. Therefore, this imagined optimization can be seen as an attempt to find implicit parallelism, and it runs into the problems of implicit parallelism that were discussed in Section 10.5.

and predictable. Its behavior is always repeatable, which can greatly simplify the task of debugging. However, it has a disadvantage in that it squanders potential parallelism since the various branches of conditionals are never executed in parallel, even though there may be no interference between them. This can be a significant performance problem for heterogeneous problems with deeply nested conditionals.

10.8 Connection Machine Lisp

CONNECTION MACHINE LISP is based on a parallel data structure called a *xapping* [SH86, WS87, Con87]. Section 8.3.2 discussed the xapping as a possible shape for a paralation field to illustrate an important point: that the shape facility could be used to create a new parallel structure with a less complicated geometry than a field. Although CONNECTION MACHINE LISP shares many concepts with PARALATION LISP, and implementation strategies that apply to one language can often be applied to the other, there is one major difference: Xappings have no concept of locality. There is no concept of elementwise locality, because each xapping is an independent entity. There is no intraxapping locality, since xappings are unordered sets of pairs. All xappings are equally distant from each other, because all xappings are compatible via a dynamic, run-time intersection of their domain elements. As a result, it is difficult to express the locality that is inherent in a problem in the notation of CONNECTION MACHINE LISP.

CONNECTION MACHINE LISP is less precise than PARALATION LISP; the programmer has much less control over the cost of communication. In fact, the programmer has little control over whether or not communication will even be required during the course of a computation. Even though a problem might not require communication, each invocation of CONNECTION MACHINE LISP's parallel computation operator might have to make use of the communications network to perform a domain intersection. This can also happen in PARALATION LISP if an implementation's storage allocator chooses not to align fields that are in the same paralation, perhaps because of a memory shortage. However, it is far less likely to be a problem in PARALATION LISP because the compiler never needs to align fields that are not in the same paralation and can therefore more evenly distribute data among processors. Lacking explicit locality advice from the programmer (because CONNECTION MACHINE LISP has no paralations), a CONNECTION MACHINE LISP compiler must make do by attempting to align xappings that have similar domains. This strategy can align unrelated xappings that simply happen to have similar domains. For example, it might request the alignment of two unrelated xectors (xapping representation of a parallel vector), just because they have overlapping numerical domains.

Since each xapping is made up of pairs, each xapping can be thought of as representing two fields. In a xapping-shaped paralation created by the paralation model's shape facility, the first member of each pair is the name of a paralation site; the second is the data at the site. The result is that a single xapping can encode certain types of information more concisely than an unshaped paralation field, since a xapping can contain twice as much information as a field. CONNECTION MACHINE LISP programs tend to be shorter than equivalent paralation programs. Of course, the paralation programmer can use the xapping shape facility to write equally concise programs, but a CONNECTION MACHINE LISP programmer cannot express algorithms and their locality with the precision of PARALATION LISP.

10.8.1   Alpha Notation

In addition to its concise data structure, CONNECTION MACHINE LISP also has a concise parallel notation, one with mathematical ties in the sense that distributive algebraic laws apply to it. To explain it, I will describe it as if it were a replacement for `elwise`, to be used with fields in paralations of xapping shape. In fact, the notation is more general than this because it does not actually cause parallel function calling like an `elwise`. Instead, it is a powerful way of creating xappings, and when xappings of functions are applied to xappings of arguments, parallel function calling occurs.

   To begin with, the functionality of `elwise` is performed by α (alpha) and the functionality of elementwise variables is replaced by • (bullet). α indicates that the LISP form following it should be executed in parallel. • can be used only within an α. The use of a • indicates that the LISP form that follows it should be executed once, rather than many times in parallel. For example, to add 1 to the elements of a field, the standard paralation notation would be:

```
(elwise (a) (+ a 1))
```

The CONNECTION MACHINE LISP notation might look like this:

α(+ •a 1)

A • is more general than `elwise`'s list of elementwise variables. Although both are lexical constructs that indicate what should be treated serially, a • can mark *any* LISP code, while the list of elementwise variables can only contain LISP symbols. For example:

```
(elwise ((b (calculate-a-field))) (+ b 1))
```

The equivalent CONNECTION MACHINE LISP notation is more compact. No intermediate name has to be invented for the field b:

α(+ •(calculate-a-field) 1)

The alpha notation obeys a kind of distributive law: α's can be spread out (or factored), and α's and •'s cancel each other out:

α(+ •(calculate-a-field) 1) $\equiv$ (α+ (calculate-a-field) α1)

The alpha notation is similar to the backquote notation of COMMON LISP. Like an ordinary quote, a backquote indicates that the following LISP form should be quoted and taken exactly as written. However, any subforms that are prefaced by a comma are not quoted, but are evaluated. A comma can only appear within a backquoted form. For example:

```
(setq thing 'b)
'(a ,thing)
   ⇒ (A B)
```

The analogy between backquote and alpha, and comma and bullet, is clear: backquote means "quote, except evaluate where there are commas" and alpha means "execute in parallel, except execute serially where there are bullets."

α can act like an `elwise` that is not told initially which are the elementwise variables. This is an appropriate notation for CONNECTION MACHINE LISP since it has no concept of a paralation, and any parallel object is compatible with any other; parallel computations can take place in any group of xappings because domain intersection is always applied as a compatibility coercion. However, in the paralation model, parallel computation can only occur on fields in the same paralation. `elwise`'s list of elementwise variables simplifies human error checking by textually localizing errors, rather than asking the user to examine the entire body in search of •'s in front of fields from two different paralations. This localized, upfront information also simplifies the task of the compiler.

The paralation user has to indicate only once that a variable is an elementwise variable, no matter how many times it is used. The CONNECTION MACHINE LISP user must bullet it each time it is used. To some degree, this violates one of the principles of programming discussed earlier, the abstraction principle, which concerns factoring out repeated patterns and stating them only once. However, occasionally a variable appears several times in an expression with different numbers of bullets in front of different occurrences. This is equivalent to using the `elwise` binding shorthand (see Section 2.6.3) to rename an elementwise variable and then using both the old and new names in the same expression (see Section 2.3.4).

The alpha notation has another problem, one that it shares with APL, in that most computer keyboards and display terminals do not have a greek character set (of course, substitute ASCII characters can be used, like a question mark for α and an exclamation point for •).

10.8.2 Fuzzy Separation between Computation and Communication

Like PARALATION LISP, CONNECTION MACHINE LISP is based upon two irreducible basis operations: α and β. α is used to replicate serial data to produce a xapping; when a xapping of functions is applied to arguments that are xappings of data, parallel computation takes place. β is used to perform communication, and acts much like a paralation `<-` according to a `collapse` mapping. Thus, there is a programmer-visible separation between computation and communication. This makes a language easier to use. However, the semantics of CONNECTION MACHINE LISP may require an implementation to perform communication (intersection) at run-time in order to apply xappings of functions to their arguments properly. In addition, a new processor layout must be created to hold the result of each β. Thus, CONNECTION MACHINE LISP's choice of primitives does not automatically lead to a simple, efficient implementation. There is no strict separation between communication and computation at the implementation level.

Although the CONNECTION MACHINE LISP's notation does not permit the user to explicitly express elementwise locality, a CONNECTION MACHINE LISP implementation can attempt to recover its efficiency benefits. For example, xappings that have identical or similar domains might be aligned in some way, and xappings produced by parallel computation on aligned domains might be aligned with their inputs. Perhaps this would be the case in general, and thus CONNECTION MACHINE LISP's lack of locality preservation is not as large an efficiency penalty as it might seem. Similarly, as with `collapse`, each application of β produces an output xapping that is unrelated (in terms of locality) to its arguments, and therefore cannot be aligned with them. However, repeated use of β on similar arguments *might* produce xappings that are aligned with each other, but not with anything else.[5] In the paralation model, `collapse` can guarantee this efficient behavior because of the availability of precise kernel concepts (`match` and the paralation).

The implementation strategy described above gives some of the benefits of preserving the elementwise locality inherent in a problem's data, but, of course, the implementation does not know when *not* to attempt to align data. It must necessarily waste time and complicate the work of its storage allocator, which may attempt to align unrelated xappings that happen to have similar domains (for example, all xectors, xapping vectors, have domains consisting of integers). There is no CONNECTION MACHINE LISP object analogous to a paralation mapping that, when used repeatedly with a communication function, explicitly calls for alignment

---

[5] A related phenomenon involves the canonicalization of xapping indices, which *might* only have to be performed once for a group of related β's. Canonicalization of xapping indices can be contrasted with the canonicalization of paralation mappings, which only has to occur once per mapping [WS87].

of output data. Further research is needed to evaluate how well a strategy of implicitly deducing locality fares when compared to explicit locality, like that of the paralation model. My own suspicion is that the situation is analogous to that of implicit versus explicit parallelism, with the explicit strategy proving to be better both in terms of efficiency on hardware and in ease of use.

CONNECTION MACHINE LISP has no way to express intraxapping locality in the form of shape, either from an ease of use or an efficiency point of view, since each communication operation produces a new xapping that is not aligned with any of its arguments. Difficulties and important tradeoffs arise in any attempt to add multidimensional array-like xappings, due to the mutability of domain elements and the fact that the communication operator compares them with the LISP eql operator (no other predicate can be specified). The only alternative is to use nested xappings to represent multidimensional data. For example, a column xapping might contain xappings representing rows. This approach imposes an unnatural and inconvenient asymmetry upon the dimensions of the structure. In the case of the xapping of rows, row-based operations are easier to perform than column-based operations.

As with C*, parallel computation in CONNECTION MACHINE LISP is completely synchronous [Con87]. Nevertheless, it is still possible to perform MIMD-like operations by applying xappings containing multiple functions to xappings containing multiple data. The same advantages and disadvantages of synchronous computing that were evident in C* appear in CONNECTION MACHINE LISP: predictability in exchange for a loss of parallelism in the branches of multi-way conditionals (due to the need to order the possibly interfering side effects of the various branches). This gives the user a more rigid control over synchronization at the price of hamstringing the implementation on a MIMD machine.[6] Of course, a requirement for synchronous execution is not ordinarily a burden on an inherently synchronized SIMD architecture; both C* and CONNECTION MACHINE LISP were designed for execution on SIMD machines.

10.9 MultiLisp

MultiLisp is a version of Scheme (a dialect of LISP) that has been extended with a small set of constructs that express concurrency [Hal85]. The central operator is future, and it returns an object also called a future. A future object, such as (future (+ x y)), is a placeholder for the eventual result of evaluating an expression. It is immediately returned to the caller, and the expression evaluation takes place concurrently with the main program. When the background expression

---

[6] Again, a compiler might attempt to prove that the branches of a conditional are independent and perhaps recover a limited amount of implicit parallelism.

evaluation terminates, the future is replaced by the result; the *undetermined* future has become determined.

Initially, the returned placeholder is an undetermined future because the expression has not yet been evaluated. Undetermined futures can be manipulated in a number of ways. For example, they can be bound to variables or passed to procedures. Of course, any use of an undetermined future that needs to use its determined value, such as adding it to another value, will block and wait until the future becomes determined. Like the paralation model, MultiLisp defines a number of library functions on top of the future construct. For example, `pcall` evaluates the arguments of a function call in parallel, like a fork-join construct.

MultiLisp can be thought of as an explicit version of dataflow, one in which the user can mark expressions that should be evaluated concurrently or with *lazy evaluation* because the programmer feels that the parallelism is worth the overhead of creating and tracking a background task. In contrast, dataflow indiscriminately places a future around *every* expression in an entire program. Unlike dataflow, MultiLisp recognizes the utility of side effects and allows side effects to occur in parallel. A number of library functions are included that address the problem of synchronization.

Like dataflow, MultiLisp has no concept of locality or shape. There is no new parallel data structure; control parallelism is the method used to speed up computations. Therefore, MultiLisp has much less of a feeling of manipulating vectors of parallel data than does the paralation model. However, control parallelism can be used to create data parallel primitives. For example, MultiLisp includes a library function called `pmapcar`. The ordinary LISP `mapcar` applies a single function to each element of a list in turn and constructs a list of the results. `pmapcar` constructs a list of items, where each item is a future for applying the function to an element of the list. Thus, the function is applied in parallel to the list.

Futures can be nested in order to take advantage of nested parallelism. Thus, both large and small-grained parallelism are addressed by `future`: One can make three futures, each of which performs a calculation that produces thousands of futures. The numerous futures are nested hierarchically by the manner in which they are created. For example, the quicksort routine described by Halstead uses nested futures to efficiently perform the partitioning of the data [Hal85]. The partition function simply returns a future for two partitioned lists. Wherever the main function selects parts of that possibly undetermined future, perhaps in preparation for a recursive call to itself, the selection takes place within another `future`. Thus, the quicksort program may quickly run to termination, returning a future connected to a complicated and wide (that is, very parallel) web of nested futures that eventually resolves itself into a sorted list of numbers.

The programmer who wrote the quicksort code did not have to be aware of that complicated web; the programmer simply annotated the program with the `future` construct in places that exploit parallelism. However, Halstead notes that "Where to put the `future` operators [within a program originally written in Scheme] is not immediately obvious." This is a problem with MultiLisp: it is difficult to determine the running time of a MultiLisp program (transparency), and it is therefore difficult to know how to write a new program so that it will run efficiently in parallel. However, like the paralation model, the language does have a small and simple basis set of constructs, and it addresses nested parallelism at any level of granularity.

10.10   Proposed Fortran 8x Array Extensions

Fortran is one of the two oldest computer languages still in widespread use. (The other is LISP.) One of the reasons for its longevity is the fact that it is periodically revised. The current standard is Fortran 77 [ANS78] (named after its 1977 release date); the next standard is currently referred to as Fortran 8x [ANS87, MR87]. An interesting part of Fortran 8x, the part that this section contrasts with the paralation model, attempts to extend Fortran to become a powerful array processing language. There are at least two reasons why Fortran is moving in this direction.

10.10.1   Motivation

The primary motivation behind the array extensions seems to be the development of new, better ideas about encapsulating array manipulation within programming language constructs. Array manipulation is important to many Fortran applications, such as numerical computation. A secondary motivation is efficiency on vector processors. It is clear to the Fortran community that vector processors are becoming an important force in the scientific application field, but vectorizing compilers have a disadvantage in that they are unable to find and vectorize all of the arrays in serial code. Thus, the secondary goal is to make Fortran easy to compile for vector processors.

According to the Jerry Wagner [Wag87], one of the co-chairs of the Fortran 8x committee, it is not the intent of the committee to evolve Fortran so that it addresses the problems of general parallel processing; that will probably happen in the next revision after 8x. The goal of the array extensions can be summarized as an attempt to capture some of the low-level array functionality of APL without imitating the esoteric notation of APL. Thus, the rigidly static nature of storage allocation in the Fortran base language carries over to parallel allocation. High-level concepts such as nested parallelism are not included in 8x. In effect, although it is ostensibly targeted for vector processors, 8x adds a group of flat, SIMD-like array processing constructs to Fortran.

10.10.2   Description of Array Extensions

The proposed Fortran 8x extensions currently consist of an extended semantics for expressions and a large number of intrinsic (built-in) functions. The expanded semantics allow the programmer to write expressions that manipulate whole arrays or portions of arrays at once, much like APL. For example, two arrays of identical shape can be added with the + operator. The result is an array containing the corresponding sums. A portion of an array may be described using triplet notation. Like a DO loop specification, a triplet includes a start element, a stride, and a stop element.

The new array intrinsic functions provide built-in support for matrix multiplication and dot products, reduction according to a fixed set of simple mathematical and logical functions, and a number of array manipulation and construction functions. For example, the PACK function performs much like a paralation move with a choose mapping; it packs selected values in an array into a new array. A number of the intrinsic functions are modeled after standard APL functions like RESHAPE (take a collection of data and reform it into a new shape, such as an array of different dimensionality) and SPREAD. Finally, there are functions that rearrange data elements within an array, such as CSHIFT (circular shift) and TRANSPOSE.

In addition to these extensions, there are a number of extensions that used to be in the draft 8x standard but have been removed to an "Appendix F". Basically, a decision was made that 8x contained too many extensions and that this would make the process of public review and eventual language acceptance more difficult. Therefore, extensions that could not garner enough support within the language committee were taken out of the language and relegated to Appendix F. The appendix would be distributed as part of the language description, thus allowing the public a chance to request the reinstatement of some of them.

Two of the most interesting removed extensions are the FORALL facility and the vector-valued subscript facility. FORALL allows one to specify the range of values that certain subscripts can assume; a boolean masking condition to eliminate some of them; and an action clause, which must be a single assignment statement, to be executed for each of the remaining subscripts.[7] The standard does not specify what takes place if the assignment statement has side effects that interfere with each other.

FORALL can act much like the elementwise evaluation of the paralation model. For example, if A is an N by M matrix, one can zero the array except for the diagonal with the following code:

---

[7]At this point, the astute reader might apply the language design principle of orthogonality to the FORALL construct and ask why it accepts a boolean mask as an argument when instead it could have accepted a more general action clause that used ordinary IF statements to control conditional execution.

```
FORALL (I=1:N, J=1:M, I.NE.J) A(I,J) = 0
```

I ranges from 1 to N and J ranges from 1 to M, but the action clause is not executed where the two subscripts are equal. FORALL is a powerful construct; it could be used to efficiently describe or implement the other extensions of Fortran 8x. But the goal of 8x is not general parallel power or mathematical clarity; the goal is to address the array manipulation problems encountered in numerical computation. Of course, from an academic programming model point of view, it seems clear that a simple and more general extension is always preferable to a number of very specific extensions.

Another removed extension, the vector-valued subscript facility, permits an integer vector to be used as a series of subscript values in an array reference. For example, if S is the vector [12 9 33] and A is another vector, A(V) accesses A(12), A(9) and A(33). Thus, this facility permits an integer cursor–based form of general communication. The vector of subscripts, S, may contain duplicates if the referenced array is being read (concurrent read is permitted), but S cannot contain duplicates if the referenced array is used as the target of an assignment statement. Thus, communications collisions are illegal.

10.10.3   Summary of Fortran 8x Array Extensions

The 8x extensions provide the Fortran user with low-level tools for array manipulation, much like a simplified and non-recursive version of the constructs of early APL. The extensions can describe certain application problems concisely. They can help compilers for parallel architectures to locate various optimization opportunities. Fortran programs often step over arrays in a parallelizable way, and the 8x extensions allow the programmer to make that parallelism explicit.

Fortran 8x succeeds in achieving its goals in a narrow sense. However, when the array extensions are measured against the broader goals of the paralation model, problems become evident. The 8x extensions are shortsighted: They address their application goal with a large library of immediately applicable machinery, when a bit more effort and refinement would lead to a more compact language that would be able to better address a broader range of applications. The extensions address interesting problems, but they do not go far enough. Moreover, due to an unfortunate lack of support, some of the most general, powerful, and concise 8x extensions have been removed, probably permanently, from the language.

10.11   Relational Database Languages

A number of the surface characteristics of relational database languages, such as SQL [Dat86], can be reminiscent of some of the features of the paralation model, especially since the data structures of both can be pictured as tables of data. However, there are several important differences. The differences begin with the fact that the goals of the two are quite different: A database system is an application, while the paralation model leads to languages that can be used to implement applications. One could bring up a simple relational database system in a paralation language by representing the tuples of a relation as the sites of a paralation[8]; it would be quite difficult to implement a paralation language in a relational database system.

10.11.1   Paralations Are Not Relations

It is true that both the relation and the paralation can be drawn as tables containing various columns (fields) of data. However, the fields of a relation are designated by name, while the fields of a paralation are anonymous data structures that may, or may not, be bound to variable names. The relations of a relational database also have names, and these relation names are used when the fields of a relation are accessed. On the other hand, paralations have no names and cannot be manipulated by the paralation programmer, any more than a LISP programmer can manipulate a list (LISP programs manipulate conses or dotted pairs, not lists).

10.11.2   User-Visible Paralations

An early version of the paralation model did represent paralations in a user-visible fashion: Paralations had names and their fields acted much like record selectors [Sab87e, Sab87a, Sab87f]. The corresponding early version of `elwise` (the `elwise-d` described in Section 2.3.4) accepted a paralation to designate where parallel execution should take place, along with a body that manipulated its fields. Thus, it did not accept a list of elementwise variables. This language turned out to be quite cumbersome. One reason was that many arguments had to be passed during function calls: one had to pass both the fields to be manipulated and their paralation, yet the only use for a paralation was when it was given to `elwise` as the paralation designator argument.

In addition, the preliminary paralation model was confusing and difficult to use because the designation of what was to be treated in parallel by `elwise` was dynamic and based upon type, like APL. Variables in the `elwise` body that happened to contain fields in the same paralation as that of the `elwise` were parallel; everything else was coerced to parallel. This made it quite difficult to request that a field be used as a whole and not as a collection of field values (see Section 2.3.4). In part,

---

[8]Of course, the simple and obvious implementation does not address the important issues of efficiency, the levels of the memory hierarchy, the various kinds of indexing that can be used, and so on.

this dynamic behavior was a consequence of `elwise` accepting a paralation as an explicit argument. The benefits of listing all of the elementwise variables lexically became more apparent when named paralations were no longer available: initially, the revised `elwise` accepted a single field as paralation designator, and that quickly was revised to be several fields in a single paralation.

One other benefit of eliminating paralations as manipulable data structures in the subsequent versions of the paralation model is the simplification of the manipulation of nested parallel objects. The reason is that it is easy to apply an operation to a group of objects without knowing or caring what nested structure those objects are a part of. A requirement to name them simply confuses the programmer by forcing him to think across several levels of nested parallelism. Without such a cumbersome requirement, a programmer can separate the various levels into separate procedures, functions, modules, or into recursive calls that divide and conquer a complex problem. Relational databases do not normally permit the nesting of data or of database operations. However, the system catalog can be thought of as a one-level deep nesting, since it contains data about the data in a system.

10.11.3 Dynamic Allocation

Another difference between relational data structures and those of the paralation model involves the dynamic nature of the fields of paralations: At any time, additional fields can be added to a paralation. Each invocation of `<-` (and, in PARALATION LISP, each invocation of `elwise`) creates and returns a new field. On the other hand, in most relational databases, a relation is created by specifying precisely the names of the fields that it will contain. To add a new field to a relation, one must create a new table. However, tuples can be added to a relation at any time, while the number of sites in a paralation cannot change once the paralation has been created.

One explanation for this difference is that the paralation is used for a new purpose that is entirely different from the way that relations are used in relational databases: Instead of containing the status of a database and maintaining its referential integrity, the paralation contains the variables, code, and status of general purpose programs. A relation is convenient for creating and updating an ever-growing database; a paralation is convenient for describing the data structures of communication-efficient algorithms. Relational databases view sets of data from a very abstract point of view, one that does not concern itself with locality. Of course, from an ease of use point of view, it would be preferable to be able to grow both the number of fields in a paralation and the number of sites. However, increasing the number of sites in a paralation leads to a number of problems. One ease of use problem is that it is not obvious what an old field should contain as values at newly created sites; the user must be provided with a convenient way to specify these new values. Efficiency and transparency problems arise when there is no more room "near" the sites of the paralation to be expanded. Should new sites be allocated far away, resulting in a paralation with an invisible rift down the middle that increases communication costs in a non-transparent manner? Alternatively, should the old site data be copied, at some hidden cost, to a new area that does have sufficient room for growth?

10.11.4   Paralation Generality

The elementwise evaluation operator is fully general in that it can perform MIMD calculations and can accommodate any base language. Code performing file I/O, dynamic memory allocation (cons), nested parallelism, and recursive code can all be performed elementwise. In contrast to this, the code that can be executed on the tuples of a relation is quite limited. The main purpose of a database is to take a query and retrieve corresponding tuples, although actual database languages provide facilities for manipulating the returned tuples. For example, one can count how many tuples match a query or average the contents of a given field.

   The equijoin communication operation of the relation database model is similar to match and <- in that it matches tuples (paralation sites) in two relations (paralations) based upon an equality predicate. However, the join returns a brand new relation and resolves collisions by appending them, forming a flat structure (almost as if expand were applied to the result of a collect). <-, on the other hand, makes use of reduction by combining according to any two-argument function. Finally, the relational databases permit vref-like reductions over relations, but only with a limited set of reduction operators, such as summing or logically or-ing.

10.11.5   Database-Specific Concepts

Relations are unordered sets of tuples. The sole means of addressing individual tuples arises from a uniqueness property: no two tuples can contain exactly the same values. This uniqueness property always applies to all of the fields in a relation as a whole; often it applies to a subset of them, a candidate or primary key. In contrast to this, the paralation model permits any values, including duplicates and null values, to appear in fields created by the user, and the values are ordered by the index field. One can think of the index field as a type of primary key, although it is closer in spirit to the concepts of array location or processor address. Conceptually, each paralation site contains a field value specifying its name; the index values are names that impose a useful ordering on the sites of a paralation. Of course, the value in this index (or the site-names) field can be ignored if a programmer wants to treat a field as an unordered set. Thus, the database concept of primary keys is not directly relevant to the paralation model. Similarly, database concepts such as foreign key, base relation, and views (a read-only security mechanism) are also not directly relevant to the paralation model.

10.12 Parallelism and Language Design

Issues involving parallelism do not affect many of the design decisions that must be made in creating a programming language or model. For example, one can imagine strongly typed and weakly typed parallel languages; one can imagine parallel languages that require explicit space management and parallel languages that rely on garbage collection. Issues such as conciseness and base data structure (APL uses arrays, SETL uses sets and tuples, LISP uses lists, CONNECTION MACHINE LISP uses xappings, Q'Nial uses nested rectangular structures) can be resolved independently of parallel issues. Many flavors of parallel languages are both possible and useful.

Given this orthogonality, it seems unnecessary to design a parallel language from the ground up; why not borrow a von Neumann language and use it as a base? Many language designers have recognized the waste involved in reinventing the wheel. For example, consider the following parallel languages: Parallel Pascal [Ree84, RB87, Pot85, BR83], MPP Pascal [Pot85], PascalL [Fer82], Actus (Pascal-based) [PCMP83], Parallel C [KS85], Refined C [DK85], C* [RS87, Thi86a, Thi86c], *Lisp [Thi86b, Thi86c], MultiLisp [Hal85], CONNECTION MACHINE LISP [SH86, Con87, WS87], PARALATION LISP, Concurrent Prolog [Sha83], Parlog [CG86], Refined Fortran [DK86], and DAP Fortran [Red73, F*77, Par86].

All of these languages have attempted to augment a preexisting base language with explicitly parallel constructs. Of course, the parallel constructs are not always well integrated into the language. Occasionally, a particular view of parallelism may require a new base language. This is the case with SETL, Actors, FP, or Occam. These languages are exploring new flavors of programming languages; only part of the new flavor is parallelism.

10.13 Comparison Summary Charts

10.13.1 General Characteristics

Language	Base Language	Small Basis Set	Computation versus Communication: Separation for User	Computation versus Communication: Separation for Compiler
APL	none	no	no	no
C*	C/C++	data structure and new statement	yes	yes
CONNECTION MACHINE LISP	COMMON LISP	data structure + 2 operators	yes	no
Fortran 8x Extensions	Fortran	no	no	no
*Lisp	COMMON LISP	no	yes	no
MultiLisp	Scheme	yes: future construct	no	no
Paralation Model	any	data structure + 3 operators	yes	yes
Parallel Pascal	Pascal	no	yes	yes

10.13.2 Data Structures

Language	Dynamic Creation of Parallel Collections	Dynamic Growth in Parallel Collections	Garbage Collection	Nested Parallel Collections	Nested Parallel Execution
APL	yes	no	yes	yes (modern extended APLs)	yes
C*	no: domain types fixed at compile-time	yes	no	yes (via pointers to subcollections)	no
CONNECTION MACHINE LISP	yes	yes	yes	yes	yes
Fortran 8x Extensions	no	no	no	no	no
*Lisp	yes	no: all collections are same size as machine	no	no	no
MultiLisp	no parallel data structure; parallel access to any serial data	n.a.	yes	n.a.	yes
Paralation Model	yes	no	according to base language	yes	yes
Parallel Pascal	yes	no	no	no	no

10.13.3   Computation

Language	Type of Synchronization	Parallel Side Effects	Nested Hierarchical Parallelism	Parallel to Parallel Coercions	Serial to Parallel Coercions
APL	n.a.	yes	yes (modern extended APLs)	none	dynamic replication
C*	every parallel function call	yes	yes (via pointers to subcollections)	none	static replication
CONNECTION MACHINE LISP	every parallel function call	yes	yes	dynamic intersection	static replication
Fortran 8x Extensions	intrinsic entry and exit	yes	no	none	static replication
*Lisp	every parallel function call	yes	no	none	none
MultiLisp	data precedence (future construct)	yes	yes	n.a.	n.a.
Paralation Model	elwise entry and exit	according to base language	yes	none	static replication
Parallel Pascal	every parallel function call	yes	no	none	static replication

10.13.4 Communication

Language	General Communication Arrows Description	Collision Control	Shape Locality	Shape Access
APL	integer cursors	fixed set of scan combiners	none	grid
C*	collections of C pointers	fixed set of reduction combiners	grid	grid
CONNECTION MACHINE LISP	eql equality test between object pairs	any combining function	any shape locality	any shape interface
Fortran 8x Extensions	none (removed extension has integer cursors)	none	none	grid
*Lisp	integer cursors	fixed set of reduction combiners	grid	grid
MultiLisp	no explicit communication operations	n.a.	none	none
Paralation Model	first class mapping; based on equality (any predicate) between object pairs	any combining function	any shape locality	any shape interface
Parallel Pascal	permutation library functions use integer cursors	no collisions are possible; global reductions by max, min, sum, product, and logical functions	grid	grid

Chapter 11

Conclusion

11.1 Summary

It is important to distinguish between *what* you want a computer to do (or appear to do) and *how* it actually does it. The issue of selecting a software model or language should be decoupled from the choice of a machine or a machine architecture. Computer scientists whose main interest is in programming parallel computers in high-level languages should be broad-minded about the various types of hardware designs. The important characteristic of parallel hardware is that there are many sites in the computer where useful work can take place, rather than just one site, and that these sites can interact. The important characteristic of parallel programming models is that they allow a programmer to transparently specify operations on collections of data objects (for example, numbers, words, tasks, processes, or even other (sub)collections).

A parallel model should be abstract and machine independent. A shared memory MIMD model seems to require expensive hardware; a one-level SIMD model seems not to take full advantage of expensive (MIMD) hardware. On the other hand, one can easily imagine general, efficient implementations of the models embodied by languages such as APL, Actors, FP, or PARALATION LISP, on a variety of parallel architectures. An abstract model should not be limited to, or restrained by, a particular architecture. A good model attempts to capture accurately and transparently the nature of parallel problems. Various machine architectures can be compared by comparing the efficiency with which they can run such models.

A parallel language should be created by combining a parallel model with a preëxisting base language, unless there is a compelling reason not to—for example, if the model requires features that are unavailable in any existing base language. If a parallel language uses a preexisting base language, it should accommodate the flavor of that base language. Thus, a parallel LISP should not require the user to deallocate parallel data structures explicitly; it should have a parallel garbage collector.

APL demonstrates many of the characteristics of a good parallel language. Although APL's concise notation and lack of modern language features can obscure it, APL has a core of interesting, useful, and abstract parallel mechanisms. For example, the distribution and collation of parallel data is handled by high-level constructs such as automatic scalar to parallel coercion, scan, and reduce, rather than by hardware primitives like broadcast, send, and get. Perhaps APL is so successful because of its origin as a notation for solving problems [Ive81], rather than as a language that has a convenient implementation on a particular kind of hardware.

The paralation model is based on similar ideas, but the model is both simpler and more abstract than APL. The model consists of a data structure and three operators that can be combined with a variety of base languages. The motivation behind the paralation model is based both on the nature of the parallelism inherent in application problems and on the nature of parallel hardware. The result is an easy to use, machine-independent model.

John Backus has warned against the trend to ever larger and larger languages, referring to it as von Neumann bloat [Bac78]. The richness of the problem of parallel computation can seduce one into bloating a parallel language in a search for complete coverage of all possible viewpoints, thus sacrificing the clean lines of a more minimal language. A balance must be created between the two. The solution chosen by the paralation model is to select a small set of operators as a central core with which the model can be described, analyzed, and efficiently implemented. The reasonable desire for other useful idioms can be satisfied with a library of fast and efficient functions that can be semantically defined in terms of the core. The paralation core acts as a unifying force that protects a paralation language from the disadvantages of von Neumann bloat.

11.2   Contributions of This Research

Perhaps the most important contribution of this research is not the paralation model per se, but the identification of a number of important issues in parallel programming and a study of the benefits to be gained by properly addressing them.

- Explicit distinction between computation and communication

- Explicit control over locality and shape

- Hierarchical nature of parallelism

- Utility of a communication pattern as a first class object

- Applicability of serial languages, concepts, and principles to parallel programming, including simplicity, machine-independence, and extensibility

- Applicability of parallel languages to problems that initially appear to be serial

11.2.1 Shortcomings

The paralation model attempts to meet its twin goals of ease of use and ease of compilability by using the welcome, but unexpected, synergy between the two goals. Of course, the model falls short in a number of areas. Perhaps the most important is the way that it sidesteps the issue of synchronization. Synchronization more complicated than the n-way fork and barrier synchronization join provided by elementwise evaluation will have to be addressed by new parallel computation operators. Perhaps such an operator would be similar to <-, like Guy Blelloch's fetch-and-op-like primitive, or perhaps it would have to be an all-new primitive, created from scratch. Without such an operator to address the problems of complex synchronization, the model is not easy to use for problems in which synchronization is central, such as transaction processing. Of course, the danger in introducing such operators is that the separation between computation and communication can become blurred, reducing transparency.

Another problem with the paralation model is the fact that the size of a paralation (in number of sites, not number of fields or their contents) is fixed once it is created. Perhaps a way of growing paralations should be provided, if a mechanism can be found that treats the related storage allocation issues of locality and transparency in a consistent manner (see Section 10.11.3).

11.2.2 Successes

The solutions to these shortcomings involve augmenting the basic operators of the model, while preserving the central data structures, in order to *better* meet the original goals. Thus, although <- may not address the problem of synchronization in sufficient detail for certain applications, it does address other important problems. For example, match introduces the concept of a communication pattern based upon symbolic equality between any type of data items, not the low-level concept of processor addresses. The ability to encapsulate and store these mappings leads both to ease of use and potential gains in efficiency. Similarly, move solves the problem of communications collision by using general computational reduction, rather than by incorporating ad hoc, hardware-related hacks that can be conveniently implemented but are hard to use. The programmer does not have to spend time implementing low-level communication algorithms for fan-in and fan-out trees. Similarly, elementwise evaluation frees the programmer from details of processor allocation, thus making it easier to exploit multiple levels of nested parallelism. Since fields can contain functions, and function calling can occur elementwise, in the paralation model "parallel program IS parallel data"—a parallel extension of a serial truism.

Even without change, the paralation model is applicable to a broad range of data-intensive applications, such as scientific numerical computing, signal and data processing, simulation, compilation, graph theoretic problems, database systems, and artificial intelligence and symbol manipulation. By example, this research demonstrates that parallel programs are not inherently more difficult to create or work with than their serial counterparts.

It is true that a machine with thousands of processors can seem overwhelming when viewed directly, without the assistance of an intervening model; this merely points out the need for a parallel programming model. The complexity of parallel hardware is misleading. Programmers should expect the same high-level features from the facilities used to program parallel computers as they have become accustomed to in the serial world; to settle for less is shortsighted. It is far easier to spend some time building a good set of general tools before attacking a problem than it is to launch directly into problem solving bare handed. Without a general set of tools, a programmer is doomed to address the same issues again and again, albeit in complex new guises.

Appendix A

Merging Into Lisp

It has been claimed that the paralation model is compatible with the flavor of any base language. In the case of PARALATION LISP, one way that compatibility is achieved is to extend transparently the standard user interface to accommodate fields. The extension is made by creating a new package that shadows the old LISP definitions of certain functions with new functions that know about paralation data structures. This appendix assumes that the reader is intimately familiar with COMMON LISP.

To begin with, a new package called PL-LISP is created; it :uses the standard LISP package, which means that all the standard functions are automatically available. This can be done by putting (in-package 'pl-lisp :use 'lisp) at the start of each file. Then, the LISP functions that must be changed are simply shadowed with new definitions. The full implementation of PARALATION LISP must worry about shadowing old definitions and then exporting the new ones to user packages that :use PL-LISP, such as PL-USER, but those details are ignored here.

One class of functions that is shadowed is the sequence manipulation functions, such as elt, sort, coerce, reverse, and length. The paralation length function in Figure A.1 is fairly typical of this class of function. It first checks to see if its argument sequence is a field. If it is, it calculates the length by fetching the value in the field's paralation's length slot; otherwise, it simply calls the standard LISP length function.

Another extension permits the user to modify fields serially using COMMON LISP's standard setf function. One simple way to extend setf is to use the defsetf function. In Figure A.2, defsetf tells COMMON LISP to call the elt-set function whenever setf is applied to elt-f. elt-set takes a field and a location, just like elt-f, but it also takes a third value. This third value is inserted into the field at

```
(shadow 'length)
(defun length (sequence)
  (if (typep sequence 'field)
      (paralation-internal-length (field-paralation sequence))
      (lisp:length sequence))))
```

Figure A.1: An implementation of `length`, a shadowed sequence function

```
(defsetf elt-f elt-set)
(defun elt-set (field location value)
  (setf (aref (field-pvector field) location) value))
```

Figure A.2: An implementation of `setf` of `elt-f`

the appropriate site. (In the actual implementation of PARALATION LISP, the user simply uses `elt` and `setf` of `elt`; `elt-f` is an internal function that is not visible to the user.)

Earlier, in the `defstruct` for a field, the name of a print function was supplied. This section defines that function, `print-field`, which causes fields to print out in the #F format. Print functions in COMMON LISP must accept three arguments: the object to be printed, a stream upon which to print, and a depth argument. The depth argument can be used to control the formatting of nested data structures, but it is ignored by the `print-field` function presented here. ((declare (ignore...)) is merely a declaration that the programmer is aware that the named variables are not ever used; its effect is to suppress error messages at compile-time.) To print out a field, the function in Figure A.3 simply prints the "#F(" header, loops through the field printing its values, and finally prints a close parenthesis. (See Section 8.2.2 for a more concise print function, `ring-printer`, which uses LISP's built-in list pretty printer to format its output.)

The counterpart to a print function can be thought of as a "read-function"; a way of telling COMMON LISP how to read in a certain typographical style. The way this is done is to create a function that can take a stream and return a field, and then to notify COMMON LISP that that function should be used whenever a #F is encountered. As with the `print-field` function, the `field-reader` in Figure A.4 function accepts and ignores certain extraneous arguments.

The `field-reader` function is called after the #F has been read in. `sub-char` is bound to the F and `rank` is bound to `nil`. `rank` is ignored by the rest of this

```
(defun print-field (field stream depth)
  (declare (ignore depth))
  (format stream "#F(")
  (dotimes (i (paralation-internal-length
                (field-paralation field)))
    (if (> i 0)
        (format stream " ~s"
                (aref (field-pvector field) i))
        (format stream "~s"
                (aref (field-pvector field) i))))
  (format stream ")"))
```

Figure A.3: An implementation of print-field

```
(defun field-reader (stream sub-char rank)
  (declare (ignore sub-char rank))
  (let* ((element-list (read stream t nil t))
         (result-par (make-paralation (length element-list)))
         (result (elwise (result-par) (elt element-list result-par))))
    result))

(set-dispatch-macro-character #\# #\F #'field-reader)
```

Figure A.4: A read function for fields

simple read function. (One might imagine a read/print format for grid-shaped
fields that made use of the rank.) What remains to be read is a sequence of LISP
objects, surrounded by a pair of parentheses. This happens to be the same format
as an ordinary LISP list. Therefore, the actual I/O can be performed by simply
calling the standard function `read` to read in and return the list, and then saving
it in the variable `element-list`. The task now becomes one of coercing a list
into a field with the same contents. The most concise way to do this would be
the form `(coerce element-list 'field)`, but a more verbose method is used by
`field-reader`. A paralation of appropriate length is created and elementwise each
site of the paralation calculates which value it should hold; the resulting field is then
returned. The call to `set-dispatch-macro-character` simply informs COMMON
LISP that whenever a # followed by a F is encountered, the function `field-reader`
should be called.

A.1   Syntactic Conveniences

In Section 2.6.3, a binding shorthand was introduced for `elwise`. Instead of supplying a simple list of symbols (the elementwise variables), the user could supply a list
that lexically rebound some of the variables to new values. This is done simply by
inserting a *pair* containing a symbol and an initial-value form into the list, rather
than just a symbol (thus saving the programmer from having to write a `let` to do
the rebinding). This section implements this syntactic extension to `elwise` on top
of the `elwise-s` defined in Section 6.2.3.

The code in Figure A.5 begins by installing a new macro that is responsible for
compiling calls to `elwise`; it will use `compile-elwise-gen` to perform the actual
work. `compile-elwise-gen` takes three arguments: the type of `let` to use, the
bindings (the list of elementwise variables and initializers), and the program `body`.
It returns a form that first binds the variables according to the `bindings` and then
executes the body with a properly formed `elwise-s`.

`compile-elwise-gen` begins by calculating `pair-bindings`: it is a list of all of
the pairs found in `bindings`, omitting any symbols (non-pairs). `var-list` is then
created; it is a list of symbols that contains both the non-pairs *and* the symbols that
are the first item in each pair. Finally, the returned result code is created. A `let`
of the proper type is applied to the `pair-bindings` and surrounds an invocation
of `elwise-s` on the `var-list` and the elementwise `body`. For example, given the
following:

```
(elwise (x (y (make-paralation 6)))
   (any-function x y))
```

```
(defmacro elwise (bindings &body body)
  (compile-elwise-gen 'let bindings body))

(defun compile-elwise-gen (let-type bindings body)
  (let ((pair-bindings
          (mapcan #'(lambda (binding)
                      (if (listp binding)
                          (list binding)
                          nil))
                  bindings))
        (var-list
          (mapcar #'(lambda (binding)
                      (if (listp binding)
                          (car binding)
                          binding))
                  bindings)))
    `(,let-type ,pair-bindings
       (elwise-s ,var-list ,.body))))
```

Figure A.5: An implementation of elwise with binding shorthand

the let in compile-elwise-gen would create the following bindings:

```
var-list ⇒ '(X Y)
pair-bindings ⇒ '((Y (MAKE-PARALATION 6)))
```

Given those bindings, the body of compile-elwise-gen would create and return the following as the macroexpansion of the elwise:

```
(let ((y (make-paralation 6)))
  (elwise-s (x y) (any-function x y)))
```

The careful reader might wonder why the variable let-type exists, since it is always used to pass the same value, let. In fact, LISP has another kind of binding special form, called let*, that is slightly different from let in terms of the order of evaluation and variable binding that it uses. (let* was described in Section 2.6.3.) elwise should be able to accommodate that difference since the difference is a part of the base language. elwise*, in Figure A.6, interprets its binding notation in a manner akin to that of let* by including a let* instead of a let in its expansion.

```
(defmacro elwise* (bindings &body body)
  (compile-elwise-gen 'let* bindings body))
```

Figure A.6: An implementation of `elwise*` with binding shorthand

Appendix B

Miscellaneous Lisp Code

B.1 Canonicalizing Match Code

The source code in Figure B.1 implements a canonicalizing `match`. It uses hash tables to perform the table lookup, as was described in Section 7.4.

B.2 Parallel Prefix Implementation

Figure B.2 contains the pointer doubling implementation of parallel prefix described in Section 7.4.1. Since combining and parallel prefix are so closely related, and because combining imposes fewer synchronization requirements on an implementation than parallel prefix, it does not seem as though there is a great need for a parallel prefix operator in a paralation language. However, it is interesting to see how a parallel prefix algorithm *could* be written using a paralation language.

```lisp
(defun match (to-field from-field)
  (canonicalized-mapping (elwise (to-field) to-field)
                         (elwise (from-field) from-field)))


(defun canonicalized-mapping (to-key-field from-key-field)
  (let* ((key-index (make-hash-table))
         (from-key-hash (make-hash-table))
         (from-p-size (paralation-internal-length
                        (field-paralation from-key-field)))
         (to-p-size (paralation-internal-length
                      (field-paralation to-key-field))))
    (dotimes (i from-p-size)
      (setf (gethash (elt-f from-key-field i) from-key-hash)
            t))
    (dotimes (i to-p-size)
      (let ((val (gethash (elt-f to-key-field i) key-index)))
        (if val
            (elt-set to-key-field i val)
            (cond ((gethash (elt-f to-key-field i) from-key-hash)
                   (setf (gethash (elt-f to-key-field i) key-index)
                         i)
                   (elt-set to-key-field i i))
                  (t (elt-set to-key-field i nil))))))
    (dotimes (i from-p-size)
      (let ((val (gethash (elt-f from-key-field i) key-index)))
        (elt-set from-key-field i val))))
  (make-mapping :to-key to-key-field
                :from-key from-key-field))
```

Figure B.1: An implementation of `match` with canonicalization

```
(defun parallel-prefix (function field)
  ;; copy field first so you can destroy it to produce the result
  (setq field (elwise (field) field))
  (let ((result (plain-parallel-prefix function field)))
    result))


;; destructive side effects
(defun plain-parallel-prefix (func data)
  (let ((psize (length data))
        (no-data (elwise (data) (cons :no-data nil)))
        (ordering (index data)))
    (do ((distance 1 (* distance 2)))
        ((> distance psize) data)
      (let ((shifted-data
              (<- data
                  :default no-data
                  :by (match ordering
                             (elwise (ordering)
                                (+ ordering distance))))))
        (elwise (data no-data shifted-data)
          (unless (eql shifted-data no-data)
            (setq data (funcall func shifted-data data)))))))))
```

Figure B.2: An implementation of parallel prefix using pointer doubling

Appendix C

Glossary

This glossary defines words unique to the paralation model, terms that are used in various specialties and enclaves in computer science (such as language design and computer architecture), and some of the constructs of COMMON LISP that were used in the PARALATION LISP programming examples.

aref A COMMON LISP function that is used for accessing the elements of an array. Its first argument is the array; the remaining arguments are subscripts.

backquote The character ' is used in COMMON LISP to create pieces of list structure. It acts much like a conventional LISP quote except that instead of a verbatim description of the desired list structure, backquote accepts a more general template. Backquote is often used by macros which must construct and return LISP programs, because LISP programs are represented as lists.

choose A paralation library function. It accepts a field of booleans and returns a mapping that connects the sites that contain true, in index order, to the sites of a new paralation of appropriate length.

collapse A paralation library function. It accepts a field of values, counts how many distinct values occur in the field, and creates a new paralation with that many sites. Collapse returns a mapping that connects each site of the input to a site of the new paralation, according to value, and in index order of each value's first occurrence.

collect A paralation library function. It accepts a field and a mapping that has that field's paralation as its source, and transfers the values in the field according to the mapping. The values that arrive at each site of the destination are collected into a field in a new paralation of appropriate length. Therefore, collect returns a field of fields.

collision Communication in the paralation model takes place according to mappings. When a mapping indicates that several values are being sent to a single destination site, the values are said to collide. Collisions are resolved according to combining functions.

combining function When a combining function is applied to two arguments, it returns a result. Through repeated application, a combining function is used to reduce a group of colliding values into a single result value. There is no guarantee as to the particular associative pairing that will be used during reduction, but the left-to-right order of combination will always be maintained. (In the case of move, this corresponds to the index order of the source sites.)

communication Transfer of data to or from a paralation site.

Connection Machine Computer A massively parallel (up to 65,536 processors) SIMD computer with a general communications network that can combine colliding message packets according to simple logical and mathematical functions. The nodes of its routing system are connected in the form of a boolean n-cube (hypercube).

defun A COMMON LISP macro used to define functions.

defstruct A COMMON LISP macro used to define named record structures. An invocation of defstruct creates a new type and defines appropriately named constructor, access, and assignment functions.

do A COMMON LISP macro used for general iteration. In general, a do loop can look like this:

```
(do ((var1 init1 step1)
     (var2 init2 step2)
     ...
     (varn initn stepn))
    (end-test . result)
  body)
```

When the loop is entered, the init values are evaluated in order and then the vars are bound to the corresponding results. On each iteration, the end-test is evaluated; if it is true, result is evaluated and returned. Otherwise, the body is executed, the step forms are evaluated in order and assigned to the vars, and the do loops back to the beginning (the end-test).

elementwise evaluation Elementwise evaluation executes a program at each of the sites of a paralation. Wherever that program names an elementwise variable, the element of its field at each local site is used as its value. There is no guarantee on synchronization between sites other than that they all must finish executing the elementwise code before the elementwise evaluation terminates. In PARALATION LISP, elwise returns a new field as its result; it contains the results returned by each paralation site.

elementwise locality Elementwise locality indicates that the field values at a particular paralation site are near each other. Thus, the ith elements of all fields in a paralation are near each other. Elementwise locality both paves the way for efficient implementations of elementwise evaluation and gives the user a tool for describing an important kind of locality.

elementwise variable The first argument to elementwise evaluation is a list of elementwise variables. Each must be bound to a field and all of the fields must be in the same paralation. Within the body of the program to be executed elementwise, those variables are treated in a special manner. The occurrence of an elementwise variable in the elementwise body refers to an individual element of a field, not to the value of the elementwise variable upon entry to the elementwise execution (at which time it was a field).

elt A COMMON LISP sequence function. Its first argument is a sequence (such as a field or a list), its second is an integer describing a position in the sequence (zero-based indexing). elt returns the specified element of the sequence. See also aref, fref, and setf.

expand A paralation library function. It accepts a field of fields, and returns a field in a new paralation, the concatenation of the subfields.

explicitly parallel Language semantics that allow the user to explicitly describe which computations are independent and can be performed in parallel. See also *implicitly parallel*.

field A field is a collection of values, much like a vector. A field belongs to a particular paralation and each of its values resides on a separate site of the paralation.

fref A function that accepts a field and a description of a paralation site and then returns the corresponding field value. In unshaped paralations in PARALATION LISP, the fref function is elt. In shaped paralations, the fref function usually appears to make use of the `site-names` field. However, depending upon the shape, the `fref` function created by the designer of the shape may be able to locate a field value in a more efficient manner, without performing an associative lookup into `site-names` (that is, without a `vref`). For example, in a grid-shaped paralation, `fref` can perform an inexpensive row-major order calculation, consisting of a small number of multiplications and additions, in order to transform grid coordinates into the index of the corresponding site. Similarly, the user can specify what action should take place when `fref` appears as a `setf` place descriptor.

general communication A type of communication, implemented with hardware, firmware, or software, in which any source can talk to any destination. This can be contrasted to local communication in a network that is not fully connected, in which sites can communicate only with the sites to which they have a direct connection.

implicitly parallel Language semantics that do not allow the user to explicitly describe which computations are independent and can be performed in parallel. The compiler for an implicitly parallel language must deduce or prove independence in order to make use of parallel hardware. It is the comparative difficulty of this deduction that separates implicitly parallel languages from explicitly parallel languages. Thus, APL can be thought of as an explicitly parallel language. See also *explicitly parallel.*

index field Every paralation has a field, the index field, that enumerates its sites. In PARALATION LISP, `index` is a function that accepts a field and returns the index field of its paralation.

inherited locality Elementwise locality indicates that the field values at a particular paralation site are near each other. Inherited locality indicates that this is true for any kind of field values, including numbers, structures, and even fields. Inherited locality is given that name because each object inherits the locality properties of the object that created it, along with any finer substructure that it itself contains.

interparalation locality The sites in a paralation are near each other but far from the sites of other unrelated (that is, non-nested) paralations.

intersite locality See *shape.*

intrasite locality See *elementwise locality.*

&key A keyword that can appear in the list of arguments of a function definition in COMMON LISP. When the function is later called, the user supplies the values of the arguments that follow the &key in the argument list in any order, prefacing each value with the appropriate keyword. For example:

```
(defun print-two-things (&key first second)
  (print first)
  (print second))

(print-two-things :second "I'm second" :first "I'm first")
```

let A COMMON LISP special form for establishing new variable bindings. A let can look like this:

```
(let ((var1 value1)
      (var2 value2)
      ...
      (varn valuen))
  body)
```

The value expressions are evaluated in order, the vars are bound to the corresponding results, and then the body is executed. The bindings have lexical scope and indefinite extent.

let* Similar to a let, except that after each value is evaluated, it is immediately bound to its corresponding var. Thus, value4 can refer to var3, even though both are in the same list of let* bindings.

locality Locality is a pragmatic concept having to do with reducing the cost of communication between objects that must communicate often. The paralation model provides several types of locality, including elementwise locality, interparalation locality, shape, and inherited locality. Paralation locality supplies the programmer with a specific set of tools that can be used to describe the locality that is inherent in a problem, while simultaneously supplying data to the paralation compiler that allows it to map data onto processors in a way that efficiently accommodates communication. However, in and of itself, the locality of the paralation model has no *semantic* content: the programmer can lay out data structures onto paralation fields in any desired fashion. The point is that certain ways of laying out data (those that relate a problem's inherent locality to the types of locality mentioned above) can lead to faster programs.

macroexpansion A LISP macro is a function that accepts LISP code as arguments and returns a piece of code as its result. Macroexpansion, the execution of a macro function, occurs at compile time. Macros make it possible to extend the syntax of a LISP. For example, the `elwise` construct of PARALATION LISP is defined as a macro.

mapping A mapping is a paralation data structure, a first class object, that encapsulates a communication pattern between two paralations. It can be thought of as a bundle of arrows that connect the sites of a source paralation to the sites of a destination paralation.

match Match accepts two key fields (destination and source) and an optional equality predicate as its arguments; it returns a mapping. The arrows of the mapping connect sites that contain equal key values. Thus, the mapping returned by match encapsulates the equality relationship between the two key fields.

MIMD Multiple Instruction Multiple Data. A type of parallel computer in which there are multiple processors of essentially conventional design along with facilities for interprocessor communication (for example, message passing, shared memory, and so on).

move (<-) Move accepts a field, a mapping that has that field's paralation as its source, an optional default field in the destination paralation, and an optional combining function. Move transfers the values in the field according to the mapping. If more than one value arrives at a site of the destination, that site reduces the multiple values into a single value according to the combining function. If no values are used, a site uses its default value. Move returns a new field in the destination paralation of the mapping; the field contains the transferred data.

nested parallelism The paralation constructs can be applied to themselves, which is useful in modeling the hierarchical structure of parallelism in real problems. Thus, fields can contain fields, and elementwise evaluations can take place elementwise. Since the paralation constructs are orthogonal to each other, one can elementwise perform matches and moves, and combining functions can themselves perform elementwise calculations. The details of how this orthogonality and nesting are implemented are hidden from the paralation programmer. Nested parallelism is a structuring tool that helps a paralation programmer concentrate his effort on solving application problems in a modular fashion.

paralation A paralation is a locality relationship among a group of fields. Every field belongs to one and only one paralation; fields that belong to the same paralation are near each other. A paralation can be thought of as an unordered collection of sites. A field in a paralation defines a value per site. In PARALATION LISP, `make-paralation` creates a new paralation with a specified number of sites and returns its index field.

parallel computer A computer that can perform multiple operations simultaneously, usually because multiple processors (that is, control units or ALU's) or memory units are available. Parallel computers containing a small number (say, less than 50) of processors are called multiprocessors; those with more than 1000 are often referred to as massively parallel. The paralation model can exploit massively parallel hardware, but it also can make efficient use of less parallel hardware: If a program produces enough work for 1000 processors, clearly there is enough work to keep 100 busy. Like APL, the paralation model is useful on serial computers because it is a clear and concise notation for describing data-intensive algorithms.

parallel prefix (also known as scan, or data-independent prefix) An operation that takes a sequence and a combining function and calculates a new sequence. Each element i of the new sequence contains the reduction, according to the combining function, of elements $0 \ldots i$ of the input sequence. Parallel prefix has efficient implementations on many different architectures and is a useful tool for implementing the communication operations of the paralation model.

pvector A data structure internal to an implementation of PARALATION LISP. A pvector is a vector that contains the actual data contents of a field, its values at each conceptual paralation site. A pvector is usually stored in a form that facilitates parallel operations upon it. For example, a pvector might be stored one value per processor.

reduction Transforms a group of values into a single value according to a combining function.

sequence A COMMON LISP data type. Lists, vectors, and fields are all sequences because they consist of an ordered set of values. COMMON LISP contains a family of generic sequence functions that can be applied to any sequence. Some useful sequence operations include `elt` (access a sequence ELemenT), `sort`, `reverse`, `concatenate`, `find`, and `remove-duplicates`.

setf A COMMON LISP macro for storing values within generalized variables. The first argument to `setf` describes a place (a place is equivalent to the left-hand side of an assignment statement in an Algol-like language); the second argument is a value to store in the place. One way to describe a place within a sequence is with a sample call to `elt`. Thus,

```
(setf (elt some-array 3) 100)
```

stores 100 in location 3 of some-array. Places can also be described with
fref, defstruct access functions, and most other COMMON LISP access functions.

shape The locality relationship between the sites of a paralation. Ordinary paralations are unshaped, but a shape facility can be used to create paralations
whose sites are arranged into shapes such as grids. Shaped paralations act
just like unshaped paralations except that certain built-in shape mappings are
available. For example, a two-dimensional grid might have built-in mappings
for shifting values north, south, east, and west. An implementation may indicate that communication according to certain shape mappings is faster than
communication according to arbitrary mappings. In addition to these shape
maps, the shape facility of PARALATION LISP also provides a way of naming
the sites of a paralation which simplifies shape access and a number of other
facilities that make it easy to build efficient implementations of other parallel
models (for example, APL, COMMON LISP, SETL) on top of PARALATION
LISP. See also site-names and fref.

SIMD Single Instruction Multiple Data. A type of parallel computer in which
there are multiple local memories, each equipped with an arithmetic logic
unit (ALU). A single control unit causes the ALU's to perform operations in
parallel on their own local data.

site-names A designated field in a paralation that contains values that are thought
of as names for the sites. In an unshaped paralation, the index field is also the
site-names field. In a shaped paralation, site-names may contain other values
that are appropriate to the shape at hand. For example, sites in a three-
dimensional grid-shaped paralation have names consisting of three numerical
coordinates, while xappings have names consisting of arbitrary LISP objects.
In PARALATION LISP, the function site-names can be applied to any field; it
finds the field's paralation and returns the paralation's site-names field (much
as index takes a field, finds its paralation, and returns the index field of the
paralation).

subfield When fields are stored within fields, the nested values can be referred to
as subfields. Similarly, one might refer to the subarrays of an array of arrays.
In both cases, the prefix *sub* arises from the perspective of the description
(at least two levels of nesting away from the bottom), not from a special
characteristic of the data structure.

transparency For the purposes of this book, transparency refers to a property of a language or its constructs that measures the ease with which a programmer can determine the cost of a language construct or group of constructs used in combination. In general, however, there are other forms of transparency, such as referential transparency.

ultracomputer A shared memory MIMD computer incorporating a perfect-shuffle interconnection network capable of combining colliding message packets according to simple logical and mathematical functions.

virtual processor An abstraction away from the physical processors of a parallel computer that permits one to program the computer as if it had more processors than are actually available.

vref A paralation library function. Vref (standing for Value REFerence) accepts a field, a combining function, and an optional default value as arguments. Vref reduces the values in the field according to the combining function and returns the result. If the field being vrefed has no elements (its paralation is of length 0), vref returns the specified default value instead. In PARALATION LISP, **vref** cannot be used as a `setf` place descriptor.

xapping The central data structure of the CONNECTION MACHINE LISP language. Also, a paralation shape that was inspired by CONNECTION MACHINE LISP.

Bibliography

[ACM84]   Association for Computing Machinery. *Proceedings of the Symposium on Theory of Computing*, 1984.

[ACM85]   Association for Computing Machinery. *Proceedings of the Symposium on Theory of Computing*, 1985.

[ACM86]   ACM. *Symposium on Theory of Computing*, 1986.

[AHU74]   Alfred V. Aho, John E. Hopcroft, and Jeffrey D. Ullman. *The Design and Analysis of Computer Algorithms*. Addison-Wesley, Reading, Massachusetts, 1974.

[AHU83]   Alfred V. Aho, John E. Hopcroft, and Jeffrey D. Ullman. *Data Structures and Algorithms*. Addison-Wesley, Reading, Massachusetts, 1983.

[AI83]   Arvind and Robert A. Iannucci. *Two Fundamental Issues in Multiprocessing: The Data Flow Solution*. Technical Report 226-2, Computation Structures Group, Laboratory for Computer Science, Massachusetts Institute of Technology, Cambridge, Massachusetts 02139, 1983.

[ANS78]   *American National Standard Programming Language FORTRAN*. American National Standards Institute, Inc., New York, New York, ANSI X3.9-1978 edition, 1978.

[ANS87]   *Draft Proposed Revised American National Standard Programming Language Fortran*. American National Standards Institute, Inc., Washington, D.C., ANSI X3.9-198x edition, 1987.

[APL84]   *APL2 Programming: Language Reference*. IBM, first edition, August 1984. Order Number SH20-9227-0.

[AT80]   Arvind and R. E. Thomas. *I-Structures: An Efficient Data Type for Functional Languages.* Technical Report TM-178, Laboratory for Computer Science, Massachusetts Institute of Technology, Cambridge, Massachusetts 02139, September 1980.

[Bac78]   John Backus. Can programming be liberated from the von Neumann style? A functional style and its algebra of programs. *Communications of the ACM*, 21(8):613–641, August 1978.

[Ble87]   Guy Blelloch. Scans as primitive parallel operations. In *International Conference on Parallel Processing*, pages 355–362, IEEE Computer Society, 1987.

[BR83]   John D. Bruner and Anthony P. Reeves. A parallel p-code for Parallel Pascal and other high level languages. In *International Conference on Parallel Processing*, pages 240–243, IEEE Computer Society, 1983.

[CG86]   K. L. Clark and S. Gregory. PARLOG: Parallel programming in logic. *ACM Transactions on Programming Languages and Systems*, 8(1):1–49, January 1986.

[Con87]   *Connection Machine Lisp Reference Manual.* Thinking Machines Corporation, Cambridge, Massachusetts 02142, February 1987.

[Dat86]   C. J. Date. *Database Systems, Volume I.* Addison-Wesley, Reading, Massachusetts, fourth edition, 1986.

[DC80]   Patrick W. Dymod and Stephen A. Cook. Hardware complexity and parallel computation. In *21st Annual Symposium on Foundations of Computer Science*, pages 360–372, IEEE, 1980.

[Den80]   Jack B. Dennis. Data flow supercomputers. *Computer*, 13(11):48–56, November 1980.

[DK85]   Henry Dietz and David Klappholz. Refined C: a sequential language for parallel programming. In *International Conference on Parallel Processing*, pages 442–449, IEEE Computer Society, 1985.

[DK86]   Henry Dietz and David Klappholz. Refined Fortran: another sequential language for parallel programming. In *Proc. 1986 International Conference on Parallel Processing*, pages 184–191, IEEE Computer Society, 1986.

[DSSD86]   R. B. K. Dewar, E. Schonberg, J. T. Schwartz, and E. Dubinsky. *Higher Level Programming: Introduction to the Use of the Set-Theoretic Programming Language SETL.* Springer-Verlag, New York, 1986.

[Ell86]   John R. Ellis. *Bulldog: A Compiler for VLIW Architectures.* The MIT Press, Cambridge, Massachusetts, 1986.

[F*77]   P. M. Flanders et al. Efficient high speed computing with the Distributed Array Processor. In *High Speed Computer and Algorithm Organization*, pages 113–127, Academic Press, 1977.

[Fer82]   Christer Fernström. Implementation of an array and vector processing language. In *International Conference on Parallel Processing*, pages 253–261, IEEE Computer Society, 1982.

[Fey85]   Richard Feynman. *Surely You're Joking, Mr. Feynman!* W. W. Norton & Company, Inc., New York, New York, 1985.

[Fis86]   James R. Fischer, editor. *Frontiers of Massively Parallel Scientific Computation*, NASA and Goodyear Aerospace Corporation, NASA Scientific and Technical Information Office, NASA/Goddard Space Flight Center, Greenbelt, Maryland 20771, September 1986. NASA Conference Publication 2478.

[Fly66]   Mark Flynn. Very high speed computers. *Proceedings of the IEEE*, 54(12):1901–1909, December 1966.

[GGK*83]   Allan Gottlieb, Ralph Grishman, Clyde P. Kruskal, Kevin P. McAuliffe, Larry Rudolph, and Marc Snir. The NYU Ultracomputer—Designing a MIMD shared memory parallel computer. *IEEE Transactions on Computers*, C-32(2):175–189, February 1983.

[GLR83]   Allan Gottlieb, B. D. Lubachevsky, and Larry Rudolph. Basic techniques for the efficient coordination of very large numbers of cooperating sequential processors. *ACM Transactions on Programming Languages and Systems*, 5(2):184–189, April 1983.

[GR76]   Leonard Gilman and Allen J. Rose. *APL: An Interactive Approach.* John Wiley & Sons, Inc, New York, revised reprinting of the second edition, 1976.

[GS87]   Ray Greenlaw and Larry Snyder. *Achieving Speedups for a Shared Memory Model Language on a SIMD Parallel Computer.* Technical Report 87-09-03, University of Washington, Department of Computer Science FR-35, Seattle, Washington 98195, September 1987.

[Hal85]   Robert H. Halstead, Jr. Multilisp: a language for concurrent symbolic computation. *ACM Transactions on Programming Languages and Systems*, 7(4):501–538, October 1985.

[Hil85]   W. Daniel Hillis. *The Connection Machine*. The MIT Press, Cambridge, Massachusetts, 1985.

[Hil86]   W. Daniel Hillis. *Why Parallel Processing is Inevitable*. Technical Report G-86-2, Thinking Machines Corporation, Cambridge, Massachusetts 02142, 1986.

[Hon84]   Jai-Wei Hong. On similarity and duality of computation. *Information and Control*, 62(2/3):109–128, August/September 1984.

[Hon86]   Jai-Wei Hong. *Computation: Computability, Similarity and Duality*. John Wiley & Sons, Inc., New York, 1986.

[HS86]   W. Daniel Hillis and Guy L. Steele Jr. Data parallel algorithms. *Communications of the ACM*, 29(12):1170–1183, December 1986.

[HW60]   Godfrey Hardy and Edward Wright. *The Theory of Numbers*. Oxford University Press, 1960.

[Ive62]   Kenneth E. Iverson. *A Programming Language*. John Wiley & Sons, Inc, New York, 1962.

[Ive81]   Kenneth E. Iverson. *The Evolution of APL*, chapter XIV, pages 661–691. *History of Programming Languages, ACM Monograph Series*, Academic Press, New York, 1981.

[Ive87]   Kenneth E. Iverson. A dictionary of APL. *APL Quote Quad*, 18(1):5–40, September 1987.

[JJ85]   Michael A. Jenkins and William H. Jenkins. *Q'Nial Reference Manual*. Nial Systems Limited, 20 Hatter Street, Kingston, Ontario, Canada K7M 2L5, first edition, July 1985.

[KKP*81]   D. J. Kuck, R. H. Kuhn, D. A. Padua, B. Leasure, and M. Wolfe. Dependence graphs and compiler optimizations. In *Conference Record of the Eighth Annual ACM Symposium on Principles of Programming Languages*, pages 207–218, 1981.

[Knu76]   Donald E. Knuth. Big omicron and big omega and big theta. *SIGACT News*, 8(2):18–24, April–June 1976.

[KRS85]   Clyde P. Kruskal, Larry Rudolph, and Marc Snir. The power of parallel prefix. In *International Conference on Parallel Processing*, pages 180–184, IEEE Computer Society, 1985.

[KRS86]   Clyde P. Kruskal, Larry Rudolph, and Marc Snir. *Efficient Synchronization on Multiprocessors with Shared Memory.* Technical Report Ultracomputer Note #105, Ultracomputer Research Laboratory, New York University, Courant Institute of Mathematical Sciences, Division of Computer Science, 251 Mercer Street, New York, New York 10012, May 1986.

[KS85]   James T. Kuehn and Howard Jay Siegel. Extensions to the C programming language for SIMD/MIMD parallelism. In *International Conference on Parallel Processing*, pages 232–235, IEEE Computer Society, 1985.

[Kuc78]   David J. Kuck. *The Structure of Computers and Computations.* Volume I, John Wiley & Sons, Inc, New York, 1978.

[Lan65]   P. J. Landin. A correspondence between ALGOL 60 and Church's lambda-notation: Parts I and II. *Communications of the ACM*, 8(2 and 3):89–101 and 158–165, February and March 1965.

[Lew81]   Harry R. Lewis. *An Introduction to Computer Programming and Data Structures using MACRO-11.* Reston Publishing Company, Inc., Reston, Virginia, 1981.

[LG87]   Boris D. Lubachevsky and Albert G. Greenberg. Simple, efficient asynchronous parallel prefix algorithms. In *International Conference on Parallel Processing*, pages 66–69, IEEE Computer Society, 1987.

[LKK85]   Gyungho Lee, Clyde P. Kruskal, and David J. Kuck. The effectiveness of automatic restructuring on nonnumerical programs. In *International Conference on Parallel Processing*, pages 607–611, IEEE Computer Society, 1985.

[LM86]   Charles E. Leiserson and Bruce M. Maggs. Communication-efficient parallel graph algorithms. In *International Conference on Parallel Processing*, pages 861–868, IEEE Computer Society, 1986.

[Luc87]   Steven E. Lucco. Parallel programming in a virtual object space. In *Object-Oriented Programming Systems, Languages and Applications*, pages 26–34, ACM, 1987.

[Mac83]   Bruce J. MacLennan. *Principles of Programming Languages: Design, Evaluation, and Implementation.* Holt, Rinehart and Winston, New York, 1983.

[MN82]   N. Metropolis and E. C. Nelson. Early computing at Los Alamos. *Annals of the History of Computing*, 4(4):348–357, October 1982.

[Mor79]   Trenchard More. The nested rectangular array as a model of data. In *APL79 Conference Proceedings*, pages 55–73, ACM, 1979.

[MR87]   Michael Metcalf and John Reid. *Fortran 8x Explained*. Oxford Science Publications, New York, 1987.

[Nil71]   Nils J. Nilsson. *Problem-Solving Methods in Artificial Intelligence*. McGraw-Hill, Inc., New York, 1971.

[Par86]   Dennis Parkinson. Experience in highly parallel processing using DAP. In James R. Fischer, editor, *Frontiers of Massively Parallel Scientific Computation*, pages 205–208, NASA and Goodyear Aerospace Corporation, NASA Scientific and Technical Information Office, NASA/Goddard Space Flight Center, Greenbelt, Maryland 20771, September 1986. Invited address.

[PBG*85] G. F. Pfister, W. C. Brantley, D. A. George, S. L. Harvey, W. J. Kleinfelder, K. P. McAuliffe, E. A. Melton, V. A. Norton, and J. Weiss. The IBM research parallel processor prototype (RP3): Introduction and architecture. In *International Conference on Parallel Processing*, pages 764–771, IEEE Computer Society, 1985.

[PCMP83] R. H. Perrott, D. Crookes, P. Milligan, and W. R. M. Purdy. Implementation of an array and vector processing language. In *International Conference on Parallel Processing*, pages 232–239, IEEE Computer Society, 1983.

[Pot85]   J. L. Potter, editor. *The Massively Parallel Processor*. The MIT Press, Cambridge, Massachusetts, 1985.

[Pot87]   J. L. Potter. An associative model of computation. In *Proc. Second International Conference on Supercomputing*, pages 1–8, International Supercomputing Institute, Inc., Santa Clara, California, May 1987.

[PR79]   Alan J. Perlis and Spencer Rugaber. Programming with idioms in APL. *APL Quote Quad*, 9(4):232–235, June 1979.

[RB87]   Anthony P. Reeves and Donna Bergmark. Parallel Pascal and the FPS hypercube supercomputer. In *International Conference on Parallel Processing*, pages 385–388, IEEE Computer Society, 1987.

[Red73]   S. F. Reddaway. DAP - A Distributed Array Processor. In *Proceedings of the First Annual Symposium on Computer Architecture*, pages 61–65, 1973.

[Ree84]   Anthony P. Reeves. Parallel Pascal: an extended Pascal for parallel computers. *Journal of Parallel and Distributed Computing*, 1(1):64–80, August 1984.

[Rey78]   John C. Reynolds. Syntactic control of interference. In *Conference Record of the Fifth Annual ACM Symposium on Principles of Programming Languages*, pages 39–46, 1978.

[RS87]   John R. Rose and Guy L. Steele Jr. C*: An extended C language for data parallel programming. In Lana P. Kartashev and Steven I. Kartashev, editors, *Proc. Second International Conference on Supercomputing*, pages 2–16, International Supercomputing Institute, Santa Clara, California, May 1987.

[Sab86]   Gary W. Sabot. Bulk processing of text on a massively parallel computer. In *24th Annual Meeting, Proceedings of the Conference*, pages 128–135, Association for Computational Linguistics, June 1986.

[Sab87a]   Gary W. Sabot. *Implementation of a Parallel Language*. Technical Report PL87-2, Thinking Machines Corporation, Cambridge, Massachusetts 02142, January 1987.

[Sab87b]   Gary W. Sabot. *Introduction to Paralation Lisp*. Technical Report PL87-10, Thinking Machines Corporation, Cambridge, Massachusetts 02142, October 1987.

[Sab87c]   Gary W. Sabot. *PAM: An Abstract Target Machine for Compilers of Parallel Languages*. Technical Report PL87-1, Thinking Machines Corporation, Cambridge, Massachusetts 02142, January 1987.

[Sab87d]   Gary W. Sabot. *Paralation Lisp Reference Manual*. Technical Report PL87-11, Thinking Machines Corporation, Cambridge, Massachusetts 02142, October 1987.

[Sab87e]   Gary W. Sabot. *The Paralation Model as a Basis for Parallel Programming Languages*. Technical Report PL87-3, Thinking Machines Corporation, Cambridge, Massachusetts 02142, January 1987.

[Sab87f]   Gary W. Sabot. *Why Current Models Distort The Way We Think About Parallel Programming, And What To Do About It*. Technical Report PL87-4, Thinking Machines Corporation, Cambridge, Massachusetts 02142, January 1987.

[SFG*84]   Guy L. Steele Jr., Scott E. Fahlman, Richard P. Gabriel, David A.
           Moon, and Daniel L. Weinreb. *Common Lisp: The Language*. Digital
           Press, Burlington, Massachusetts, 1984.

[SH86]   Guy L. Steele Jr. and W. Daniel Hillis. Connection Machine LISP:
           fine-grained parallel symbolic processing. In *Proc. 1986 ACM Confer-
           ence on Lisp and Functional Programming*, pages 279–297, ACM SIG-
           PLAN/SIGACT/SIGART, Cambridge, Massachusetts, August 1986.

[Sha83]   Ehud Shapiro. *A Subset of Concurrent Prolog and its Interpreter*. Tech-
           nical Report TR-003, ICOT—Institute for New Generation Computer
           Technology, Tokyo, 1983.

[SKS81]   Howard Jay Siegel, Frederick C. Kemmerer, and Harold E. Smalley, Jr.
           PASM: a partitionable SIMD/MIMD system for image processing and
           pattern recognition. *IEEE Transactions on Computers*, C-30(12):934–
           947, December 1981.

[Sny87]   November 1987. Larry Snyder, personal communication.

[SSKI87]   Howard Jay Siegel, Thomas Schwederski, James T. Kuehn, and
           Nathaniel J. Davis IV. An overview of the PASM parallel process-
           ing system. In D. D. Gajski, V. M. Milutinovic, H. J. Siegel, and B. P.
           Furht, editors, *Tutorial: Computer Architecture*, pages 387–407, IEEE
           Computer Society Press, 1987.

[Ste78]   Guy L. Steele Jr. *RABBIT: A Compiler for Scheme*. Master's the-
           sis, Massachusetts Institute of Technology, Cambridge, Massachusetts
           02139, May 1978. AI-TR-474.

[Str86]   Bjarne Stroustrup. *The C++ Programming Language*. Addison-Wesley,
           Reading, Massachusetts, 1986.

[Thi86a]   Thinking Machines Corporation. *C* Programming Manual*. Cam-
           bridge, Massachusetts 02142, 1986.

[Thi86b]   Thinking Machines Corporation. *The Essential *Lisp Manual*. Cam-
           bridge, Massachusetts 02142, 1986.

[Thi86c]   Thinking Machines Corporation. *Introduction to Data Level Paral-
           lelism*. Cambridge, Massachusetts 02142, 1986. Technical Report 86.14.

[Tou84]   David S. Touretzky. *A Gentle Introduction to Symbolic Computing*.
           Harper & Row, Publishers, New York, 1984.

[Tra85]   Joseph F. Traub, editor. *Annual Review of Computer Science.* Volume 1, Annual Reviews Inc., Palo Alto, California, 1985.

[Wag87]   August 1987. Jerry Wagner, telephone conversation with the author.

[Win77]   Patrick Henry Winston. *Artificial Intelligence.* Addison-Wesley, Reading, Massachusetts, 1977.

[WS87]   Skef Wholey and Guy L. Steele Jr. Connection Machine Lisp: a dialect of Common Lisp for data parallel programming. In *Proc. Second International Conference on Supercomputing*, pages 45–54, International Supercomputing Institute, Inc., Santa Clara, California, 1987.

[Yan87]   Chyan Yang. *An Investigation of Multigauge Architectures.* PhD thesis, University of Washington, Seattle, Washington 98195, September 1987.

[YT87a]   Yasuhiko Yokote and Mario Tokoro. Experience and evolution of ConcurrentSmalltalk. In *Object-Oriented Programming Systems, Languages and Applications*, pages 406–415, ACM, 1987.

[YT87b]   Akinori Yonezawa and Mario Tokoro, editors. *Object-Oriented Concurrent Programming.* The MIT Press, Cambridge, Massachusetts, 1987.

Index

–O–

–N–

–W–

–X–

–Y–

–Z–

The MIT Press Series in Artificial Intelligence
Edited by Patrick Henry Winston and J. Michael Brady

Robotics Research: The Third International Symposium edited by O.D. Faugeras and Georges Giralt, 1986

Machine Interpretation of Line Drawings by Kokichi Sugihara, 1986

ACTORS: A Model of Concurrent Computation in Distributed Systems by Gul A. Agha, 1986

Knowledge-Based Tutoring: The GUIDON Program by William Clancey, 1987

AI in the 1980s and Beyond: An MIT Survey edited by W. Eric L. Grimson and Ramesh S. Patil, 1987

Visual Reconstruction by Andrew Blake and Andrew Zisserman, 1987

Reasoning about Change: Time and Causation from the Standpoint of Artificial Intelligence by Yoav Shoham, 1988

Model-Based Control of a Robot Manipulator by Chae H. An, Christopher G. Atkeson, and John M. Hollerbach, 1988

A Robot Ping-Pong Player: Experiment in Real-Time Intelligent Control by Russell L. Andersson, 1988

Robotics Research: The Fourth International Symposium edited by Robert C. Bolles and Bernard Roth, 1988

The Paralation Model: Architecture-Independent Parallel Programming by Gary Sabot, 1988